Off-road routes

Back cover photograph: Looking towards Stenbury Down, north of Ventnor

Acknowledgements
Nick Cotton: *back cover, 67, 105, 107, 111* • Comstock (Simon McBride): *129* • Spectrum Colour Library: *61* • Andy Williams: *25, 37, 48-49, 73, 91, 97, 122-123, 130-131*

First published by

Ordnance Survey and Hamlyn, an imprint of Reed Consumer Books Ltd

Ordnance Survey	Hamlyn, an imprint of
Romsey Road	Reed Consumer Books Ltd
Maybush	Michelin House
Southampton	81 Fulham Road
SO9 4DH	London SW3 6RB

First edition 1993
First impression 1993

A catalogue record for this atlas is available from the British Library

ISBN 0 600 57915 8
(Ordnance Survey ISBN 0 319 00343 4)

Made, printed and published in Great Britain

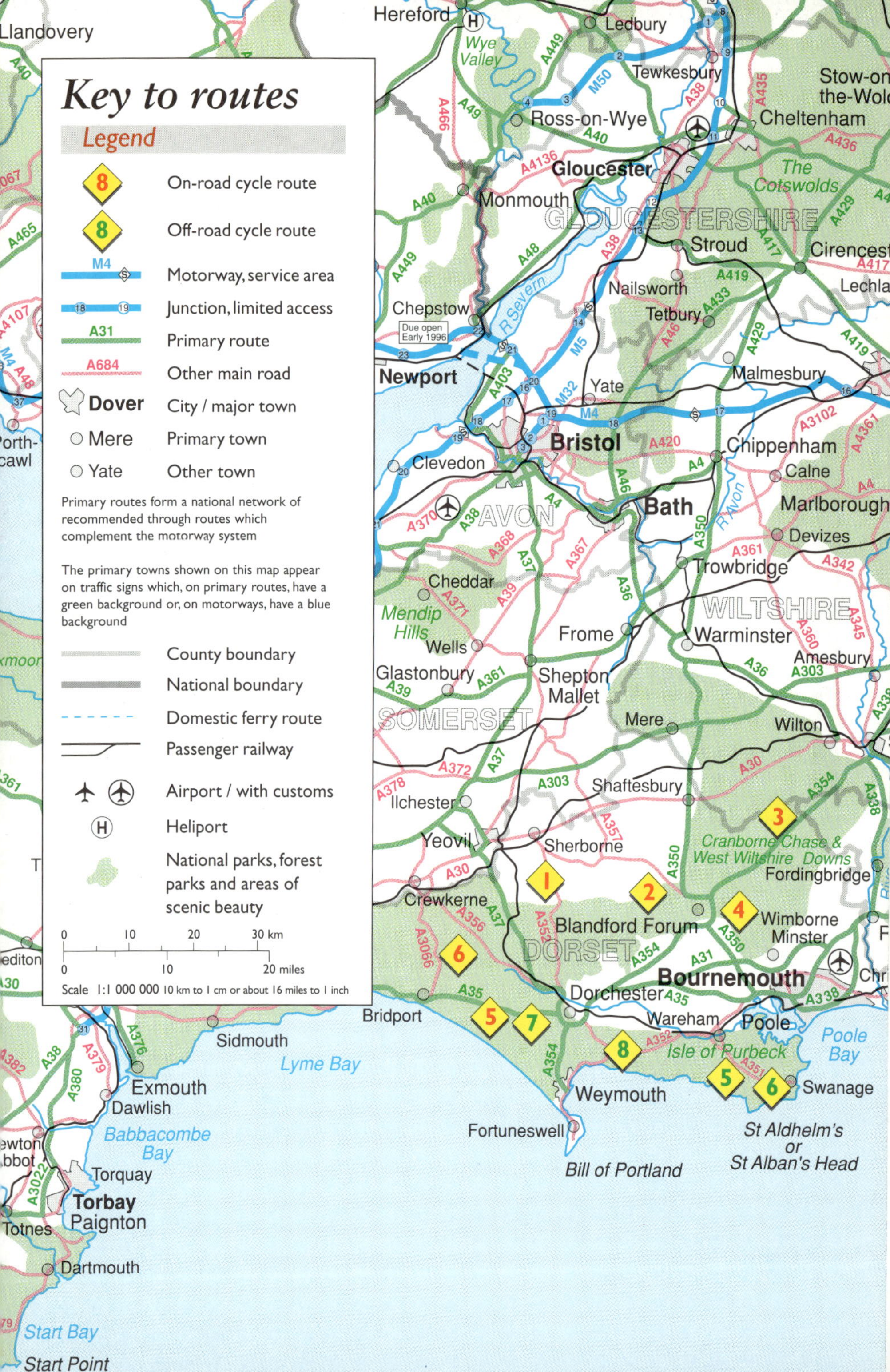

Key to routes
Legend
On-road cycle route
Off-road cycle route
Motorway, service area
Junction, limited access
Primary route
Other main road
Dover City / major town
Mere Primary town
Yate Other town
Primary routes form a national network of recommended through routes which complement the motorway system
The primary towns shown on this map appear on traffic signs which, on primary routes, have a green background or, on motorways, have a blue background
County boundary
National boundary
Domestic ferry route
Passenger railway
Airport / with customs
Heliport
National parks, forest parks and areas of scenic beauty
Scale 1:1 000 000 10 km to 1 cm or about 16 miles to 1 inch
Llandovery
Hereford
Ledbury
Wye Valley
Tewkesbury
Ross-on-Wye
Stow-on-the-Wold
Cheltenham
Gloucester
The Cotswolds
Monmouth
GLOUCESTERSHIRE
Stroud
Cirencester
Nailsworth
Lechlade
Chepstow
Due open Early 1996
Tetbury
R Severn
Newport
Yate
Malmesbury
Bristol
Chippenham
Porthcawl
Clevedon
Calne
AVON
Bath
Marlborough
R Avon
Devizes
Cheddar
Trowbridge
Mendip Hills
WILTSHIRE
Wells
Frome
Warminster
Amesbury
Glastonbury
Shepton Mallet
SOMERSET
Mere
Wilton
Exmoor
Ilchester
Shaftesbury
Yeovil
Sherborne
Cranborne Chase & West Wiltshire Downs
Fordingbridge
Crewkerne
Blandford Forum
Wimborne Minster
DORSET
Bournemouth
Dorchester
Bridport
Wareham
Poole
Sidmouth
Lyme Bay
Isle of Purbeck
Poole Bay
Exmouth
Weymouth
Swanage
Dawlish
Babbacombe Bay
Fortuneswell
St Aldhelm's or St Alban's Head
Bill of Portland
Torquay
Torbay
Paignton
Totnes
Dartmouth
Start Bay
Start Point

ORDNANCE SURVEY

Cycle Tours

24 one-day routes in

Dorset, Hampshire & Isle of Wight

Compiled by Nick Cotton

HAMLYN

Contents

ENGLISH CHANNEL

Quick reference chart

	Route	Page	Distance (miles)	Grade (easy/moderate/strenuous)	Links with other routes [1]	Tourist information centres [2]
	On-road routes					
1	*South from Sherborne to Cerne Abbas*	18	35	■■■■	2,5	Sherborne 0935-815341
2	*From Sturminster Newton over Bulbarrow Hill to Milton Abbas*	24	28	■■■	1,4	Blandford Forum 0258-454770
3	*Chalk downland and river valleys through three counties*	30	33	■■■	4	Wimborne 0202-886116
4	*From Blandford Forum to Wimborne Minster via the Tarrant and Stour valleys*	36	30	■	2,3	Blandford Forum 0258-454770
5	*Southwest from Dorchester to Abbotsbury and along the top of the Downs*	42	32	■■■■	1,6	Dorchester 0305-267992
6	*Through west Dorset hills from Bridport to Beaminster and Rampisham*	48	33	■■■■■	5	Bridport 0308-24901
7	*Northwest from Whitchurch over the North Hampshire Downs*	54	33	■■	8,9	Andover 0264-324320
8	*From Whitchurch to Kingsclere via Hampshire lanes and Watership Down*	60	36	■■	7,9, 10	Andover 0264-324320
9	*Along the beautiful Test Valley from Stockbridge*	66	31	■■	7,8	Winchester 0962-840500
10	*Rolling hills and woodland north from New Alresford to Odiham*	72	38	■■■	8,11, 12	Winchester 0962-840500
11	*New Alresford to Bishop's Waltham, along the Meon Valley and over the Downs*	78	31	■■	10,12	Winchester 0962-840500
12	*From Petersfield west through the Meon Valley and north to Selborne*	84	31	■■■	10,11	Petersfield 0730-68829

Route	Page	Distance (miles)	Grade (easy/moderate/ strenuous)	Links with other routes [1]	Tourist information centres [2]
13 *Newport to Cowes and Yarmouth via three cycle paths*	90	38	●●●	14	Cowes 0983-291914
14 *From Newport to Brading and south to Niton*	96	28	●●●	13	Newport 0983-525450
Off-road routes					
1 *Chalk ridges and woodland tracks south of Hungerford*	102	21	●●●●	2	Andover 0264-324320
2 *Watership Down, south of Newbury*	106	19	●●	1	Basingstoke 0256-817618
3 *A gentle journey in the heart of Hampshire north of New Alresford*	110	18	●	4	Winchester 0962-840500
4 *Easy tracks south of New Alresford*	114	19	●●	3	Winchester 0962-840500
5 *Corfe Castle southwest to Swyre Head, returning via Knowle Hill*	118	12	●●●●	6	Swanage 0929-422885
6 *Corfe Castle to Worth Matravers via Brenscombe Hill and the Priests Way*	122	17	●●●●	5	Swanage 0929-422885
7 *From Dorchester via Maiden Castle and Hardy Monument to Abbotsbury*	126	28	●●●●	8	Dorchester 0305-267992
8 *Chalk ridges near the Dorset coast southeast from Dorchester*	130	18	●●●●	7	Dorchester 0305-267992
9 *Superb chalk ridges with sea views on the west of the Isle of Wight*	134	19	●●●●●	10	Yarmouth 0983-760015
10 *Rough riding on the southern downlands of the Isle of Wight*	138	22	●●●●●	9	Newport 0983-525450

[1] ***Links with other routes*** Use this information to create a more strenuous ride or if you are planning to do more than one ride in a day or on a weekend or over a few days. The rides do not necessarily join: there may be a distance of up to three miles between the closest points. Several rides are in pairs, sharing the same starting point, which may be a good place to base yourself for a weekend.

[2] ***Tourist Information Centres*** You can contact them for details about accommodation. If they cannot help, there are many books that recommend places to stay. If nothing is listed for the place where you want to stay, try phoning the post office or the pub in the village to see if they can suggest somewhere.

Dorset, Hampshire and the Isle of Wight

East of Poole there are hardly any areas on the coast that are not built-up, so Hampshire's cycling joys lie inland, on the downland in the north of the county, along the beautiful valleys of the Test and Meon Rivers, or starting from attractive towns such as New Alresford and Petersfield. It is a predominantly rolling agricultural landscape, dotted with small villages of stone and half-timbered, sometimes thatched, buildings.

Dorset is Thomas Hardy country and many people are drawn there to explore the settings of famous novels. There are many attractive towns, such as Sherborne, Dorchester, Shaftesbury and Bridport, and myriad picturesque villages. Easy cycling can be found in the Blackmoor Vale, but in general, Dorset provides some tough challenges, with steep climbs to the top of the Dorset Downs. There is good off-road cycling near the coast, with magnificent views out to sea.

Shaped like a diamond, the Isle of Wight is a real delight for cyclists. The cost of transporting a car on the ferry may encourage you to leave the vehicle on the mainland and travel with just a bike and panniers. There is excellent on-road and off-road cycling, with some fine ridges offering views of all the Solent to the north and the English Channel to the south. The trails are well signposted and the local authority is very pro-cycling and has already created three cycleways on dismantled railways.

Abbreviations and instructions

Instructions are given as concisely as possible to make them easy to follow while you are cycling. Remember to read one or two instructions ahead so that you do not miss a turning. This is most likely to occur when you have to turn off a road on which you have been riding for a fairly long distance and these junctions are marked ***Easy to miss*** to warn you.

If there appears to be a contradiction between the instructions and what you actually see, always refer to the map. There are many reasons why over the course of a few years instructions will need updating as new roads are built and priorities and signposts change.

If giving instructions for road routes is at times difficult, doing so for off-road routes can often be almost impossible, particularly when the route passes through woodland. With few signposts and buildings by which to orientate yourself, more attention is paid to other features, such as gradient and surface. Most of these routes have been explored between late spring and early autumn and the countryside changes its appearance very dramatically in winter. If in doubt, consult your map and check your compass to see that you are heading in the right direction.

Remember, there is a big difference between temporarily losing the route and being completely lost.

Where I have encountered mud I have mentioned it, but this may change not only from summer to winter but also from dry to wet weather at any time during the year. At times you may have to retrace your steps and find a road alternative.

Some routes have small sections that follow footpaths. The instructions will highlight these sections where you must get off and push your bike. You may only ride on bridleways and byways so be careful if you stray from the given routes.

Directions	
L	left
LH	left-hand
RH	right-hand
SA	straight ahead or straight across
bear L or R	make less than a 90-degree (right-angle) turn at a fork in the road or track or at a sharp bend so that your course appears to be straight ahead; this is often written as *in effect SA*
sharp L or R turn	is more acute than 90 degrees
sharp R/L back on yourself	an almost U-turn
sharp LH/RH bend	a 90-degree bend
R then L or R	the second turning is visible then immediately L from the first
R then 1st L	the second turning may be some distance from the first; the distance may also be indicated: *R, then after 1 mile L*

Junctions

T-j	T-junction, a junction where you have to give way
X-roads	crossroads, a junction where you may or may not have to give way
offset X-roads	the four roads are not in the form of a perfect cross and you will have to turn left then right, or vice versa, to continue the route

Signs

'Placename 2'	words in quotation marks are those that appear on signposts; the numbers indicate distance in miles unless stated otherwise
NS	not signposted
trig point	a trigonometrical station

Instructions

An example of an easy instruction is:

4 *At the T-j at the end of Smith Road by the White Swan PH R on Brown Street 'Greentown 2, Redville 3'.*

There is more information in this instruction than you would normally need, but things do change: pubs may close down and signs may be replaced, removed or vandalised.

An example of a difficult instruction is:

8 *Shortly after the brow of the hill, soon after passing a telephone box on the right next L (NS).*

As you can see, there is no T-junction to halt you in your tracks, no signpost indicating where the left turn will take you, so you need to have your wits about you in order not to miss the turning.

Fact boxes

The introduction to each route includes a fact box giving useful information:

Start

This is the suggested start point coinciding with instruction 1 on the map. There is no reason why you should not start at another point if it is more convenient

Distance and grade

The distance is, of course, that from the beginning to the end of the route. However, if you wish to shorten the ride because of tiredness, mechanical problems or a change in the weather, the maps enable you to do so.

Page diagrams

The on-road routes occupy four pages of mapping each. The page diagrams on the introductory pages show how the map pages have been laid out, how they overlap and if any inset maps have been used.

This section of the route is shown on pages 92 and 93

This overlap area appears at the foot of pages 92 and 93 and at the top of pages 94 and 95

This area is shown as an inset on page 94

This section of the route is shown on pages 94 and 95

92

93

94

95

The number of drinks bottles indicates the grade:
Easy
Moderate
Strenuous
The grade is based on the amount of climbing involved and, for off-road rides, the roughness of the surface rather than the distance covered.

Remember that conditions may vary dramatically with the weather and seasons; especially along off-road routes

Terrain

This brief description of the terrain covered by the route may be read in conjunction with the cross-profile diagram at the foot of the page to help you to plan your journey.

Nearest railway

This is the distance to the nearest station from the closest point on the route, not necessarily from the start. Before starting out you should check with British Rail for local restrictions regarding the carrying of bicycles.
(See page 15)

Before you go

Preparing yourself

Fitness

- Cycling uses muscles in a different way from walking or running, so if you are beginning or returning to it after a long absence you will need time to train your muscles and become accustomed to sitting on a saddle for a few hours. Build up your fitness and stamina gradually and make sure you are using a bicycle that is the right size for you and suits your needs.

Equipment

- Attach the following items to the bike: bell, pump, light-brackets and lights, lock-holder and lock, rack and panniers or elastic straps for securing things to the rack, map holder. Unless it is the middle of summer and the weather is guaranteed to be fine, you will need to carry extra clothes, particularly a waterproof, with you, and it is well worth investing in a rack for this purpose.
- Wearing a small pouch around your waist is the easiest and safest way of carrying small tools and personal equipment. The basics are: Allen keys to fit the various Allen bolts on your bike, chainlink extractor, puncture repair kit, reversible screwdriver (slot and crosshead), small adjustable spanner, spare inner tube, tyre levers (not always necessary with mountain bike tyres), coins and a phonecard for food and telephone calls, compass
- Additional tools for extended touring: bottom bracket extractor, cone spanners, freewheel extractor, headset spanners, lubricant, socket spanner for pedals, spare cables, spoke-key

Clothing

- What you wear when you are cycling should be comfortable, allowing you, and most especially your legs, to move freely. It should also be practical, so that it will keep you warm and dry if and when the weather changes.
- ***Feet*** You can cycle in just about any sort of footwear, but bear in mind that the chain has oil on it, so do not use your very best shoes. Leather tennis shoes or something similar, with a smooth sole to slip into the pedal and toe clip are probably adequate until you buy specialist cycling shoes, which have stiffer soles and are sometimes designed for use with specialist pedals.
- ***Legs*** Cycling shorts or padded cycling underwear worn under everyday clothing make long rides much more comfortable. Avoid tight, non-stretch trousers, which are very uncomfortable for cycling and will sap your energy, as they restrict the movement of your legs; baggy tracksuit bottoms, which can get caught in the chain and will sag around your ankles

if they get wet. Almost anything else will do, though a pair of stretch leggings is probably best.

- ***Upper body*** What you wear should be long enough to cover your lower back when you are leaning forward and, ideally, should have zips or buttons that you can adjust to regulate your temperature. Several thin layers are better than one thick layer.
- ***Head*** A helmet may protect your head in a fall.
- ***Wet weather*** If you get soaked to your skin and you are tired, your body core temperature can drop very quickly when you are cycling. A waterproof, windproof top is essential if it looks like rain. A dustbin bag would be better than nothing but obviously a breathable waterproof material is best.
- ***Cold weather*** Your extremities suffer far more when you are cycling than when you are walking in similar conditions. A hat that covers your ears, a scarf around your neck, a pair of warm gloves and a thermal top and bottom combined with what you would normally wear cycling should cover almost all conditions.
- ***Night and poor light*** Wearing light-coloured clothes or reflective strips is almost as important as having lights on your bike. Reflective bands worn around the ankles are particularly effective in making you visible to motorists.

Preparing your bicycle

- You may not be a bicycle maintenance expert, but you should make sure that your bike is roadworthy before you begin a ride.
- If you are planning to ride in soft, off-road conditions, fit fat, knobbly tyres. If you are using the bike around town or on a road route, fit narrower, smoother tyres.
- Check the tyres for punctures or damage and repair or replace if necessary or if you are in any doubt. Keep tyres inflated hard (recommended pressures are on the side wall of the tyre) for mainly on-road riding. You do not need to inflate tyres as hard for off-road use; slightly softer tyres give some cushioning and get better traction in muddy conditions.
- Ensure that the brakes work efficiently. Replace worn cables and brake blocks.
- The bike should glide along silently. Tighten and adjust any part that is loose or rubbing against a moving part. Using a good-quality bike oil lubricate the hubs, bottom bracket, pedals where they join the cranks, chain and gear-changing mechanism from both sides. If the bike still makes grating noises, replace the bearings.
- Adjust the saddle properly. You can raise or lower it, move it forwards or backwards or tilt it up or down. The saddle height should ensure that your legs are working efficiently: too low and your knees will ache; too high and your hips will be rocking in order for your feet to reach the pedals.
- Some women find the average bike saddle uncomfortable because the female pelvis is a different shape from the male pelvis and needs a broader saddle for support. Some manufacturers make saddles especially for women.

Cross-profile diagrams

The introduction to each route includes a cross-profile diagram. The vertical scale is the same on each diagram but the horizontal scale varies according to the length of the route

Corfe Castle
Start / finish
Blashenwell Farm
Kingston
Swyre Head
Kimmeridge

Tips for touring

The law

England and Wales have 120 000 miles of rights of way, but under the Wildlife and Countryside Act of 1968 you are allowed to cycle on only about 10 percent of them, namely on bridleways, byways open to all traffic (BOATS) and roads used as public paths (RUPPS). The other 90 percent of rights of way are footpaths, where you may walk and push your bike, but not ride it.

- You are not allowed to ride where there is no right of way. If you lose the route and find yourself in conflict with a landowner, stay calm and courteous, make a note of exactly where you are and then contact the Rights of Way Department of the local authority. It has copies of definitive maps and will take up the matter on your behalf if you are in the right.

Cycling techniques

If you are not used to cycling more than a few miles at a stretch, you may find initially that touring is tiring. There are ways of conserving your energy, however:

- Do not struggle in a difficult gear if you have an easier one. Let the gears help you up the hills. However, no matter how many gears a bike has, ultimately it is leg power that you need to get you up a hill. You may decide to get off and walk uphill with your bike to rest your muscles.
- You can save a lot of energy on the road by following close behind a stronger rider in his or her slipstream, but do not try this offroad. All the routes are circular, so you can start at any point and follow the instructions until you return to it. This is useful when there is a strong wind, as you can alter the route to go into the wind at the start of the ride, when you are fresh, and have the wind behind you on the return, when you are more tired.
- The main difference in technique between on-road and off-road cycling lies in getting your weight balanced correctly. When going down steep off-road sections, lower the saddle, keep the pedals level, stand up out of the saddle to let your legs absorb the bumps and keep your weight over the rear wheel. Control is paramount: keep your eyes on what lies ahead.

Steeple Hill
Grange Arch
Ridgeway Hill
Knowle Hill
Start / finish

Traffic

The rides in this book are designed to minimise time spent on busy roads, but you will inevitably encounter some traffic. The most effective way to avoid an accident with a motor vehicle is to be highly aware of what is going on around you and to ensure that other road users are aware of you.

- Ride confidently
- Indicate clearly to other road users what you intend to do, particularly when turning right. Look behind you, wait for a gap in the traffic, indicate, then turn. If you have to turn right off a busy road or on a difficult bend, pull in and wait for a gap in the traffic or go past the turning to a point where you have a clear view of the traffic in both directions, then cross and return to the turning.
- Use your lights and wear reflective clothing at night and in poor light
- Do not ride two-abreast if there is a vehicle behind you. Let it pass. If it cannot easily overtake you because the road is narrow, look for a passing place or a gate entrance and pull in to let it pass.

Maintenance

Mountain bikes are generally stronger than road bikes, but any bike can suffer. To prevent damage as far as possible:

- Watch out for holes and obstacles
- Clean off mud and lubricate moving parts regularly
- Replace worn parts, particularly brake blocks

Riders also need maintenance:

- Eat before you get hungry, drink before you get thirsty. Dried fruit, nuts and chocolate take up little space and provide lots of energy.
- Carry a water bottle and keep it filled, especially on hot days. Tea, water and well-diluted soft drinks are the best thirst-quenchers.

Breakdowns

The most likely breakdown to occur is a puncture.

- Always carry a pump
- Take a spare inner tube so that you can leave the puncture repair until later
- Make sure you know how to remove a wheel. This may require an adjustable spanner or, in many cases, no tool at all, as many bikes now have wheels with quick-release skewers that can be loosened by hand.

Security

Where you park your bike, what you lock it with and what you lock it to are important in protecting it from being stolen.

- Buy the best lock you can afford
- Lock your bike to something immovable in a well-lit public place
- Locking two bikes together is better than locking them individually
- Use a chain with a lock to secure the wheels and saddle to the frame. Keep a note of the frame number and other details, and insure, photograph and code the bike.

Lost and Found

The detailed instructions and the Ordnance Survey mapping in this book minimise the chances of getting lost. However, if you do lose your way:

- Ask someone for directions
- Retrace the route back to the last point where you knew where you were
- Use the map to rejoin the route at a point further ahead

Code of Conduct

- Enjoy the countryside and respect its life and work
- Only ride where you know you have a legal right
- Always yield to horses and pedestrians
- Take all litter with you
- Don't get annoyed with anyone; it never solves any problems
- Guard against all risk of fire
- Fasten all gates
- Keep your dogs under close control
- Keep to public paths across farmland
- Use gates and stiles to cross fences, hedges and walls
- Avoid livestock, crops and machinery or, if not possible, keep contact to a minimum
- Help keep all water clean
- Protect wildlife, plants and trees
- Take special care on country roads

Transporting your bike

There are three ways of getting you and your bike to the start of a ride:

Cycle to the start or to a point along a route near your home.

Take the train. Always check in advance that you can take the bike on the train. Some trains allow only up to two bikes and you may need to make a reservation and pay a flat fee however long the journey. Always label your bike showing your name and destination station.

Travel by motor vehicle. You can carry the bikes:

- Inside the vehicle. With the advent of quick release mechanisms on both wheels and the seatpost, which allow a quick dismantling of the bike, it is possible to fit a bike in even quite small cars. It is unwise to stack one bike on top of another unless you have a thick blanket separating them to prevent scratching or worse damage. If you are standing them up in a van, make sure they are secured so they cannot slide around.
- On top of the vehicle. The advantages of this method are that the bikes are completely out of the way and are not resting against each other, you can get at the boot or hatch easily and the bikes do not obscure the number plate or rear lights and indicators. The disadvantages are that you use up more fuel, the car can feel uncomfortable in a crosswind and you have to be reasonably tall and strong to get the bikes on and off the roof.
- On a rack that attaches to the rear of the vehicle. The advantages are that the rack is easily and quickly assembled and disassembled, fuel consumption is better and anyone can lift the bikes on and off. The disadvantages are that you will need to invest in a separate board carrying the number plate and rear lights if they are obstructed by the bikes, you cannot easily get to the boot or hatch once the bikes have been loaded and secured, and the bikes are resting against each other so you must take care that they don't scrape off paint or damage delicate parts.
- Whichever way you carry the bikes on the outside of the vehicle, ensure that you regularly check that they are secure and that straps and fixings that hold them in place have not come loose. If you are leaving the bikes for any length of time, be sure they are secure against theft; if nothing else lock them to each other

Legend to 1:50 000 maps

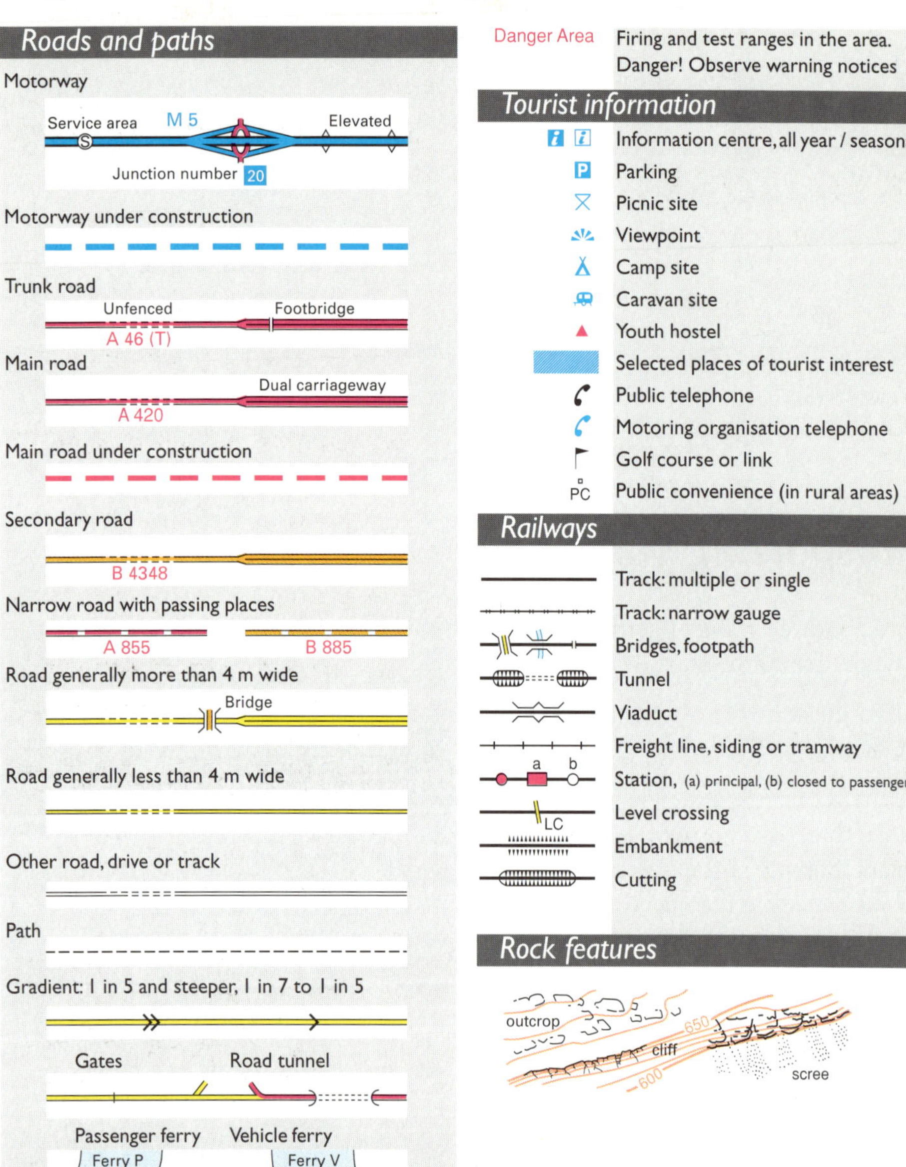

Public rights of way (Not applicable to Scotland)

Footpath

Bridleway

Road used as a public footpath

Byway open to all traffic

Public rights of way indicated by these symbols have been derived from Definitive Maps as amended by the latest enactments or instruments held by Ordnance Survey and are shown subject to the limitations imposed by the scale of mapping. Further information may be obtained from the appropriate County or London Borough Council

The representation on this map of any other road, track or path is no evidence of the existence of a right of way

Water features

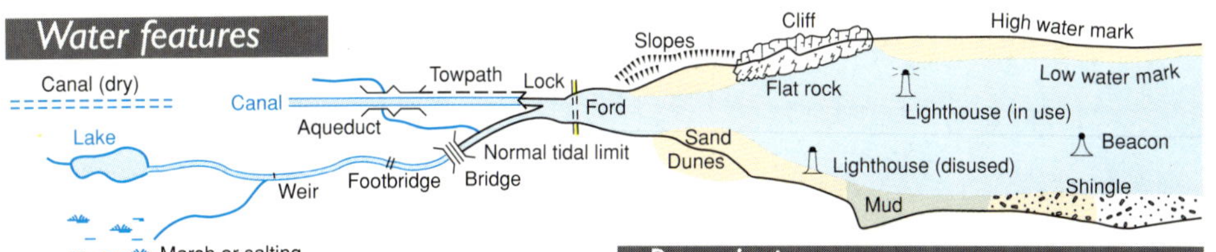

General features

Electricity transmission line (with pylons spaced conventionally)

Pipeline (arrow indicates direction of flow)

ruin

Buildings

Public buildings (selected)

Bus or coach station

Coniferous wood

Non-coniferous wood

Mixed wood

Orchard

Park or ornamental grounds

Quarry

Spoil heap, refuse tip or dump

Radio or TV mast

Church or chapel with tower

Church or chapel with spire

Church or chapel without tower or spire

Chimney or tower

Glasshouse

Graticule intersection at 5' intervals

Heliport

Triangulation pillar

Windmill with or without sails

Windpump

Boundaries

National

London borough

National park or forest park

National Trust — NT open access; NT limited access

County, region or islands area

District

Abbreviations

P	Post office
PH	Public house
MS	Milestone
MP	Milepost
CH	Clubhouse
PC	Public convenience (in rural areas)
TH	Town hall, guildhall or equivalent
CG	Coastguard

Antiquities

VILLA	Roman
Castle	Non-Roman
⚔	Battlefield (with date)
☆	Tumulus
+	Position of antiquity which cannot be drawn to scale
𝔐	Ancient monuments and historic buildings in the care of the Secretaries of State for the Environment, for Scotland and for Wales and that are open to the public

Heights

50	Contours are at 10 metres vertical interval
·144	Heights are to the nearest metre above mean sea level

Heights shown close to a triangulation pillar refer to the station height at ground level and not necessarily to the summit

South from Sherborne to Cerne Abbas

Sherborne is a most attractive town close to the border of Dorset and Somerset. There is plenty to see here, including two castles and an abbey, and there are lots of pubs and tea shops. The ride starts gently along quiet lanes through Bradford Abbas, Yetminster and Chetnole. The hills loom ahead and the gradual climb becomes more pronounced beyond Redford. You really feel as though you are cutting across the grain of the land as you climb up and over two ridges before swooping down into Cerne Abbas. There are lots of reasons for stopping here, not least of which is to gaze at the giant carved into the chalk. Prepare yourself for the steepest of the three major climbs up to the ridge road. Although it is fairly busy, you will have magnificent views in all directions and then a fantastic descent down to Middlemarsh. Two more short climbs as the route passes through Milborne Port and you are back in Sherborne.

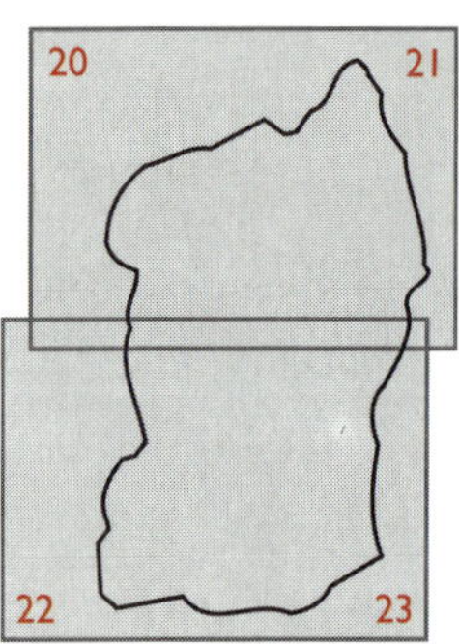

Refreshments

White Hart PH, Yetminster
Chetnole Arms PH, Chetnole
Red Lion PH, New Inn PH, Royal Oak PH, Cerne Abbas
White Hart PH, Bishop's Caundle

Start

Tourist Information Centre, Sherborne

Parking: Follow signs

Distance and grade

35 miles

Moderate/strenuous

Terrain

The ride is divided into three parts: the flatter, northern part of Blackmoor Vale south of Sherborne; a very hilly middle section where you climb to the top of three ridges; and a stretch along a ridge that descends back down to Blackmoor Vale. The three major climbs are 650 feet from Bradford Abbas to the A37 at Stagg's Folly, 320 feet from Sydling St Nicholas to Rowden Hill and 380 feet east from Cerne Abbas

Nearest railway

Sherborne

Sherborne
Bradford Abbas
Yetminster
Chetnole
Redford
Frome St Quintin
Stagg's Folly
Sydling St N

Places of interest

Sherborne (1)

This small market town is full of historic buildings, notably the abbey which is now partly occupied by the famous Sherborne School. Medieval, Georgian and Victorian shopfronts line the streets but there are also remains of some Roman buildings.

Abbey Church (1)

The oldest surviving parts of the abbey church are the Saxon west wall and the north-west doorway; the external buttresses and south porch are Norman but much of the rest was rebuilt in the 15th century.

Almshouse of Saints John the Baptist and John the Evangelist (1)

Founded in 1437, this cloister courtyard and the original stone buildings are still used as an almshouse. Shut off from the hall by a 15th-century screen is a small chapel which houses a 15th-century Flemish altar triptych.

Sherborne Old Castle (25)

Very little remains of the castle built by Roger de Caen in the 11th century. It was almost entirely reduced to ruins by Parliamentary forces in the Civil War and only the gatehouse, one of the central buildings and sections of the curtain wall survived.

Cerne Abbas (11)

This village is known for the Cerne Abbas Giant, a huge figure cut into the chalky hillside and believed to be a fertility figure dating from Roman times. The name Cerne Abbas derives from the Benedictine Abbey founded here in the 10th century but only the Abbot's Porch, a 15th-century guest house and a well remain.

Sherborne New Castle (25)

Constructed in the 16th century by Sir Walter Raleigh, the last resident of the Old Castle, the New Castle stands on a hill on the other side of the river in grounds laid out by 'Capability' Brown. Sir John Digby acquired the estate in 1617 and added the turreted wings and the Digby family crest wherever possible; the estate has belonged to the family ever since. Very little of the original interior survived extensive 'Jacobean style' redecoration in the 19th century, however; only the Georgian library and the Jacobean oak-panelled room remain.

Cerne Abbas

Middlemarsh

Holt Hill

Goathill

Oborne

1 At the T-j by the Tourist Information Centre facing the abbey L towards 'No entry' signs. At T-j just past Britannia Inn R on Lower Acreman Street

2 At T-j with A30 L, then 1st L on Bradford Road 'Bradford Abbas 3¼'

3 At X-roads SA onto Bradford Road 'Bradford Abbas 3'

4 After 2 miles, shortly before pylons, on gentle RH bend L 'Bradford Abbas 1, Clifton Maybank 2, Yetminster 3½'

5 After almost 2 miles R 'Yetminster 1½, Chetnole 3'

page 22

16 At T-j by triangle of grass L 'Bishop's Caundle 1¼, Allweston 2¾, Sherborne 5¾'

17 Just after bridge R on Milburn Lane 'Bishop's Caundle ¾'

18 At X-roads with A3030 SA onto Holt Lane 'Milborne Port 4¾, Purse Caundle 3½'. At T-j L (NS)

19 Follow signs for Milborne Port, round sharp RH then LH bend, then shortly L 'Goathill 1, Milborne Port 2¼'

20 At T-j at bottom of hill R 'Goathill ¼, Milborne Port 1½'

21 At end of Goathill Road, at T-j with A30 R (NS), then 1st L on Gainsborough 'Tannery'

22 At T-j L 'Oborne 1, Sherborne 3'

23 At T-j with A30 R. ***Take care***

24 1st L 'Sherborne town centre, Longburton 3½'

25 Follow signs for town centre along Long Street to return to Tourist Information Centre

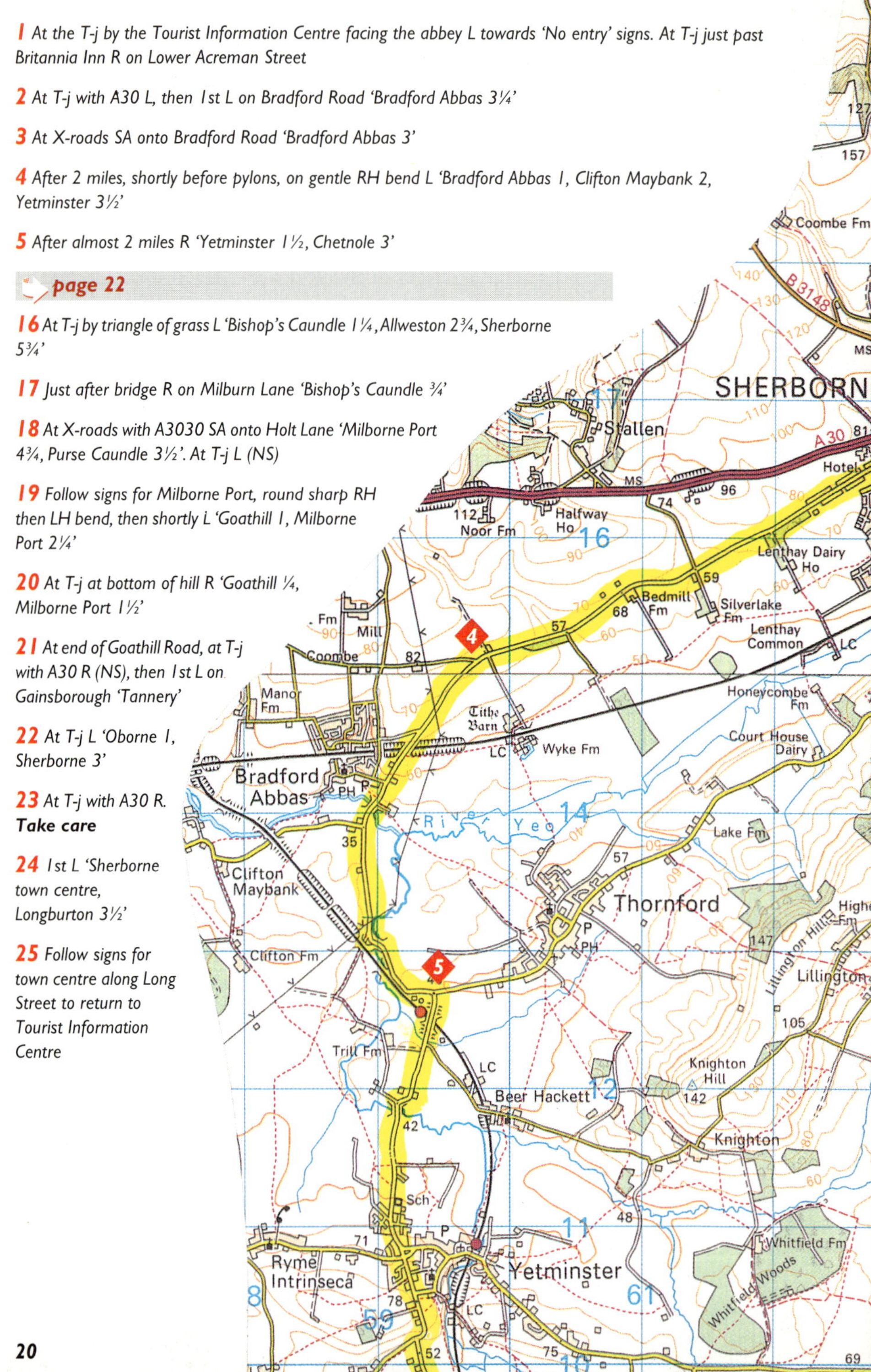

Red Post
Poyntington
Clatcombe Fm
Ambrose Hill
Oborne
Kingsbury Regis
New Town
Milborne Port
Spurles Fm
Gospel Ash Fm
Crendle
Vartenham Hill
Blackmarsh Fm
Clatcombe Fm
Hospl
Pinford
Goathill
Hanover Wood
Hanover Hill
Manor Fm
Manor Ho
Sherborne Castle
Sherborne Lake
Castle
Sherborne Park
Deer Park
Trip's Fm
Plumley Wood
Haydon
Home Fm
The Kennels
Dancing Hill
Limekiln Fm
Rue Fm
Ashcombe Fm
Church
North Wootton
Wenlock
Westhill Lodge
Honeycombe Wood
Tut Hill Fm
Holt Hill
Alweston
Marsh Court
Leweston Fm
Font le Roi
Hawkins's Fm
Folke
Caundle Marsh
West Hall
Longburton
Kitford Br
Cornford Bridge
St Antony's-Leweston Sch
Broke Wood
Bishop's Down
Barnes Cross
Densham Fm
Hunters Br
The Cam
Buckshaw Ho
Stockbridge Fms
Burton Hill Wood
Butterwick
Westrow
Stockbridge Oak
Ryewater Fm
Boys Hill
Sandhills
Manor Ho
The Holm Bushes
B 3145
A 30
A 3030
1
2
3
16
17
18
19
20
21
22
23
24
25
63
64
65
66
67
68
69

6 *Follow signs for Melbury Bubb out of Chetnole*

7 *Do not turn off to Melbury Bubb. Continue to T-j, turn R 'Evershot 2¾'*

8 *At T-j R 'Evershot 1½'. At T-j with A37 L 'Dorchester', then 1st R 'Frome St Quintin 1, Chantmarle 1¾'*

9 *At T-j by triangle of grass L 'Sydling St Nicholas, Cerne Abbas'*

10 *At T-j with A37 SA through gate onto disused road. At T-j L (NS)*

11 *At X-roads with A352 SA 'Village Centre, Buckland Newton 5'*

12 *Through village and climb steeply to ridge. At T-j L 'Buckland Newton 3, Sherborne 10'*

13 *Follow signs for Middlemarsh. In Middlemarsh just before A352 R at X-roads (NS)*

14 *At T-j L 'Glanvilles Wotton ¼, Sherborne 7'*

15 *On LH bend by a memorial stone R 'Holwell 2½, Bishop's Caundle 3¾'*

page 20

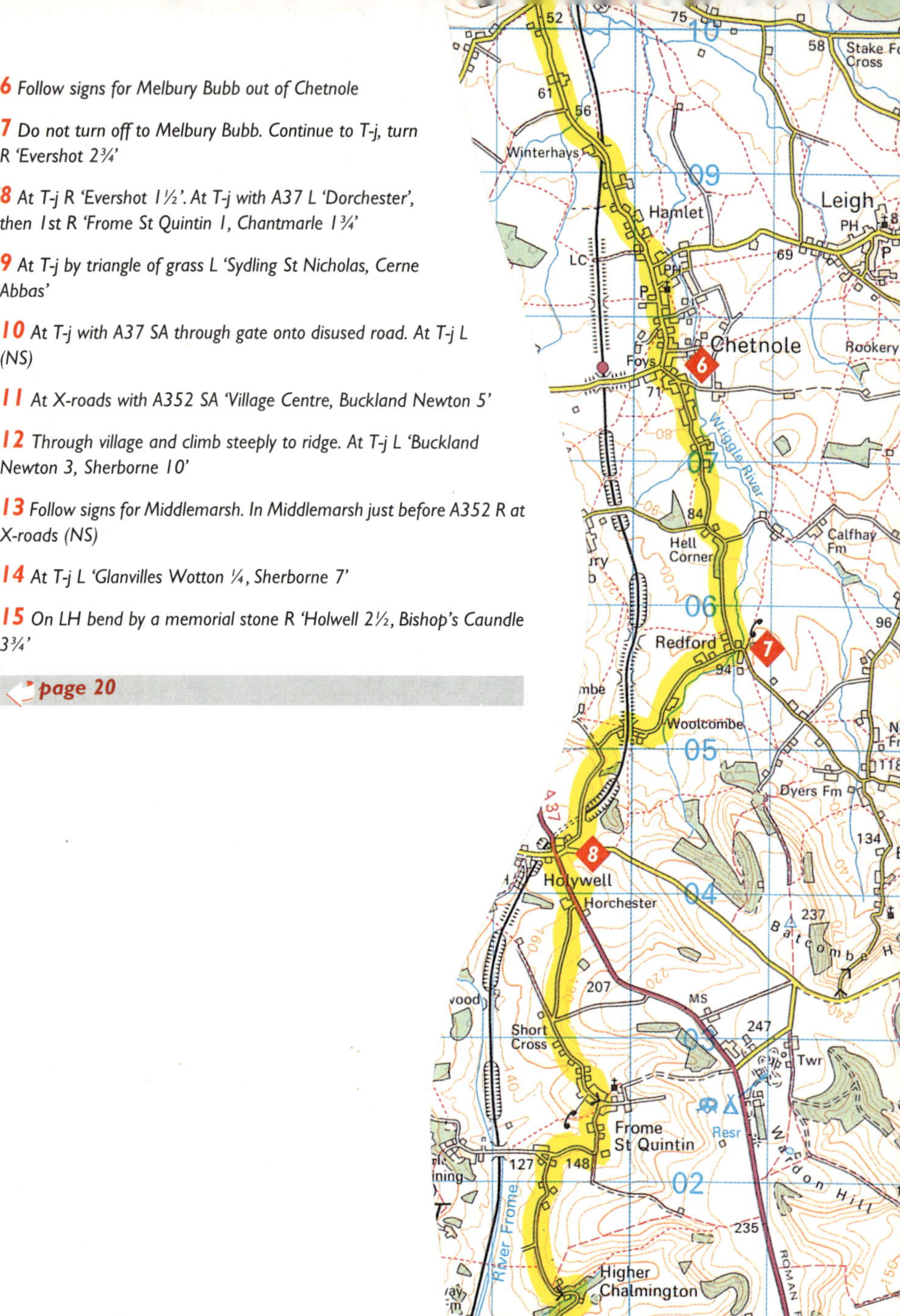

Holnest
Bailey Ridge Fms
White House Fm
Dyer's Fm
Osehill Green
Blackmore Ford Br
Round Chimneys Fm
Hotel
Holnest Park
Higher Holnest
Totnell
White House Common
Almshouse Fm
Stock Hill
Manor Ho
Glanvilles Wootton
A 352
Middlemarsh Common
Manor Fm
Court Fm
Great Wood
The Castle
Three Gates
Manor Fm
Hermitage
Middlemarsh
B 3146
Tiley
Prince's Wood
Grange Woods
Hilfield Manor
Stone's Fm
Lady's Well
Hartley Manor Fm
Pond Fm
Lyon's Hill Fm
Lyon's Gate
Lower Revels Fm
Spring Head
Knapps Hill Fm
Cosmore
Manor Fm
High Stoy
Clinger Fm
Dogbury Gate
Dogbury Enclosure
Hilfield
Telegraph Hill
Ridge Hill
Court Fm
PH
Tumulus
The Friary of St Francis
Park Pale
Minterne Magna
East Hill
Little Minterne Hill
Bladeley Hill
Minterne Ho
Weirs
Cross & Hand
Gore Hill
Bazon Hill
Row Hill
Wether Hill
High Cank
Tumulus
Minterne Parva
Holcombe Dairy
Up Cerne
Manor Ho
Giants Head
Eastcombe Bottom
Wancombe Hill
Tumulus
Settlement
Giant Hill
Cross Hill
Ellston Hill
Weam Common Hill
Tumulus
The Giant
NT
Earthwork
Yelcombe Bottom
Tumuli
Park Pale
Cerne Abbey
Cemy
Up Sydling
Cerne Park
Field System
Higher Down
Cerne Abbas
Higher Southco
Rowden Hill
Tithe Barn
Inn
Field Hill
Tumulus
Hog Hill
Settlement
Dickley Hill
Black Hill
River Cerne
Tumulus
Peak End Hill
Cowdown Hill
Green
11
12
13
14
15
63
64
65
66
67
68

2 From Sturminster Newton over Bulbarrow Hill to Milton Abbas

Starting from the quiet charm of the small town of Sturminster Newton, the ride passes through the attractive villages of Child Okeford and Okeford Fitzpaine before the first ascent of Bulbarrow Hill. At almost 900 feet, Bulbarrow is the highest point in Dorset and the views, particularly to the northwest over the Vale of Blackmoor, are spectacular. This ride gives you a double dose of Bulbarrow, with a lovely long descent through the shallow valley of the River Winterborne. The village of Milton Abbas is quite extraordinary in its precise picturesqueness, exact rows of thatched cottages set against a wooded backdrop.

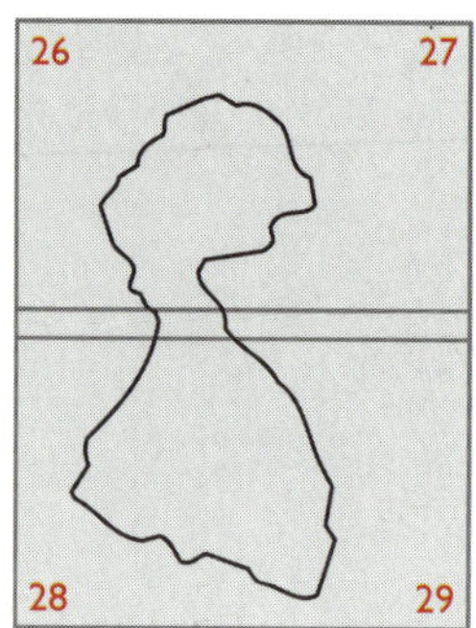

Start

The Swan Hotel, Sturminster Newton

Parking: Station Road, off the B3091 Shaftesbury Road

Distance and grade

28 miles

 Moderate

Terrain

Two major climbs, both towards the ridge of Bulbarrow Hill. The first, of 500 feet, lies south from Okeford Fitzpaine; the second is in two stages, from Winterborne Whitechurch to Milton Abbas (340 feet) then from Milton to the viewpoint (430 feet)

Nearest railway

Gillingham, 8 miles north of Sturminster Newton, or Wool, 9 miles south of Winterborne Whitechurch

Sturminster Newton
Manston
Child Okeford
Shillingstone
Okeford Fitzpaine
Bulbarrow Hill Ridge
Winterborne Stickland

Refreshments

Red Lion PH, Sturminster Newton
Saxon Arms PH, Baker Arms PH, Child Okeford
Royal Oak PH, Okeford Fitzpaine
Shire Horse PH, Winterborne Stickland
Milton Arms PH, Winterborne Whitechurch
Hambro Arms PH, Milton Abbas

Milton Abbas

Winterborne Whitechurch
Milton Abbas
Hilton
Bulbarrow Hill Ridge
Belchalwell
The Common

Marnhull
Mounters
Hotel
Triangle Fm
Todgoods Fm
Gomershay Fm
Walton Elm
White Way Hill
Lushes Fm
Thornton Fm
Pleck
Yardgrove Fm
Crib-House Fm
King's Mill Br
Chivrick's Brook
Ram's Hill Fm
Northwood Fm
Marsh Fm
Cutt Mill
Manor Fm
Ryalls Fm
Hinton St Mary
Bagber Br
Manor Fm
Twinwood Coppice
Hosey Br
Manston
Colber Fm
Stour View Ho
Rixon
River Stour
Hammoon
Mullins Fm
Bagber Common
Sewage Wks
Sturminster Newton
dismantled railway
Woodlands Fm
Weir
Mill
The Bridge
Fiddleford Mill
Bagber
Road Lane Fm
Cemy
Fiddleford
Roll Mill
Newton
Piddles Wood
Tan-hill Copse
Rivers' Corner
Broad Oak
Puxey
Sturminster Common
New Cross Gate
Angiers Fm
Haydon
Salkeld Br
Banbury Hill
Fort
Conygar Coppice
Plumber Manor
Darknoll Fm
Haydon Fm
Okeford Common
Etheridge Fm
Deadmoor Common
Knackers Hole
Roome Fm
Mill Fm
Cookwell Brook
Fifehead Neville
The Common
Okeford Fitzpaine
Woodrow
River Divelish
Cemy
Fifehead St Quintin
Stroud Fm
Whitmore Coppice
Hartcliff Fm
Tumulus
Kingston
Belchalwell
Okeford Hill
Cross Dyke
Lowbrook Fm
NORTH DORSET DISTRICT
Belchalwell Street
Turnworth Down
Kitford
Locketts Fm
Leigh
Ringmoor Settlement & Field System
A 357
B 3092
B 3091

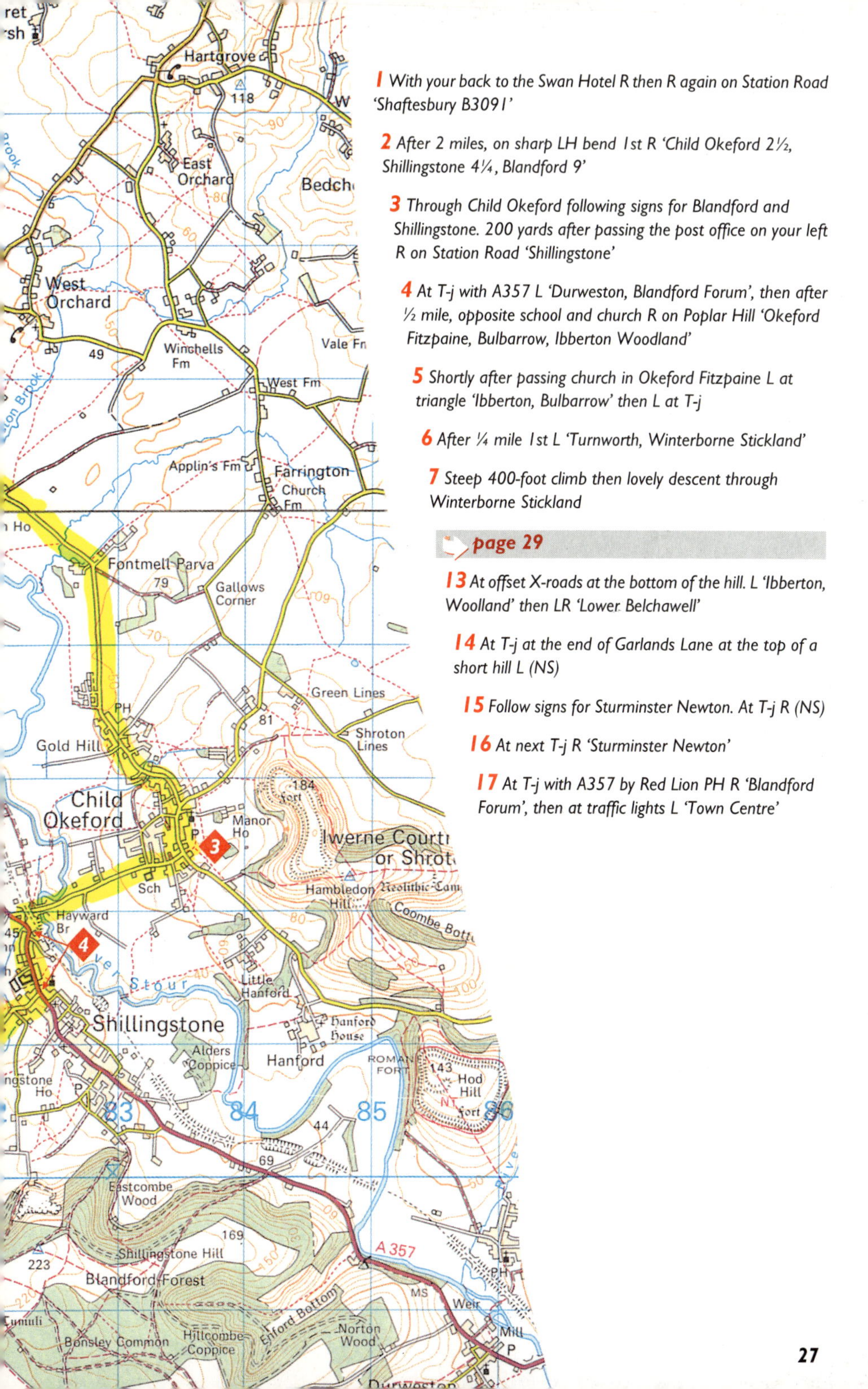

1 *With your back to the Swan Hotel R then R again on Station Road 'Shaftesbury B3091'*

2 *After 2 miles, on sharp LH bend 1st R 'Child Okeford 2½, Shillingstone 4¼, Blandford 9'*

3 *Through Child Okeford following signs for Blandford and Shillingstone. 200 yards after passing the post office on your left R on Station Road 'Shillingstone'*

4 *At T-j with A357 L 'Durweston, Blandford Forum', then after ½ mile, opposite school and church R on Poplar Hill 'Okeford Fitzpaine, Bulbarrow, Ibberton Woodland'*

5 *Shortly after passing church in Okeford Fitzpaine L at triangle 'Ibberton, Bulbarrow' then L at T-j*

6 *After ¼ mile 1st L 'Turnworth, Winterborne Stickland'*

7 *Steep 400-foot climb then lovely descent through Winterborne Stickland*

page 29

13 *At offset X-roads at the bottom of the hill. L 'Ibberton, Woolland' then LR 'Lower Belchawell'*

14 *At T-j at the end of Garlands Lane at the top of a short hill L (NS)*

15 *Follow signs for Sturminster Newton. At T-j R (NS)*

16 *At next T-j R 'Sturminster Newton'*

17 *At T-j with A357 by Red Lion PH R 'Blandford Forum', then at traffic lights L 'Town Centre'*

NORTH DORSET DISTRICT
Pidney
Hazelbury Bryan
Locketts Fm
Droop
Mount Pleasant Fm
Kitford
Leigh
Marsh Fm
Belchalwell Street
Bell Hill
Ringmoor Settlement & Field System
Turnworth Clump
Turnworth Ho
Ibberton
Cross Dyke
Ibberton Long Down
Coombe Bottom
Long Wood
Skinners Fm
Park Gate
Crate Wood
Manor Ho
Woolland
Ibberton Hill
South Down
Stoke Common
Hill Fm
Stoke Wake
Skinners Fm
Woolland Hill
Rawlsbury Camp
Bulbarrow Hill
Bul Barrow
Delcombe Wood
Houghton North Down
Hatherly Fm
Bulbarrow Fm
Heath Bottom
Delcombe Manor
Higher Houghton Fm
Winterborne Houghton
Moots Copse
Hilton Bottom
Delcombe Bottom
Park Wood
Pleck or Little Ansty
Field System
Breach Wood
Higher Ansty
Manor Fm
Green Hill
Delcombe Fm
Dunbury
Chilmore
Ansty Cross
Cothayes Fm
Inn
Lower Ansty
Broadfield
Crincombe Bottom
Hilton
Melcombe Bingham
Aller
Milton Park Fm
Mus
Higher Melcombe
Milton Abbey (Sch)
St Catherine's Chapel
Burgham's Melcombe
Combe Hill
Monmouth's Hill
Hotel
Hoggen Down
Cross Lanes
Great Down Clump
Milton Abbas
Highdon
Giant's Grave
Henning Hill
Coombe Bottom
Newton Fm
Luccombe Down
Luccombe Fm
Bramblecombe
Long Close Fm
Manor Ho
Gallows Corner
Streetway Lane
Hewish Fm
Cheselbourne
Stable Barrow
Bagber Fm
Tumulus
PH
P
NT
9
10
11
12
13
75
76
77
78
79
80
81
09
08
07
06
05
04
02
01
00
99

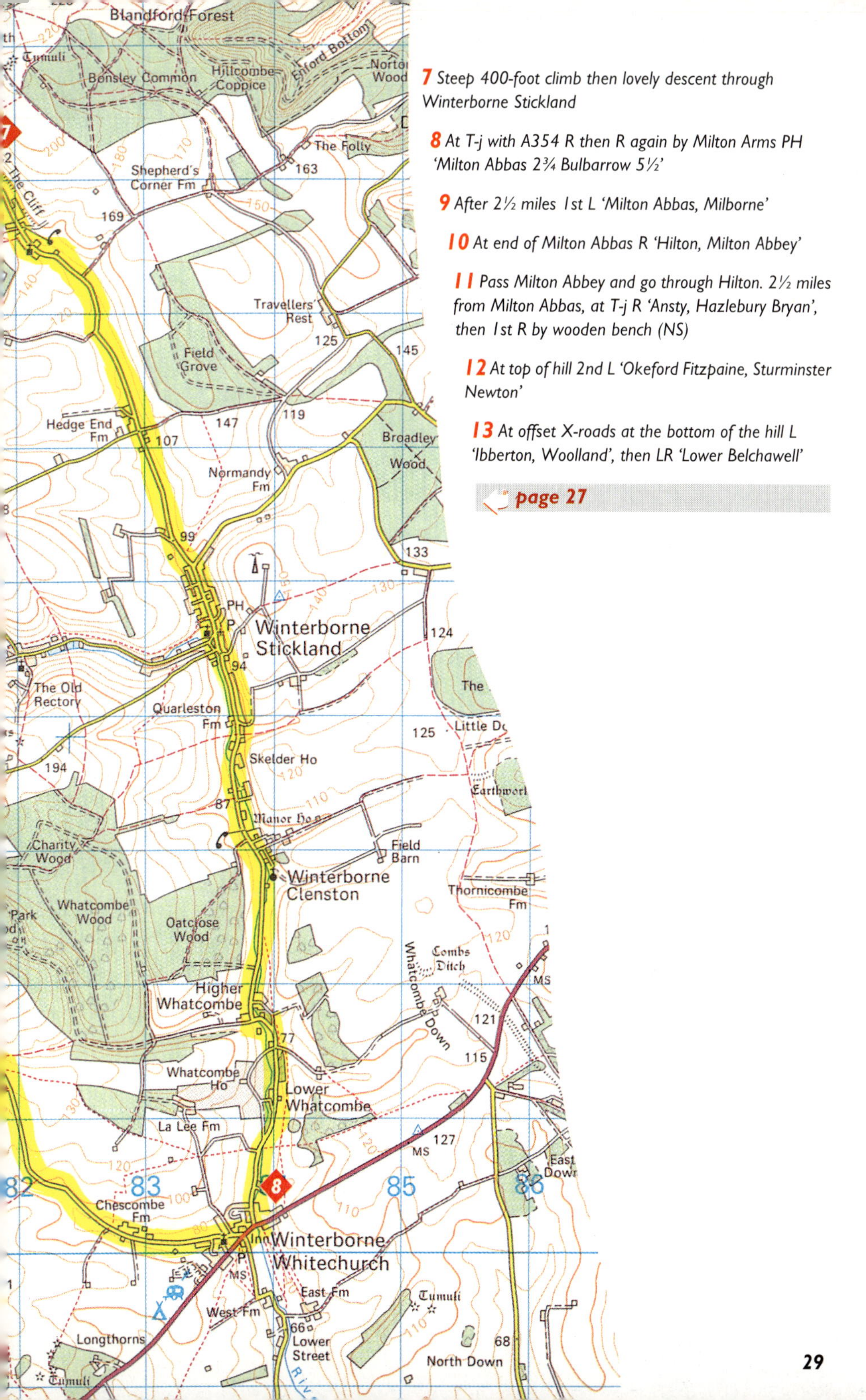

7 Steep 400-foot climb then lovely descent through Winterborne Stickland

8 At T-j with A354 R then R again by Milton Arms PH 'Milton Abbas 2¾ Bulbarrow 5½'

9 After 2½ miles 1st L 'Milton Abbas, Milborne'

10 At end of Milton Abbas R 'Hilton, Milton Abbey'

11 Pass Milton Abbey and go through Hilton. 2½ miles from Milton Abbas, at T-j R 'Ansty, Hazlebury Bryan', then 1st R by wooden bench (NS)

12 At top of hill 2nd L 'Okeford Fitzpaine, Sturminster Newton'

13 At offset X-roads at the bottom of the hill L 'Ibberton, Woolland', then LR 'Lower Belchawell'

page 27

Chalk downland and river valleys through three counties

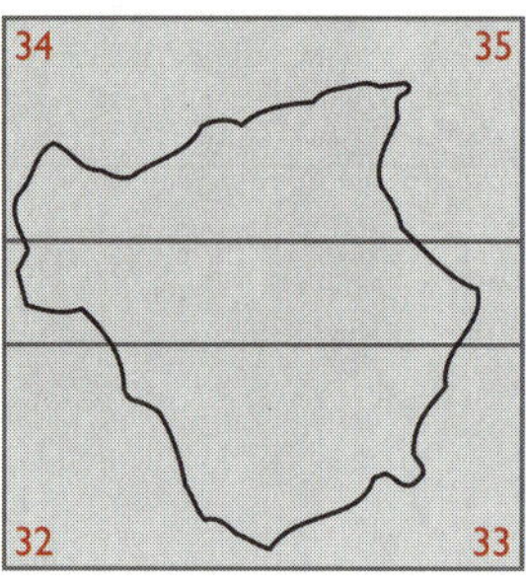

Passing though Hampshire and Dorset, this ride also takes in a slice of Wiltshire to form a lovely circuit over the chalk downs and along the Ebble Valley. Starting in the small village of Cranborne, it crosses two ridges, with especially fine views from the second one on Knowle Hill. The ride descends into the Ebble Valley at Broad Chalke and gently climbs through the charming villages of Ebbesborne Wake, Alvediston and Berwick St John. The big climb nearly to the top of Win Green lies ahead. You can now feast your eyes on the magnificent views all around and look forward to a gentle descent almost all the way to Gussage All Saints and only a gentle rise back to Cranborne.

Start

The Fleur de Lys PH, Cranborne, on the B3078 between Fordingbridge and Wimborne Minster

Parking: In Water Street, off the road to Damerham, near the fire station

Distance and grade

33 miles

Moderate

Terrain

Three climbs, the first one out of the Crane Valley to Martin Wood (280 feet), the second from Martin over Knowle Hill (465 feet) and the last and longest from Broad Chalke, gently then more steeply up to Ashmore Down, beneath Win Green (630 feet)

Nearest railway

Tisbury, 5 miles from the route at Alvediston

Cranbourne
Martin Wood
Tidpit
Martin
Knowle Hill
Broad Chalke
Fifield Bavant
Ebbesborne Wake
Alvediston
Berwick

Places of interest

Cranborne Manor Gardens (1)

Laid out in the 17th century, these gardens contain some very interesting plants. There is a pergola walk, a church walk, a herb garden and a river garden with borders full of unusual bulbs. A Jacobean mount garden looks down to a small garden containing 16th- and 17th-century flowers.

Refreshments

Fleur de Lys PH, Sheaf of Arrows PH, Beehive tea shop, Cranborne
Horseshoes Inn, Ebbesbourne Wake
Talbot Inn, Berwick St John
King John PH, Tollard Royal
Drovers Inn, Gussage All Saints

Cranborne Chase (14-15)

This large area of grassland and beechwoods was once a royal hunting forest before the hunting rights passed to the earls of Salisbury and Shaftesbury.

Chettle House (18)

Slightly off the route, this house was built by Thomas Archer in 1710 and although much of it has been modified, the staircase remains as a fine example of English Baroque architecture.

Ashmore Down
Tollard Royal
Farnham
Gussage All Saints
Wimborne St Giles

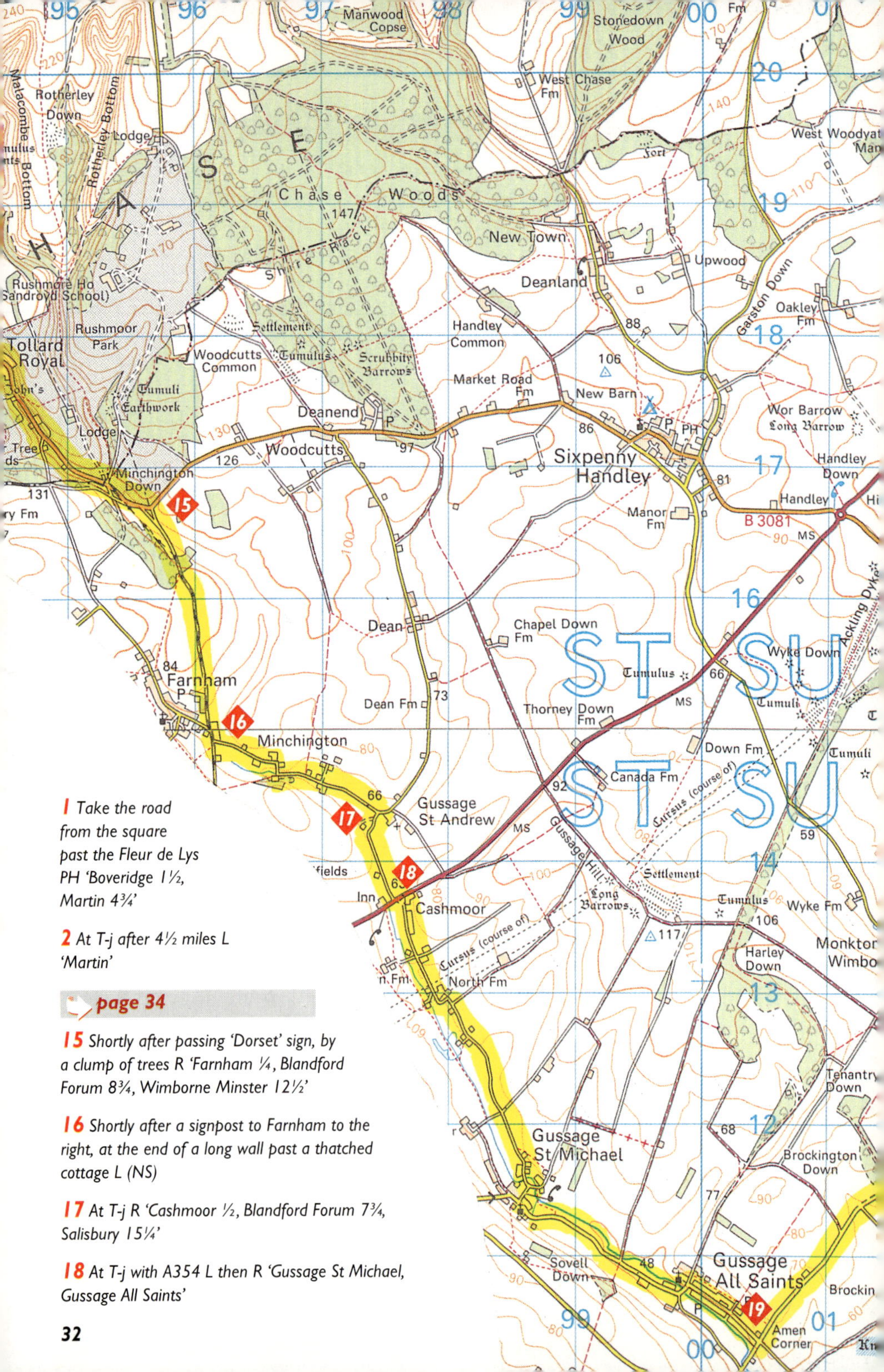

1 Take the road from the square past the Fleur de Lys PH 'Boveridge 1½, Martin 4¾'

2 At T-j after 4½ miles L 'Martin'

page 34

15 Shortly after passing 'Dorset' sign, by a clump of trees R 'Farnham ¼, Blandford Forum 8¾, Wimborne Minster 12½'

16 Shortly after a signpost to Farnham to the right, at the end of a long wall past a thatched cottage L (NS)

17 At T-j R 'Cashmoor ½, Blandford Forum 7¾, Salisbury 15¼'

18 At T-j with A354 L then R 'Gussage St Michael, Gussage All Saints'

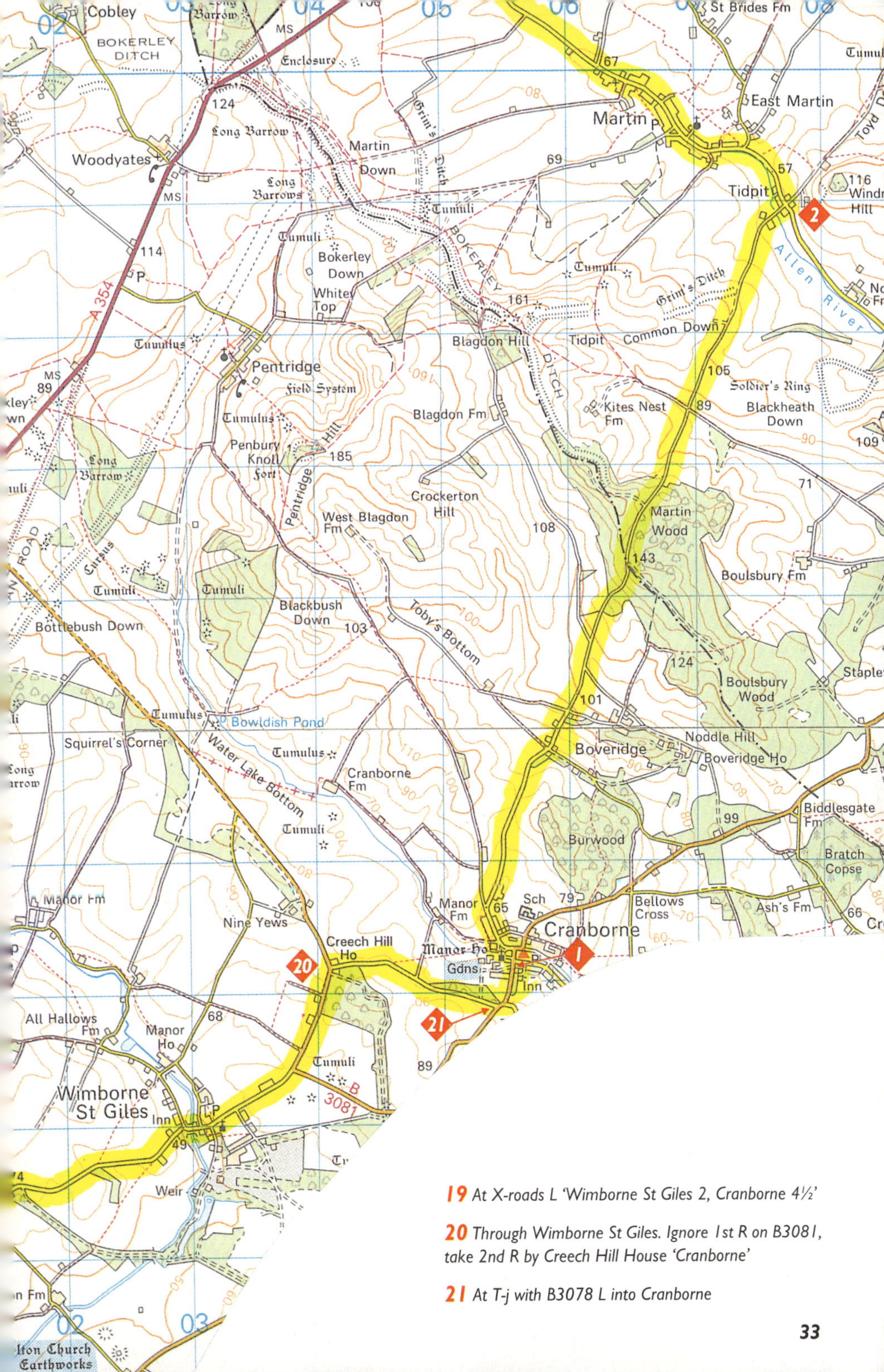

19 *At X-roads L 'Wimborne St Giles 2, Cranborne 4½'*

20 *Through Wimborne St Giles. Ignore 1st R on B3081, take 2nd R by Creech Hill House 'Cranborne'*

21 *At T-j with B3078 L into Cranborne*

3 ***Take care.*** *At X-roads with A354 dual carriageway SA 'Broad Chalke 3½'*

4 *At junction at bottom of hill L 'Bowerchalke, Shaftesbury'*

5 *At T-j by church L 'Bowerchalke' (or R for PH)*

6 *At end of village by a small triangle of grass R*

7 *After short, steep hill at T-j L*

8 *Follow signs for Ebbesborne Wake and 'Village' past Three Horseshoes PH*

9 *At T-j L 'Shaftesbury'*

10 *In Berwick St John past the Talbot Inn bear R on Church Street 'Shaftesbury A30'*

11 *20 yards* ***before*** *A30 L '7.5T except for access'*

12 *At T-j L 'Tollard Royal, Farnham'*

13 *At X-roads L 'Tollard Royal, Ringwood'*

14 *Follow the road for 3½ miles passing through Tollard Royal*

page32

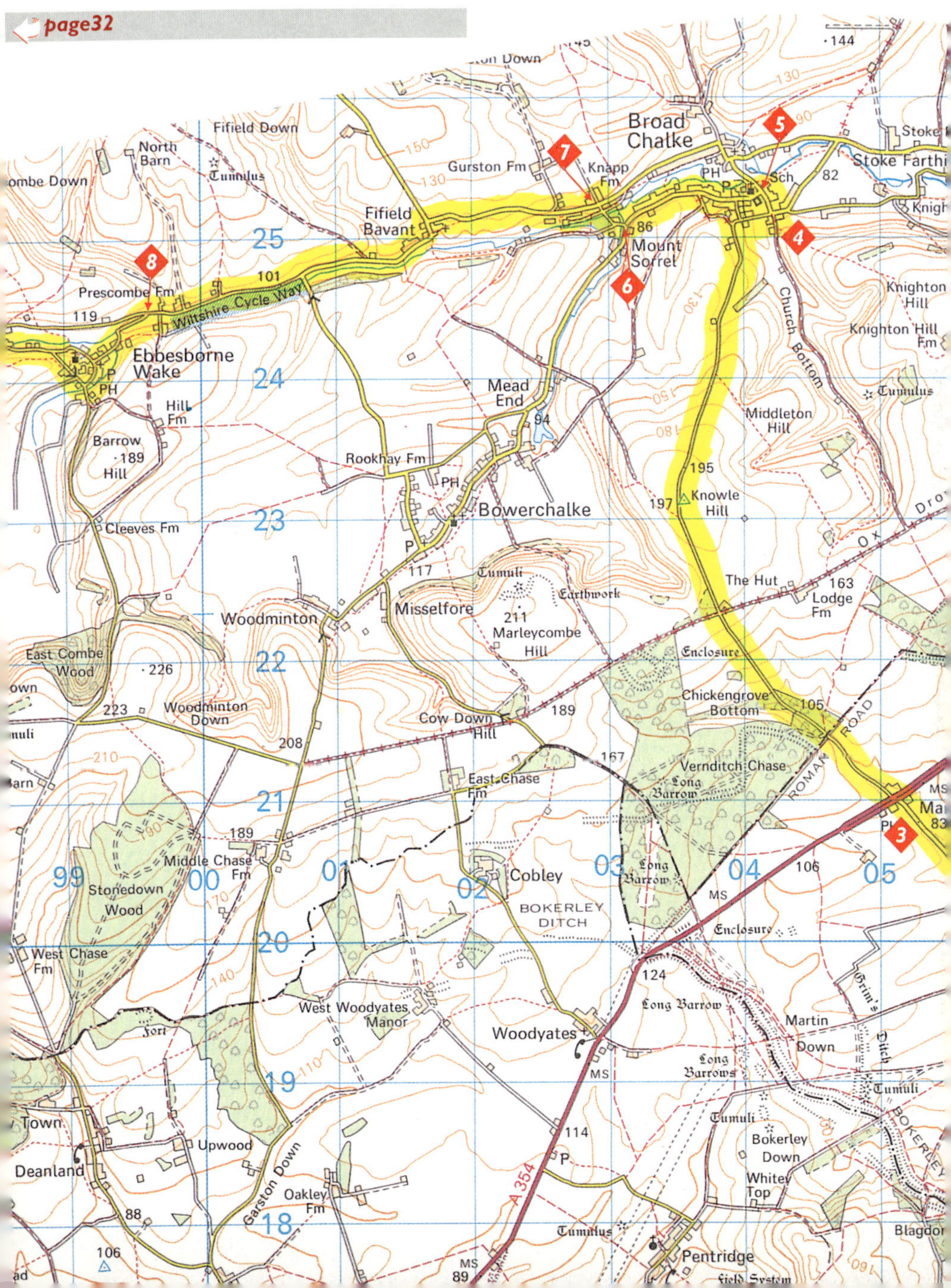

From Blandford Forum to Wimborne Minster via the Tarrant and Stour valleys

The elegant Georgian appearance of Blandford Forum is the result of a fire that devastated the centre of town in the summer of 1731. The town was rebuilt by the Bastard brothers. The ride goes north, then east to cross the hills separating the valleys of the rivers Stour and Tarrant. The Tarrant, really little more than a stream, gives rise to no fewer than eight hamlets and villages named after it in a stretch of 8 miles. The route joins the valley at the first of these, Tarrant Gunville, and proceeds via Tarrant Hinton, Launceston and Monkton before leaving the valley, climbing The Cliff and proceeding to the attractive market town of Wimborne Minster. The return is on quiet, delightful lanes close to the River Stour, with the opportunity of a fine tea stop near Tarrant Crawford.

38 39 40 41

Start

Tourist Information Centre, Blandford Forum

Parking: Adjacent to the Tourist Information Centre

Distance and grade

30 miles
Easy

Terrain

One long, steady climb of 300 feet between Blandford Forum and Tarrant Gunville, a short steep climb out of the Tarrant Valley, otherwise very easy gradients

Nearest railway

Poole, 6 miles south of Wimborne Minster

Blandford Forum
Tarrant Gunville
Tarrant Hinton
Tarrant Monkton
Hogstock
Witchar

Wimborne

Refreshments

Plenty of choice in Blandford Forum
Bugle Horn PH, Tarrant Gunville
Langton Arms PH, Tarrant Monkton
Stocks Inn, Furzehill
Lost Keys PH, Wimborne Minster
Anchor Inn, Shapwick
Keyneston Mill tea shop, near Tarrant Crawford

Wimborne Minster

Shapwick

1 With your back to the Tourist Information Centre R on Salisbury Street following signs for Salisbury and one-way system to L at 1st traffic lights. Stay in middle lane at 2nd traffic lights

2 After ¾ mile, shortly after D'Amory Arms PH on your right and just before church on your left turn L 'Melbury Abbas, Shaftesbury, Industrial Estate'

3 At roundabout with A354 SA 'Sunrise Business Park, Melbury Abbas 8'

4 Following signs for Melbury and Shaftesbury, after 2½ miles 2nd R (shortly after Paradise Farm Stud on your right) 'Tarrant Gunville'

5 In Tarrant Gunville at T-j R 'Tarrant Hinton 1½, Blandford Forum 6, Salisbury 19'

6 At T-j with A354 R 'Blandford', then L 'Tarrant Launceston 1, Tarrant Monkton 1½'

7 At T-j in Tarrant Monkton R 'Langton Arms PH'. Go past church and PH. At T-j R 'Tarrant Rawston, Rushton, Keyneston'

8 After 1¼ miles 1st L sharply back on yourself 'Witchampton'

page 40

19 At T-j with A354 L onto pavement and through underpass by the river. Follow this road (Langton Road) to the end

20 At T-j L following signs for Dorchester to return to Tourist Information Centre

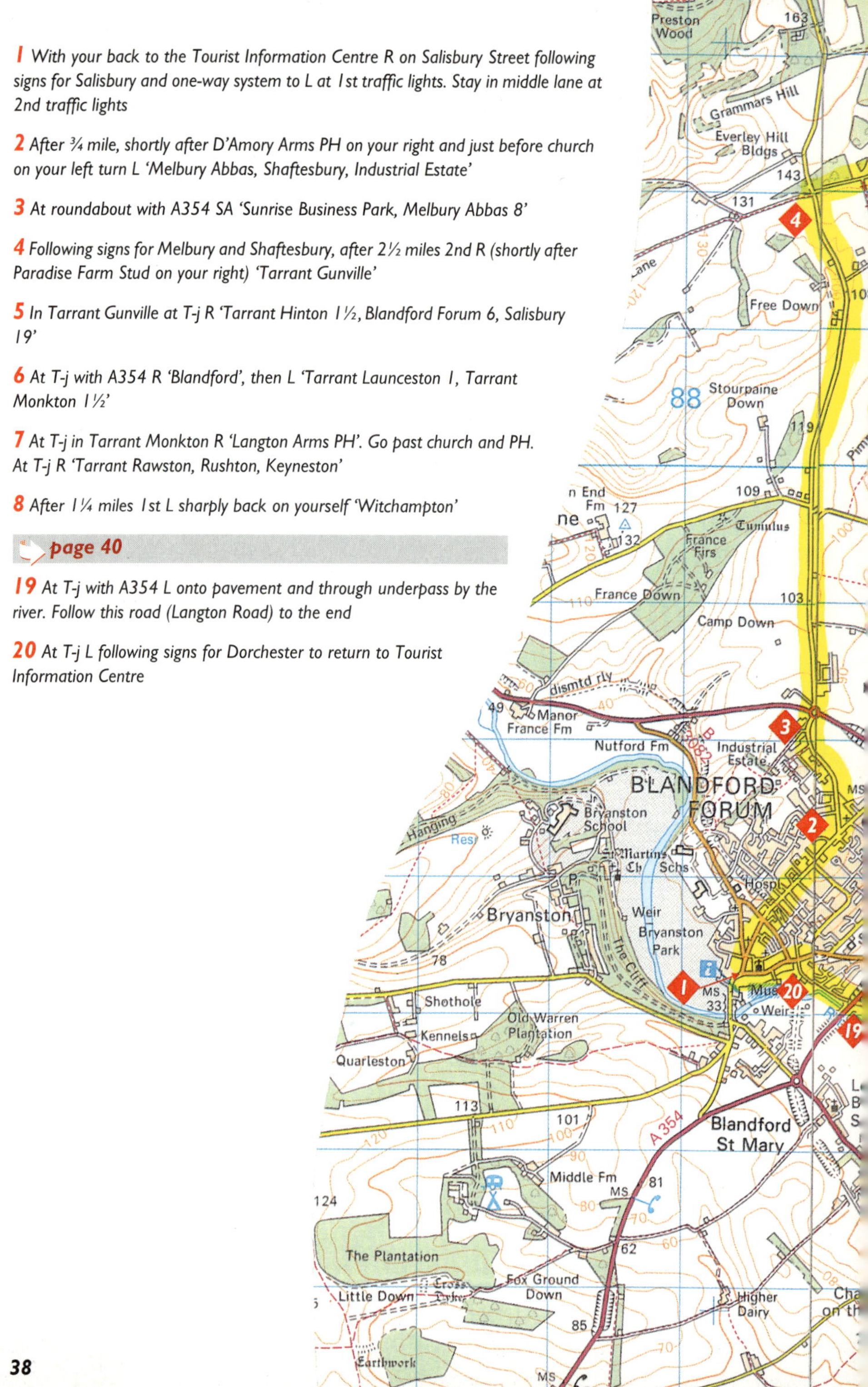

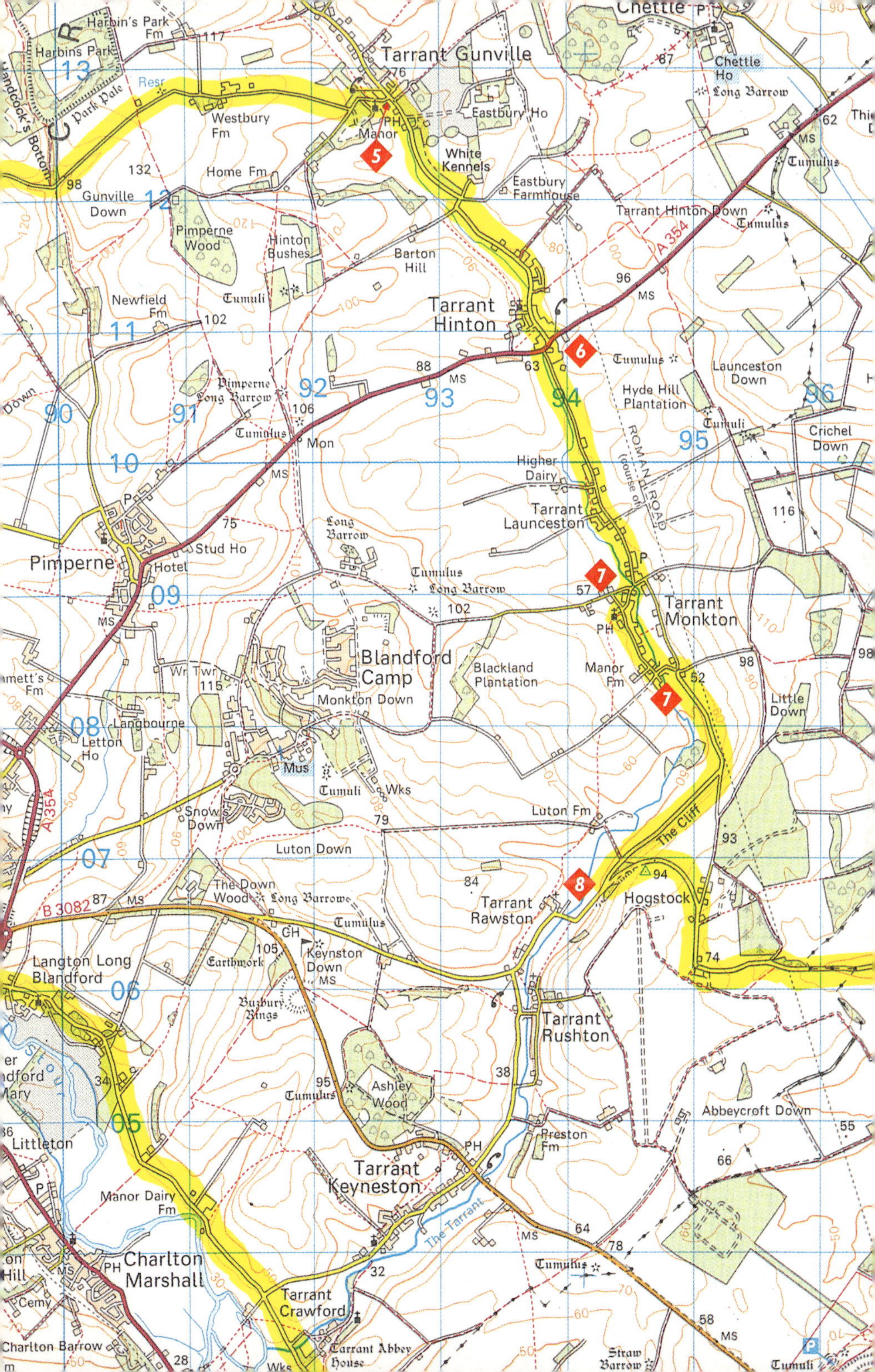

Harbin's Park Fm
Harbins Park
Chettle
Chettle Ho
Long Barrow
Tarrant Gunville
Westbury Fm
Manor
PH
Eastbury Ho
White Kennels
Eastbury Farmhouse
Home Fm
Gunville Down
Pimperne Wood
Hinton Bushes
Barton Hill
Tarrant Hinton Down
Tumulus
A 354
Newfield Fm
Tumuli
Tarrant Hinton
Tumulus
Launceston Down
Hyde Hill Plantation
Pimperne Long Barrow
Tumulus
Mon
Tumuli
Crichel Down
Higher Dairy
ROMAN ROAD (course of)
Tarrant Launceston
Pimperne
Hotel
Stud Ho
Long Barrow
Tumulus
Long Barrow
Tarrant Monkton
Blandford Camp
Blackland Plantation
Manor Fm
Monkton Down
Little Down
Wr Twr
Langbourne
Letton Ho
Mus
Tumuli
Wks
Snow's Down
Luton Fm
The Cliff
Luton Down
The Down Wood
Long Barrow
Tarrant Rawston
Hogstock
B 3082
Tumulus
Earthwork
Keynston Down
Langton Long Blandford
Buzbury Rings
Tarrant Rushton
Abbeycroft Down
Ashley Wood
Tumulus
Littleton
Preston Fm
Tarrant Keyneston
Manor Dairy Fm
The Tarrant
Charlton Marshall
Tumulus
Tarrant Crawford
Tarrant Abbey House
Charlton Barrow
Straw Barrow
Tumuli
Cemy
5
6
7
7
8

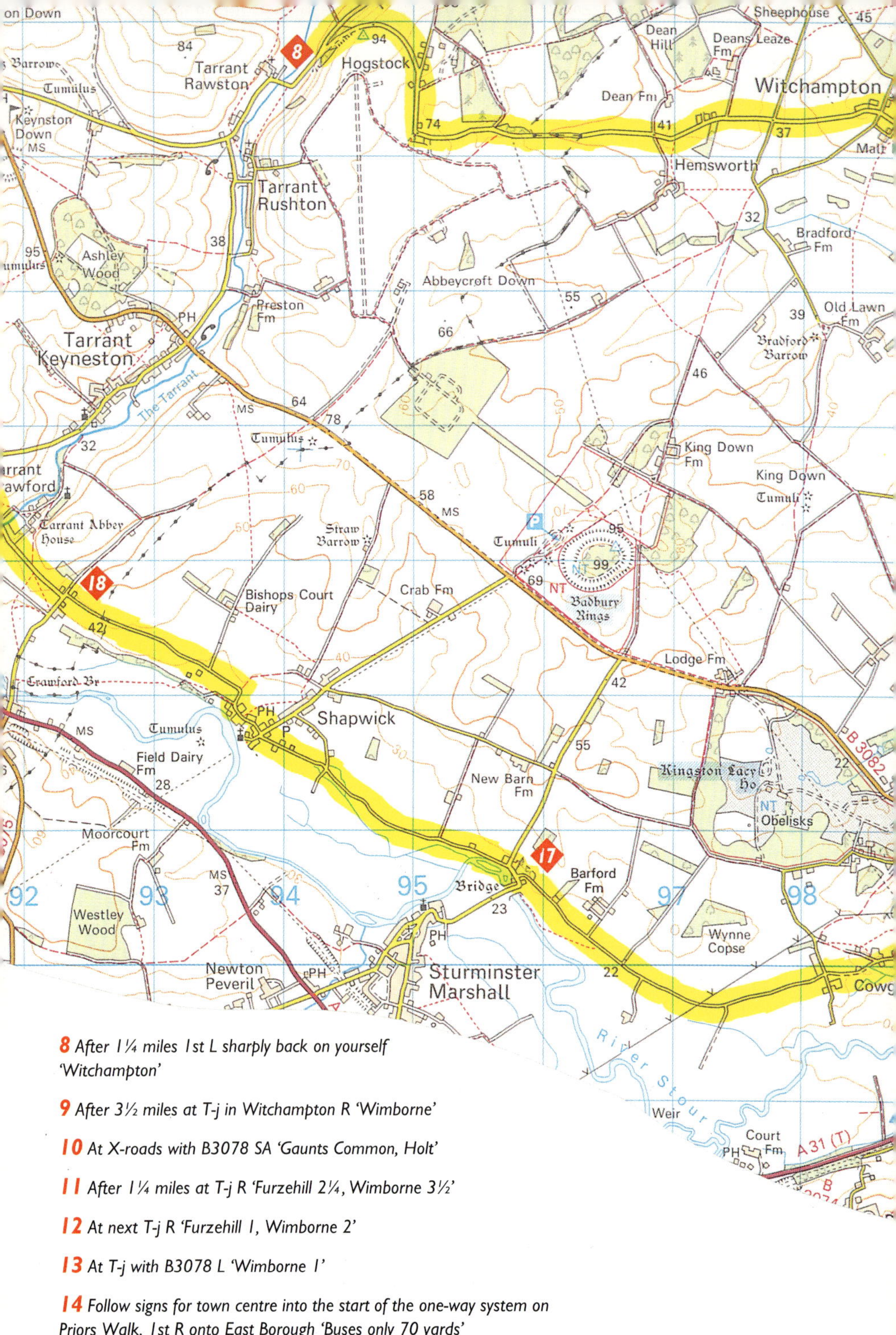

8 *After 1¼ miles 1st L sharply back on yourself 'Witchampton'*

9 *After 3½ miles at T-j in Witchampton R 'Wimborne'*

10 *At X-roads with B3078 SA 'Gaunts Common, Holt'*

11 *After 1¼ miles at T-j R 'Furzehill 2¼, Wimborne 3½'*

12 *At next T-j R 'Furzehill 1, Wimborne 2'*

13 *At T-j with B3078 L 'Wimborne 1'*

14 *Follow signs for town centre into the start of the one-way system on Priors Walk. 1st R onto East Borough 'Buses only 70 yards'*

15 In the square, L onto High Street. At T-j R onto King Street, following signs for Blandford B3082 over roundabout by Pudding and Pye PH

16 After 400 yards, opposite the cemetery L on Cowgrove Road

17 After 3 miles, at T-j R 'Shapwick, Crawford', then L (NS)

18 1½ miles after passing Anchor Inn in Shapwick 1st R by memorial cross 'Blandford Forum'

page 38

5 Southwest from Dorchester to Abbotsbury and along the top of the Downs

Dorchester is a bustling county town with plenty of interest, but it is nevertheless very easy to escape from into the countryside. The ride takes you south out of town along the southern edge of the imposing earthworks of Maiden Castle and through the delightful stone-and-thatch hamlet of Friar Waddon, and enters Abbotsbury the back way via the Swannery. Abbotsbury offers many excuses for stopping, both visual and gastronomic. You will need plenty of energy to get up the hill out of Abbotsbury. Depending on the season, the road may be busy but the views out to sea justify the climb. All the height is lost on a lovely long descent into Swyre and down to cross the River Bride. The longest climb now starts and will take you up to the top of Eggardon Hill. You could, of course, break your journey at the Spyway Inn. From the trig point at the top a long gentle descent of several miles, with views to both sides, drops you close to the A35. This very busy road is avoided by heading north to Muckleford and following the Frome Valley back into Dorchester.

46 47 44 45

Start

The roundabout at the west end of High Street West, Dorchester

Parking: Follow signs

Distance and grade

32 miles

Moderate/strenuous

Terrain

Out of the Frome Valley, over the hills and along the coast, down into the valley of the River Bride, up and over the hills to drop into the Frome Valley again. Three major climbs: 250 feet south of Winterborne Monkton, 600 feet from Abbotsbury west to the Fort, 750 feet between Swyre and Eggardon Hill

Nearest railway

Dorchester

Dorchester
Winterborne Monkton
Coryates
Rodden
Abbotsbury
fort

Places of interest

Dorchester (1)

Originally an important Roman town, Dorchester has some interesting remains although much was destroyed in a fire in 1613. A 4th-century town house has been excavated and the Roman layout of the town influenced the modern street plan. The Monmouth Rebellion and the Tolpuddle Martyrs were also connected with Dorchester, the notorious trial of the participants in the former took place in the Antelope Hotel and the latter were condemned to transportation in the Shire Hall further along the High Street. Thomas Hardy brought fame to Dorchester as the setting of many of his novels (calling it Casterbridge) and the streets of Georgian and Victorian houses are easily recognizable from his books. He was born in a village nearby and worked as an apprentice architect in the town; the Dorset County Museum contains much about him.

Refreshments

Elm Tree PH, just off the route, Langton Herring
Ilchester Arms PH, Abbotsbury
Bull Inn PH, Swyre
The Spyway PH, Askerwell

Abbotsbury (10)

An ancient Benedictine monastery stood here but only a 12th-century wall and a large 15th-century tithe barn remain. The Church of St Nicholas has bullet marks from the Civil War. Nearby, the Abbotsbury Gardens occupy a sheltered spot, free from frost, which has an almost sub-tropical climate. The plants grown, especially the trees, are appropriate to the unusual climate and there is a great variety of flowers. A swannery lies to the south of the village and was established by the monks in the late 14th century to provide food for the monastery and the village; it is now the home of over 500 swans as well as wild geese, ducks and other water birds.

Nine Stones, Winterbourne Abbas (19)

Slightly off the route, this ancient stone circle is the most important in the area.

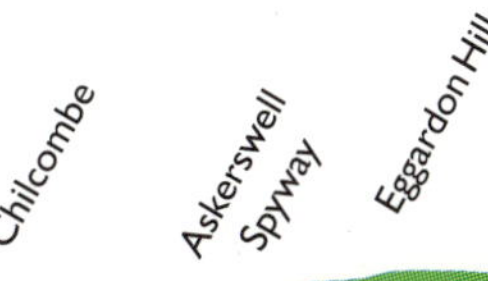

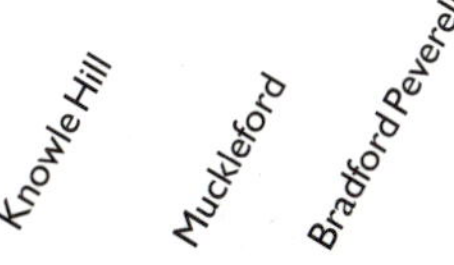

Compton Valence
Tout Hill
Muckleford
New Littlewood Fm
Town Hill Fm
Hogtleaze Fm
Roman Road
Roman Road Dairy
Kingston Russell Fm
Black Down
Bank Barrows
Cross Dyke
The Broad Stone
Winterbourne Abbas
Nine Stones
Inn
North Hill
Knowle Hill
Higher Skipp Fm
Bradford Down
Lambert's Hill
Long Barrow
Longlands
Whatcombe Down
Pitcombe
Littlebredy
Bridehead
Old Warren
Foxholes Fm
Hut Circle
Tenants Hill
White Hill
Sheep Down
Loscombe Fm
Strip Lynchets
Winterbourne Steepleton
Rew
Rew Manor
Rew Hill
Martinstow
Grove Hill
Pen Barn Fm
Littlebredy Fm
Enclosure
Crow Hill
Valley of Stones
Black Down
Hardy Monument
NT
Goldcombe Fm
Shorn Hill
Bronkham Hill
Great Hill
Corton Down
The Grey Mare & her Colts Long Barrow
Portesham Hill
Hell Stone
Stone Circle
White Hill
Dorset Coast Path
Abbotsbury Plains
Bench
Portesham Fm
Waddon House
Cemy
Portesham
Waddon
Coryates
Corton Farm
Friar Waddon
dismantled railway
Marsh Fm
Clover
Goose Hill
B 3157
St Peter's Abbey
Abbey Barn
Nunnery Grove
Elworth
Rodden Barn Fm
Linton Hill
Shilvinghampton
Clayhanger Fm
Merry Hill
Rodden House
Rodden
Abbotsbury Swannery
Chesters Hill
Wyke
Hewish
18
19
20
10
9
8
7

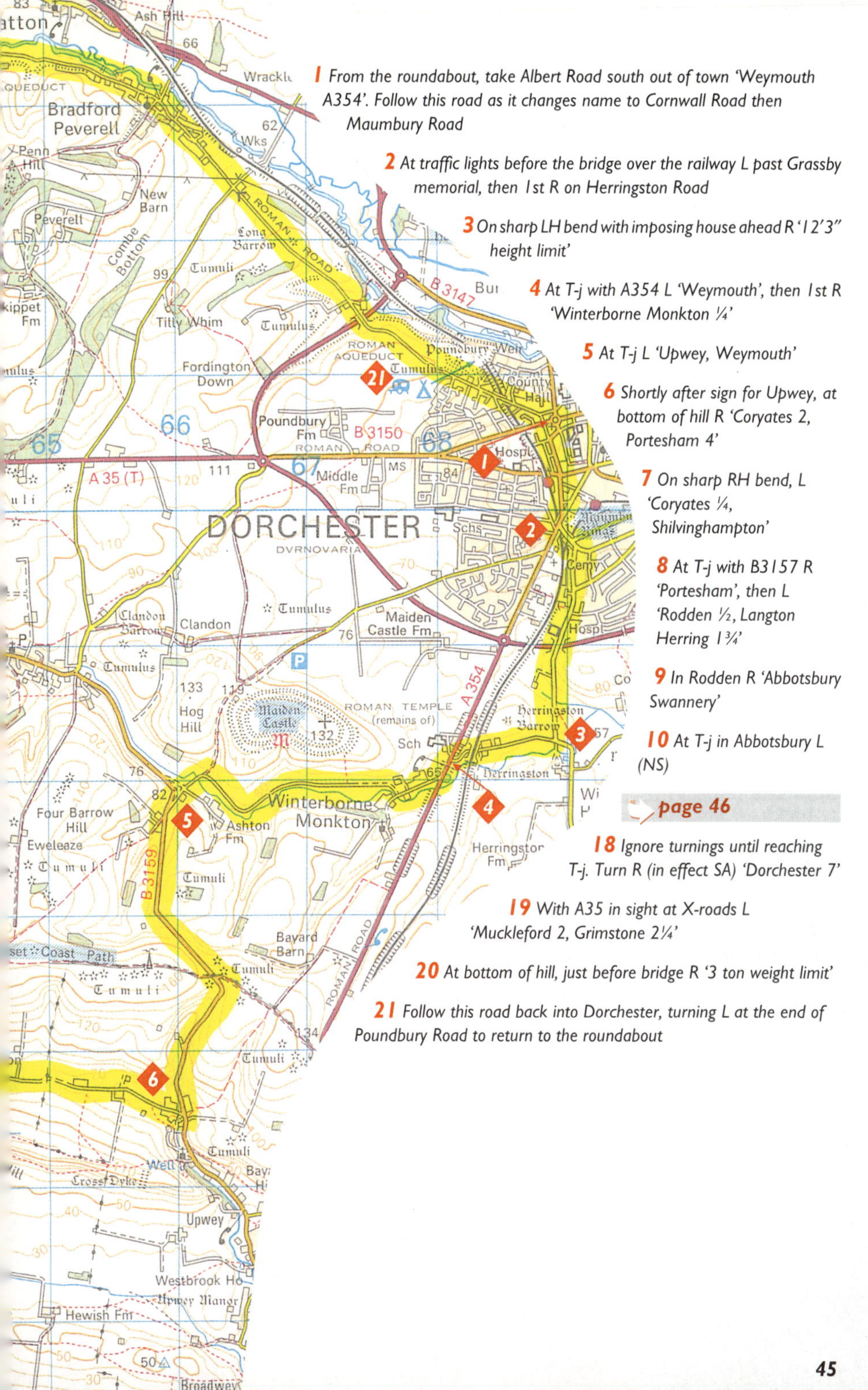

1 From the roundabout, take Albert Road south out of town 'Weymouth A354'. Follow this road as it changes name to Cornwall Road then Maumbury Road

2 At traffic lights before the bridge over the railway L past Grassby memorial, then 1st R on Herringston Road

3 On sharp LH bend with imposing house ahead R '12'3" height limit'

4 At T-j with A354 L 'Weymouth', then 1st R 'Winterborne Monkton ¼'

5 At T-j L 'Upwey, Weymouth'

6 Shortly after sign for Upwey, at bottom of hill R 'Coryates 2, Portesham 4'

7 On sharp RH bend, L 'Coryates ¼, Shilvinghampton'

8 At T-j with B3157 R 'Portesham', then L 'Rodden ½, Langton Herring 1¾'

9 In Rodden R 'Abbotsbury Swannery'

10 At T-j in Abbotsbury L (NS)

page 46

18 Ignore turnings until reaching T-j. Turn R (in effect SA) 'Dorchester 7'

19 With A35 in sight at X-roads L 'Muckleford 2, Grimstone 2¼'

20 At bottom of hill, just before bridge R '3 ton weight limit'

21 Follow this road back into Dorchester, turning L at the end of Poundbury Road to return to the roundabout

10 *At T-j in Abbotsbury L (NS)*

11 *Follow the B3157 uphill out of Abbotsbury (at times busy) for 3½ miles. Just past the Bull Inn in Swyre R opposite stone cross 'Puncknowle ¾, Litton Cheney 3'*

12 *On sharp RH bend just before Puncknowle L 'Litton Cheney 2½, Dorchester 11'*

13 *At X-roads SA (NS)*

14 *At A35 R then L 'Askerwell 1½'*

15 *In Askerwell bear L downhill to a junction of roads by stream. SA, passing a cottage with a thatched porch on your right*

16 *At T-j R (NS) (Spyway Inn to your left)*

17 *Shortly after trig point R at X-roads 'Dorchester 10'*

18 *Ignore turnings until reaching T-j. Turn R (in effect SA) 'Dorchester 7'*

page 45

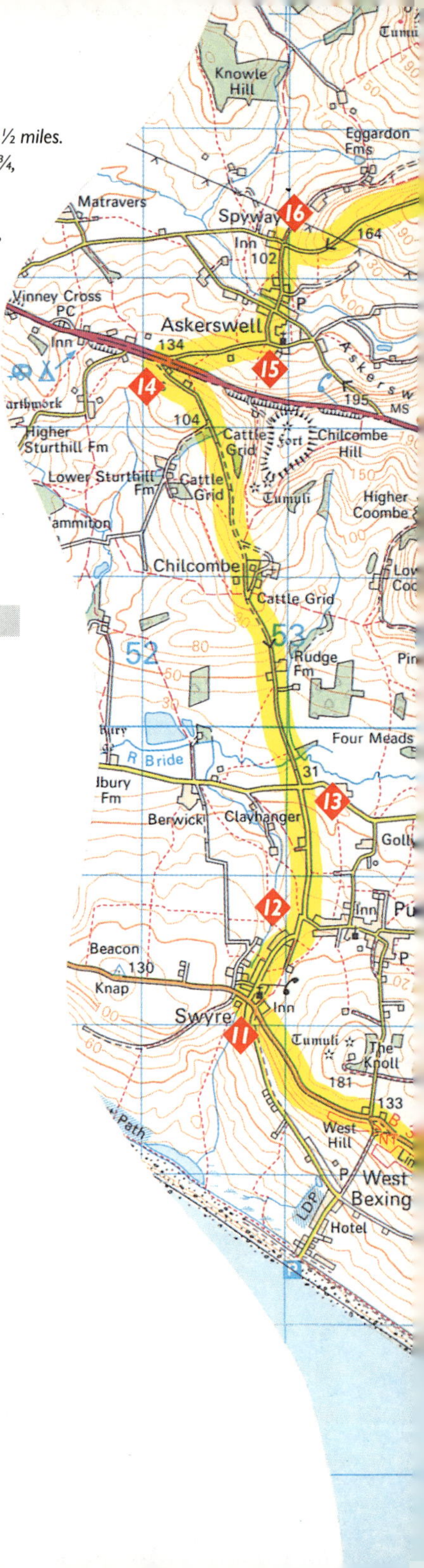

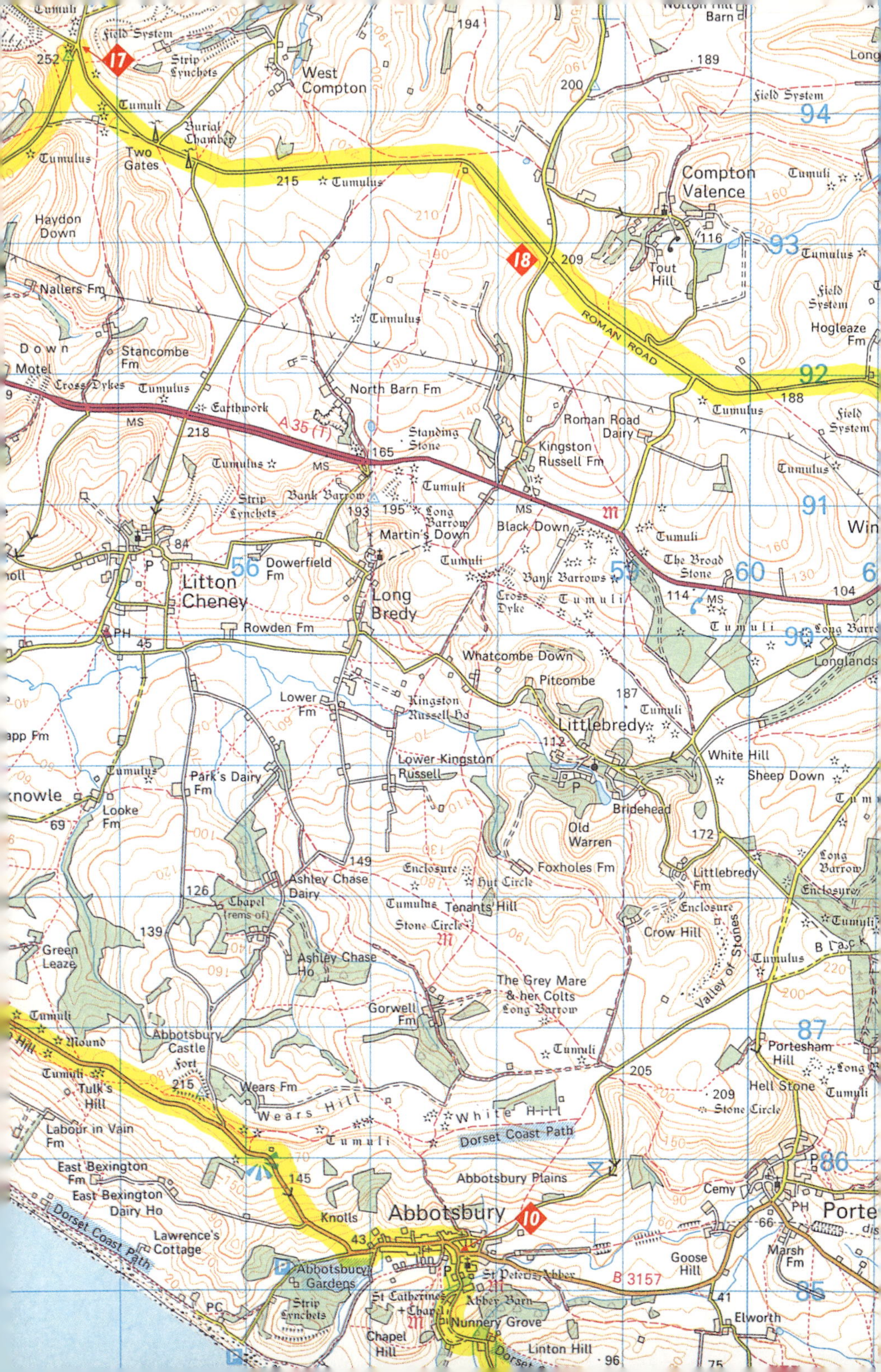

West Compton
Field System
Strip Lynchets
Tumuli
Burial Chamber
Two Gates
Tumulus
215
Haydon Down
Nallers Fm
Stancombe Fm
Motel
Cross Dykes
Earthwork
A 35 (T)
North Barn Fm
Standing Stone
165
Bank Barrow
Strip Lynchets
193
195
Long Barrow
Martin's Down
Litton Cheney
Dowerfield Fm
Long Bredy
Rowden Fm
45
84
Compton Valence
Tout Hill
116
Roman Road
209
Roman Road Dairy
Kingston Russell Fm
Black Down
Bank Barrows
Cross Dyke
The Broad Stone
Tumuli
104
Long Barrow
Longlands
Hogleaze Fm
Field System
188
Whatcombe Down
Pitcombe
187
Littlebredy
Lower Fm
Kingston Russell Ho
Lower Kingston Russell
White Hill
Sheep Down
Bridehead
Old Warren
Looke Fm
Park's Dairy Fm
69
149
Enclosure
Hut Circle
Foxholes Fm
172
Littlebredy Fm
Ashley Chase Dairy
126
Chapel (rems of)
139
Tenants' Hill
Stone Circle
Crow Hill
Valley of Stones
Green Leaze
Ashley Chase Ho
The Grey Mare & her Colts Long Barrow
Gorwell Fm
Portesham Hill
Hell Stone
Abbotsbury Castle
Fort
Mound
Tulk's Hill
Wears Fm
Wears Hill
White Hill
205
209
Stone Circle
Labour in Vain Fm
Dorset Coast Path
East Bexington Fm
East Bexington Dairy Ho
145
Abbotsbury Plains
Knolls
Abbotsbury
Lawrence's Cottage
Abbotsbury Gardens
Strip Lynchets
St Catherine's Chapel
Chapel Hill
St Peter's Abbey
Abbey Barn
Nunnery Grove
Linton Hill
B 3157
Goose Hill
Cerny
Marsh Fm
Elworth
Porte

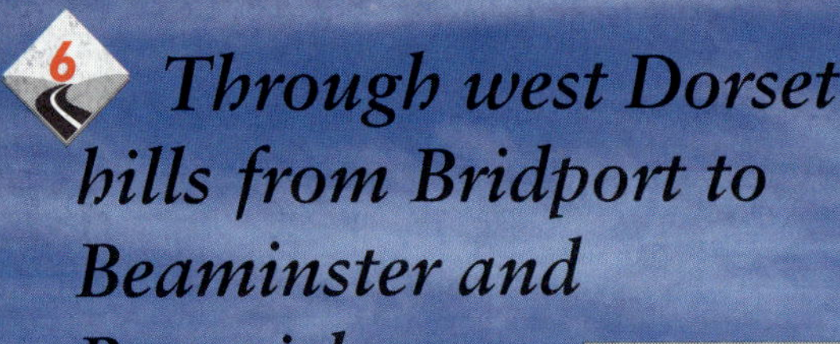

6 Through west Dorset hills from Bridport to Beaminster and Rampisham

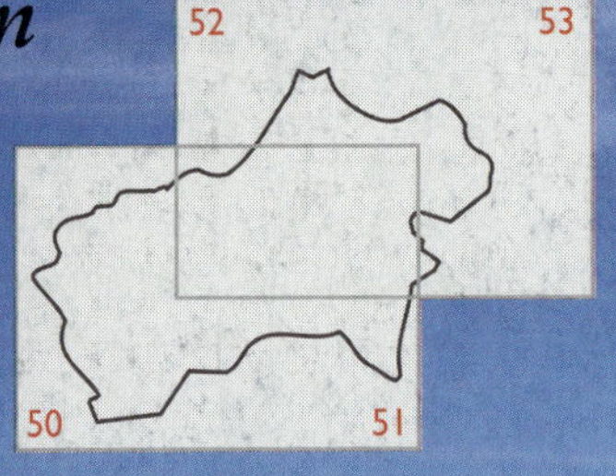

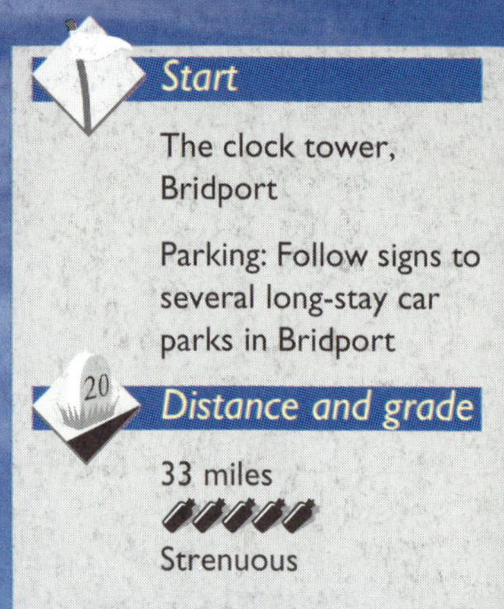

A challenging ride through the beautiful crumpled green landscape of west Dorset.

Background picture: Dorset landscape near Bridport

With a never-ending supply of hills this is not a route for the faint-hearted. However, the quiet lanes and magnificent views, the charm of villages such as Stoke Abbott and Powerstock and the variety of watering holes in Beaminster make it a thoroughly satisfying tour. The climb from Beaminster is the toughest described in this book, so be aware of this on your second helping of chocolate fudge cake. Perhaps you will prefer to walk. The views from the ridge above Corscombe are worth the climb, but the best is still to come: the stretch of road along the north side of Eggardon Hill must be one of the most beautiful in all of southern England.

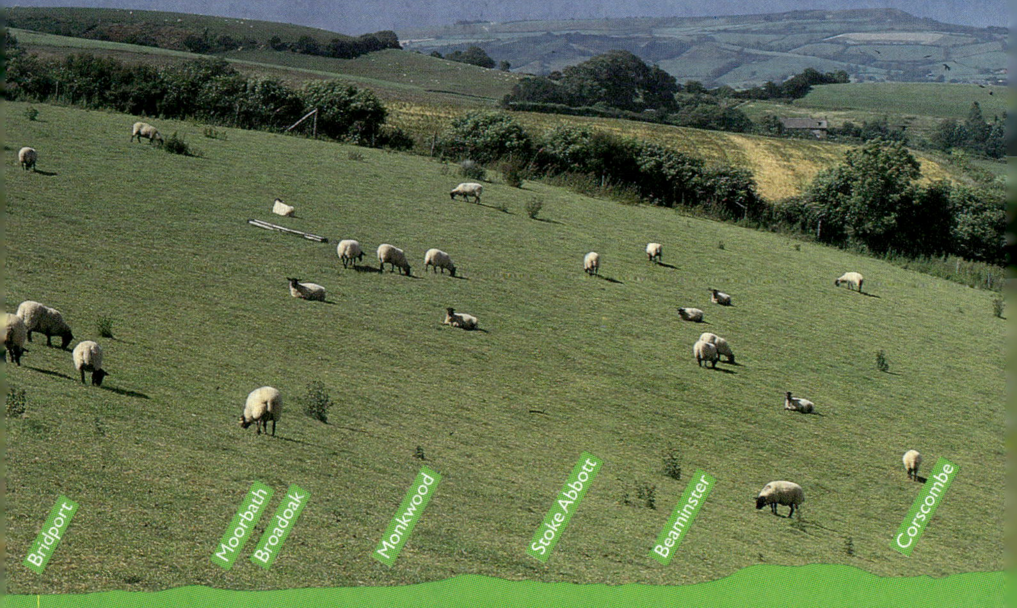

Bridport
Moorbath
Broadoak
Monkwood
Stoke Abbott
Beaminster
Corscombe

Terrain

Over 2500 feet of climbing, with three major hills: 400 feet to the ridge west of Stoke Abbott, 600 feet from Beaminster northeast towards Corscombe and 450 feet from Toller Porcorum to Eggardon Hill

Nearest railway

Crewkerne, 6 miles north of Beaminster

Refreshments

George PH, Bridport
Ilchester Arms PH, Symondsbury
New Inn, Stoke Abbott
Robins Bakery tea shop, Beaminster
Fox Inn, Corscombe
Talbot Inn, Benville
Swan Inn, Toller Porcorum
Three Horseshoes PH, Powerstock
Marqius of Lorne PH, Nettlecombe

nville
Uphall
Rampisham
Toller Porcorum
Bradford Peverell
Eggardon Hill
Powerstock
West Milton
Mangerton
Bradpole

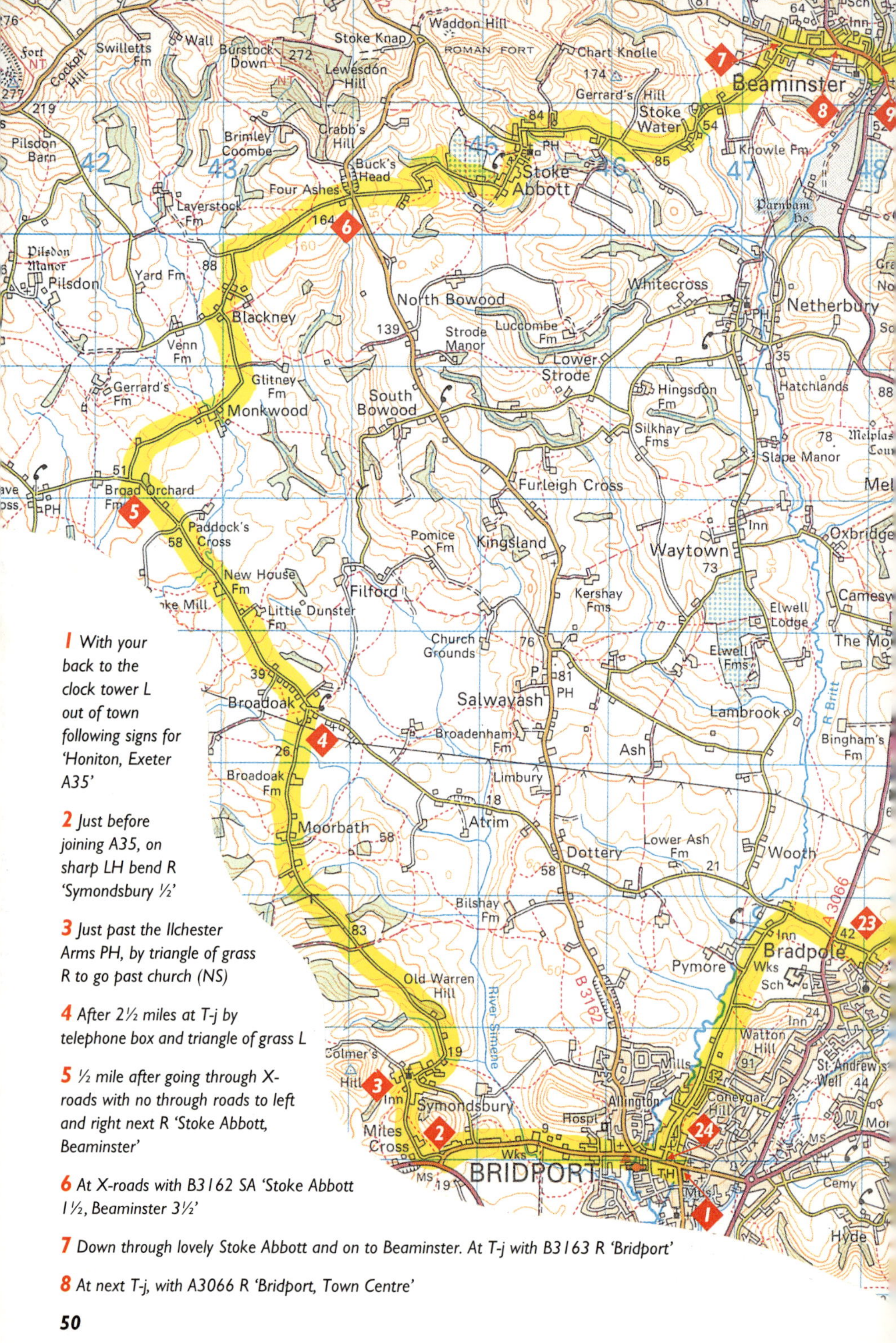

1 With your back to the clock tower L out of town following signs for 'Honiton, Exeter A35'

2 Just before joining A35, on sharp LH bend R 'Symondsbury ½'

3 Just past the Ilchester Arms PH, by triangle of grass R to go past church (NS)

4 After 2½ miles at T-j by telephone box and triangle of grass L

5 ½ mile after going through X-roads with no through roads to left and right next R 'Stoke Abbott, Beaminster'

6 At X-roads with B3162 SA 'Stoke Abbott 1½, Beaminster 3½'

7 Down through lovely Stoke Abbott and on to Beaminster. At T-j with B3163 R 'Bridport'

8 At next T-j, with A3066 R 'Bridport, Town Centre'

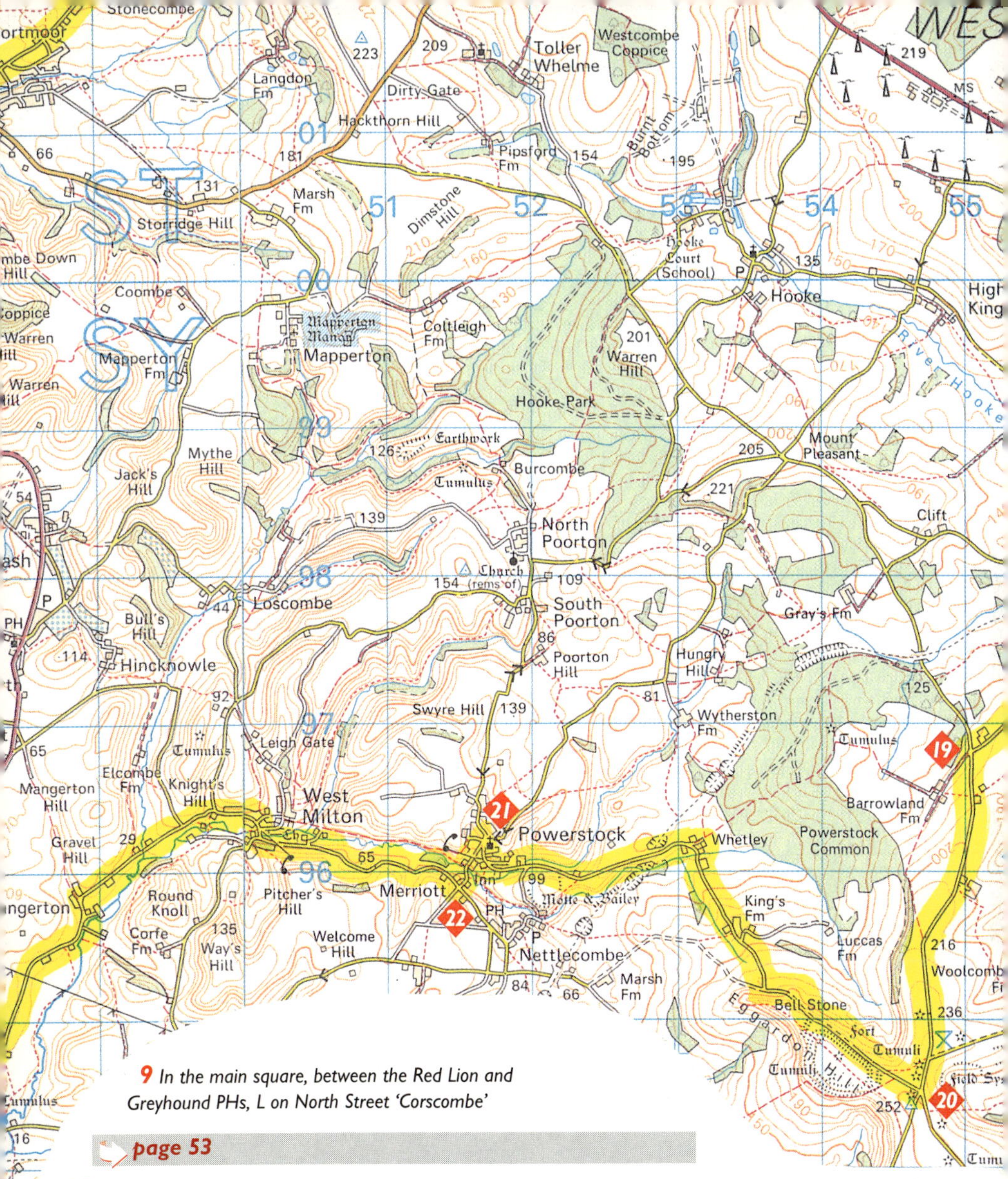

9 In the main square, between the Red Lion and Greyhound PHs, L on North Street 'Corscombe'

page 53

19 At X-roads L 'Askerwell 3¼, Bridport 7¼'

20 At X-roads at top of hill R 'Powerstock, West Milton' (It is worth continuing SA for 200 yards, past the trig point, for good views out to sea. At these X-roads the ride touches the Dorchester to Abbotsbury ride should you wish to link the two and go beyond the merely challenging to the fiercesomely tough)

21 Fantastic views and descent. At X-roads in Powerstock L 'West Milton, Bridport'

22 At T-j R 'West Milton, Bridport'

23 Follow signs for Bridport. At X-roads with A356 SA 'Pymore ¼, Dottery 1½', then 1st L (NS)

24 At T-j in Bridport L to return to clock tower

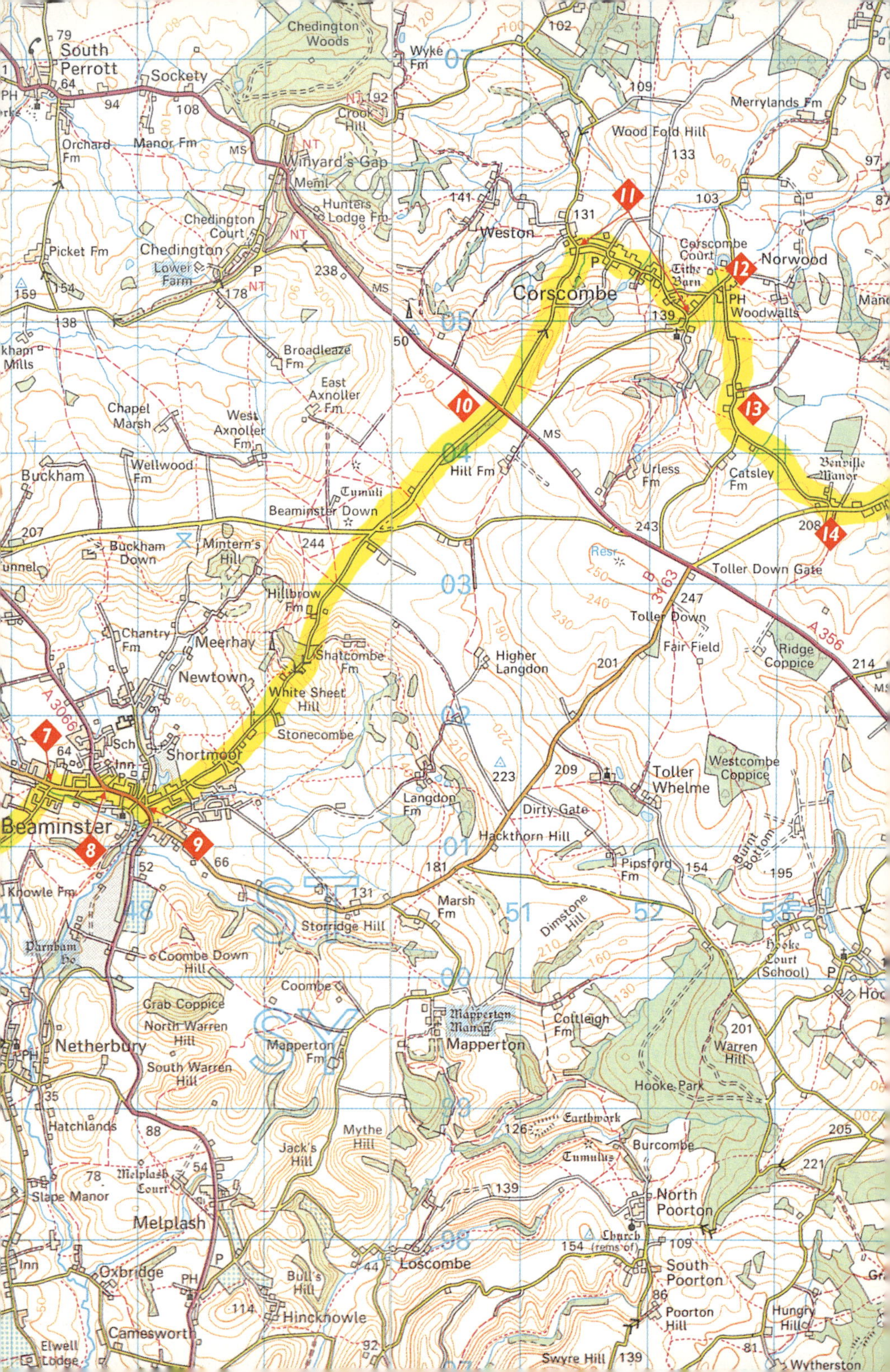

South Perrott
Sockety
Chedington Woods
Wyke Fm
Crook Hill
Orchard Fm
Manor Fm
Winyard's Gap
Meml
Hunters Lodge Fm
Chedington Court
Chedington
Lower Farm
Picket Fm
Weston
Corscombe
Corscombe Court
Tithe Barn
Norwood
Woodwalls
Wood Fold Hill
Merrylands Fm
Broadleaze Fm
East Axnoller Fm
West Axnoller Fm
Chapel Marsh
Wellwood Fm
Buckham
Hill Fm
Urless Fm
Catsley Fm
Benville Manor
Tumuli
Beaminster Down
Buckham Down
Mintern's Hill
Toller Down Gate
Toller Down
Fair Field
Ridge Coppice
Hillbrow Fm
Chantry Fm
Meerhay
Newtown
Shatcombe Fm
Higher Langdon
White Sheet Hill
Stonecombe
Shortmoor
Beaminster
Langdon Fm
Toller Whelme
Westcombe Coppice
Dirty Gate
Hackthorn Hill
Pipsford Fm
Burnt Bottom
Knowle Fm
Storridge Hill
Marsh Fm
Dimstone Hill
Hooke Court (School)
Parnham Ho
Coombe Down Hill
Coombe
Crab Coppice
North Warren Hill
South Warren Hill
Mapperton Manor
Mapperton
Mapperton Fm
Coltleigh Fm
Warren Hill
Hooke Park
Netherbury
Hatchlands
Mythe Hill
Jack's Hill
Earthwork
Tumulus
Burcombe
Slape Manor
Melplash Court
Melplash
North Poorton
Church (rems of)
South Poorton
Poorton Hill
Oxbridge
Bull's Hill
Loscombe
Hinckhowle
Camesworth
Elwell Lodge
Hungry Hill
Swyre Hill
Wytherston
A 356
A 3066
B 3163

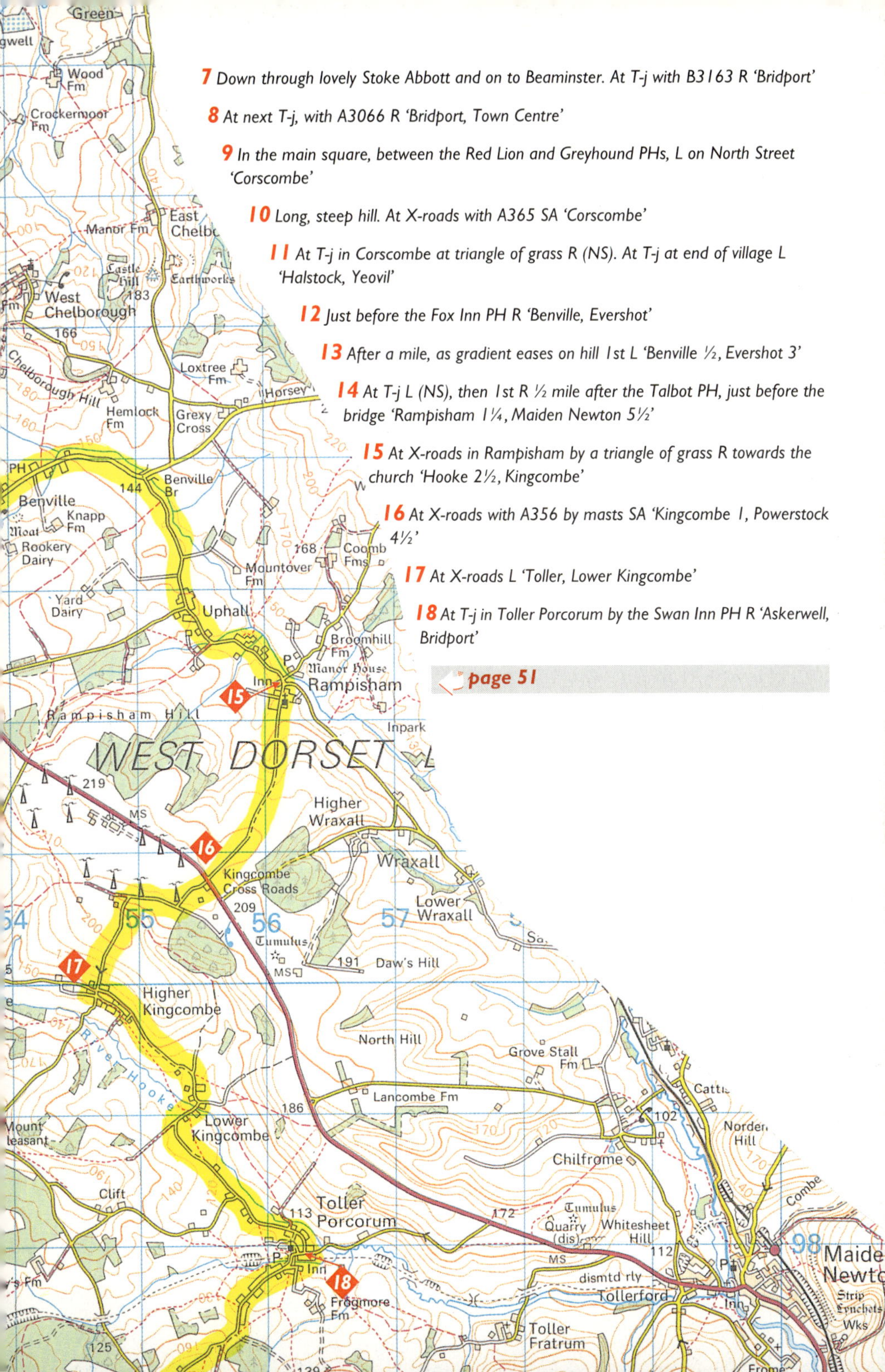

7 Down through lovely Stoke Abbott and on to Beaminster. At T-j with B3163 R 'Bridport'

8 At next T-j, with A3066 R 'Bridport, Town Centre'

9 In the main square, between the Red Lion and Greyhound PHs, L on North Street 'Corscombe'

10 Long, steep hill. At X-roads with A365 SA 'Corscombe'

11 At T-j in Corscombe at triangle of grass R (NS). At T-j at end of village L 'Halstock, Yeovil'

12 Just before the Fox Inn PH R 'Benville, Evershot'

13 After a mile, as gradient eases on hill 1st L 'Benville ½, Evershot 3'

14 At T-j L (NS), then 1st R ½ mile after the Talbot PH, just before the bridge 'Rampisham 1¼, Maiden Newton 5½'

15 At X-roads in Rampisham by a triangle of grass R towards the church 'Hooke 2½, Kingcombe'

16 At X-roads with A356 by masts SA 'Kingcombe 1, Powerstock 4½'

17 At X-roads L 'Toller, Lower Kingcombe'

18 At T-j in Toller Porcorum by the Swan Inn PH R 'Askerwell, Bridport'

page 51

7 Northwest from Whitchurch over the North Hampshire Downs

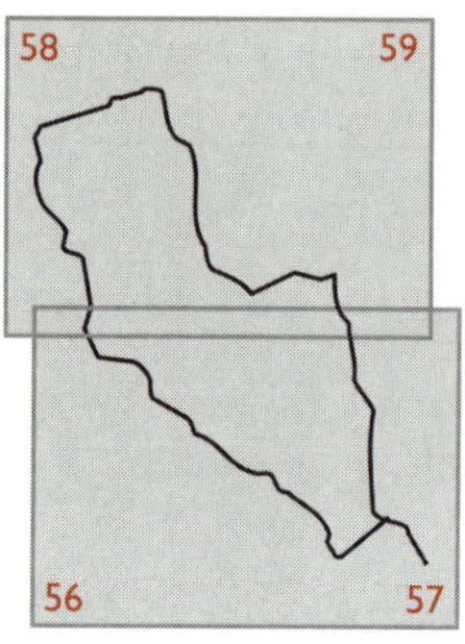

The ride passes several lovely villages of thatched stone-built houses, notably St Mary Bourne, Stoke and Hurstbourne Tarrant. Climbing gently on quiet lanes you reach the edge of the Downs at Ham Hill, with splendid views north into the valley formed by the River Kennett. After meandering through the lanes below the scarp face, the return requires some leg power to climb 500 feet back onto the top. Views once again open up, and you can look forward to a fabulous, gentle descent from Crux Easton.

Start

The roundabout in the centre of Whitchurch

Parking: Follow signs from centre of Whitchurch to two long-term car parks

Distance and grade

33 miles

 Easy/moderate

Terrain

A gentle climb of 500 feet over 12 miles takes you from St Mary Bourne up the valley formed by the Bourne Rivulet onto the Downs. The ride drops off, then climbs back onto the escarpment. A third climb from Faccombe to the A343 leaves you with a long gentle descent almost to Whitchurch

Nearest railway

Whitchurch

Whitchurch

St Mary Bourne

Hurstbourne Tarrant

Littledown

Ham

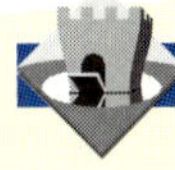

Places of interest

Hurstbourne Tarrant (4)

A pretty village with thatched cottages overlooking a stream and a church. The old farmhouse, Rookery Farm, is associated with two interesting characters: Joseph Blount and William Cobbett (the author of 'Rural Rides'). The latter left his initials and the date 1825 on the garden wall; this wall is known as 'Wayfarers' Table' because Blount would leave food out for the agricultural labourers. The artist Anna Lee Merritt lived in the village in the early 20th century and her studio stands in one of the gardens.

Combe (12)

Slightly off the route near Walbury Hill, Combe comprises a few cottages, a manor and a 12th- to 13th-century church containing what is thought to be a Saxon font (the stand is 14th-century). On the summit of Combe Hill is Combe Gibbet where George Broomham and Dorothy Newman were hanged in 1676 for murdering two of their children. The gibbet is now maintained by a local farmer. Walbury Hill, the highest hill in the area, is the site of a large prehistoric camp and there are fantastic views over the region.

Refreshments

George PH, Coronation Arms PH, St Mary Bourne
White Hart PH, Stoke
George and Dragon PH, Hurstbourne Tarrant
Crown Inn, Upton *George PH,* Vernham Dean
Crown & Anchor PH, Ham
Swan Inn, Inkpen *Jack Russell PH,* Faccombe
The Plough PH, Ashmansworth

Upper Green
Walbury Hill
Combe Hill
Faccombe
Ashmansworth
Woodcott
Egbury

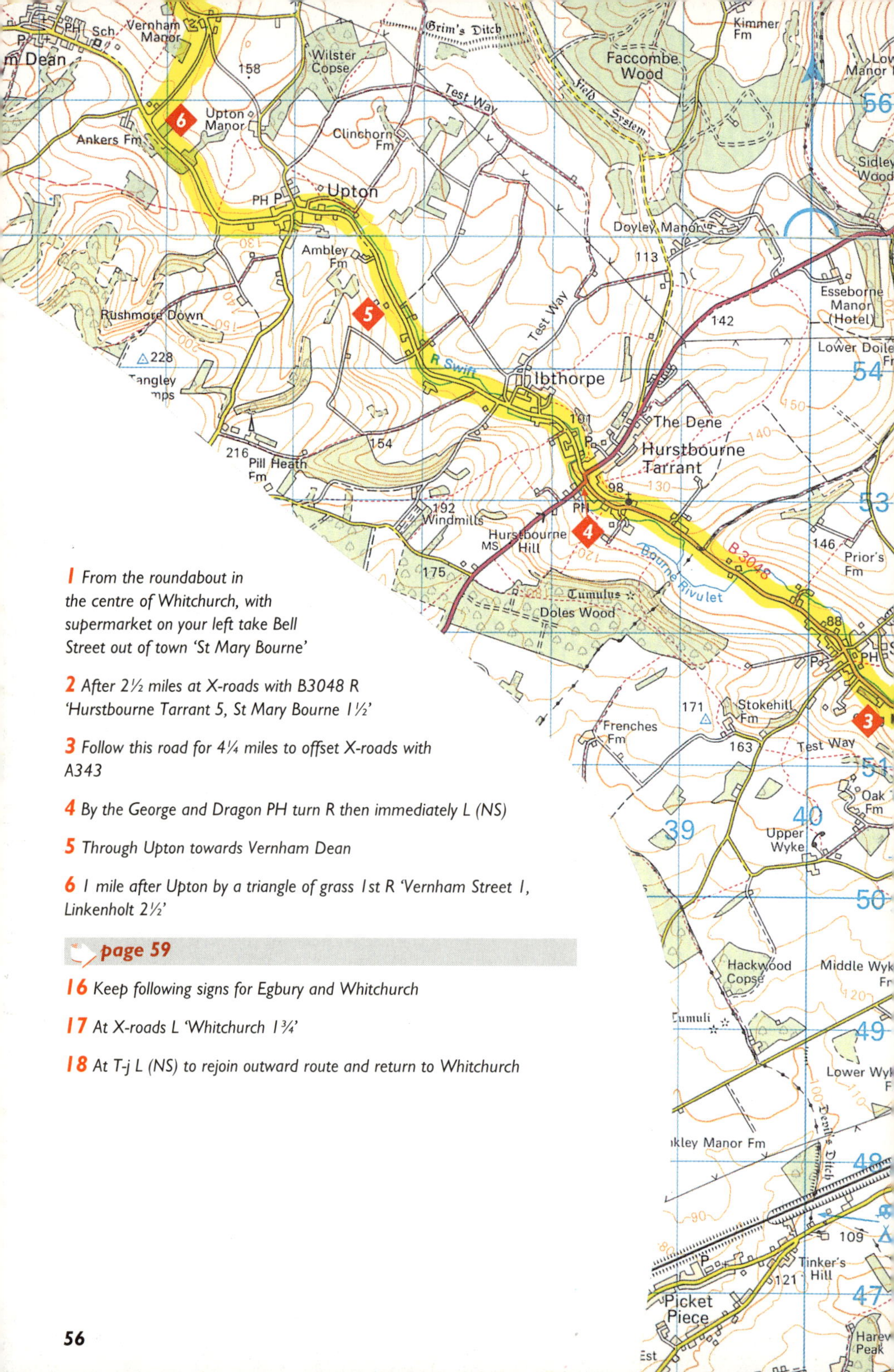

1 *From the roundabout in the centre of Whitchurch, with supermarket on your left take Bell Street out of town 'St Mary Bourne'*

2 *After 2½ miles at X-roads with B3048 R 'Hurstbourne Tarrant 5, St Mary Bourne 1½'*

3 *Follow this road for 4¼ miles to offset X-roads with A343*

4 *By the George and Dragon PH turn R then immediately L (NS)*

5 *Through Upton towards Vernham Dean*

6 *1 mile after Upton by a triangle of grass 1st R 'Vernham Street 1, Linkenholt 2½'*

page 59

16 *Keep following signs for Egbury and Whitchurch*

17 *At X-roads L 'Whitchurch 1¾'*

18 *At T-j L (NS) to rejoin outward route and return to Whitchurch*

Alexander Fm
Crux Easton
Mopper's Barn
Tumulus
Upper Woodcott Down
Down Fm
Great Litchfield Down
Beech Hanger Copse
Hook Copse
Lower Woodcott Down
Seven Barrows
Field System
Lye Fm
Easton Park Wood
Long Barrow
Woodcott
Lower Woodcott Fm
Earthwork
Woodcott Ho
Sladen Green
Highfield Ho
Paul's Copse
Stubb's Copse
16
Buckets Down Fm
Litchfield
Dunley
Binley
PH
Wadwick
Bradley Hill
Angledown Copse
Tumulus
Slade Bottom Fm
Elm Fm
Egbury
Bradley Wood Fm
Bradley Wood
Clap Gate
Downhams Fm
Egbury
Egbury Castle Fm
Cole Henley Manor Fm
Wakeswood
Cold Harbour
Swampton
Jamaica Fm
Hogdigging Copse
Cole Henley
St Mary Bourne
Bourne Court
Inn
17
Down Fm
Derrydown Fm
Dirty Corner
18
New Barn Fm
Berehill Fm
Watercress Beds
Chapmansford Fm
2
Cowdown Copse
Wr Twr
The Mansion
Manor Fm
Cemy
Inn
Lynch Hill
The Gable
Apsley Fm
Statue
Hurstbourne Park
Mill
Whitchurch
1
Faulkner's Down Fm
Sch
The Common
Test Way
Tumulus
dismtd rly
Fox Cotts
Manor Ho
Tufton
Wks
MS

Wallingtons
Titcomb Manor
Anvilles
Moat
Balsdon Fm
Titcomb
Wergs Copse
Kintbury Cross Ways
Prosperous Home Fm
Totterdown Ho
Little Common
The Folly
Cemy
Forbury
Sadlers
Anville's Copse
Northcroft Fm
Foxs Hill
Holt Lodge
New Mill
Mount Prosperous
Lower Green
Sch
Inkpen
Hell Corner
Manor Fm
Inkpen Common
Earthwork
Lower Spray Fm
Upper Green
Trapshill
Kirby Ho
West Woodhay Ho
Wood
Park Ho
Manor Ho
Ham
Ham Spray Ho
Manor Fm
Long Barrow
Highwood Fm
Cumulus
Inkpen Hill
Combe Gibbet
West Woodhay Down
Ham Hill
Fort
Walbury Hill
Wright's Fm
Summer Hill
Town Fm
Test Way
Buttermere
Grange Fm
Combe
Lower Fm
Earthwork
Manor Fm
Combe Hill
Manor Fm
Bishop's Barn
Eastwick
Ballyack Ho
Buttermere Wood
Sheepless Hill
Moordown Fm
Rockmoor Down
Combe Wood
Hogs Hole
Upper Horns Fm
Field System
Hart Hill Down
Upper Row Fm
Winterside Fm
Manor Ho
Linkenholt
Faccombe
Littledown
Manor Fm
Netherton
Vernham Row
Box Fm
Vernham Street
Rymer's Barn
Vernham Bank
Vernham Manor
Grim's Ditch
Vernham Dean
Wilster Copse
Faccombe Wood
Test Way
Field System
Upton Manor
Clinchorn
1
2
3
4
5
6
7
8
9
10
11
12
13
33
34
35
36
37
38
39

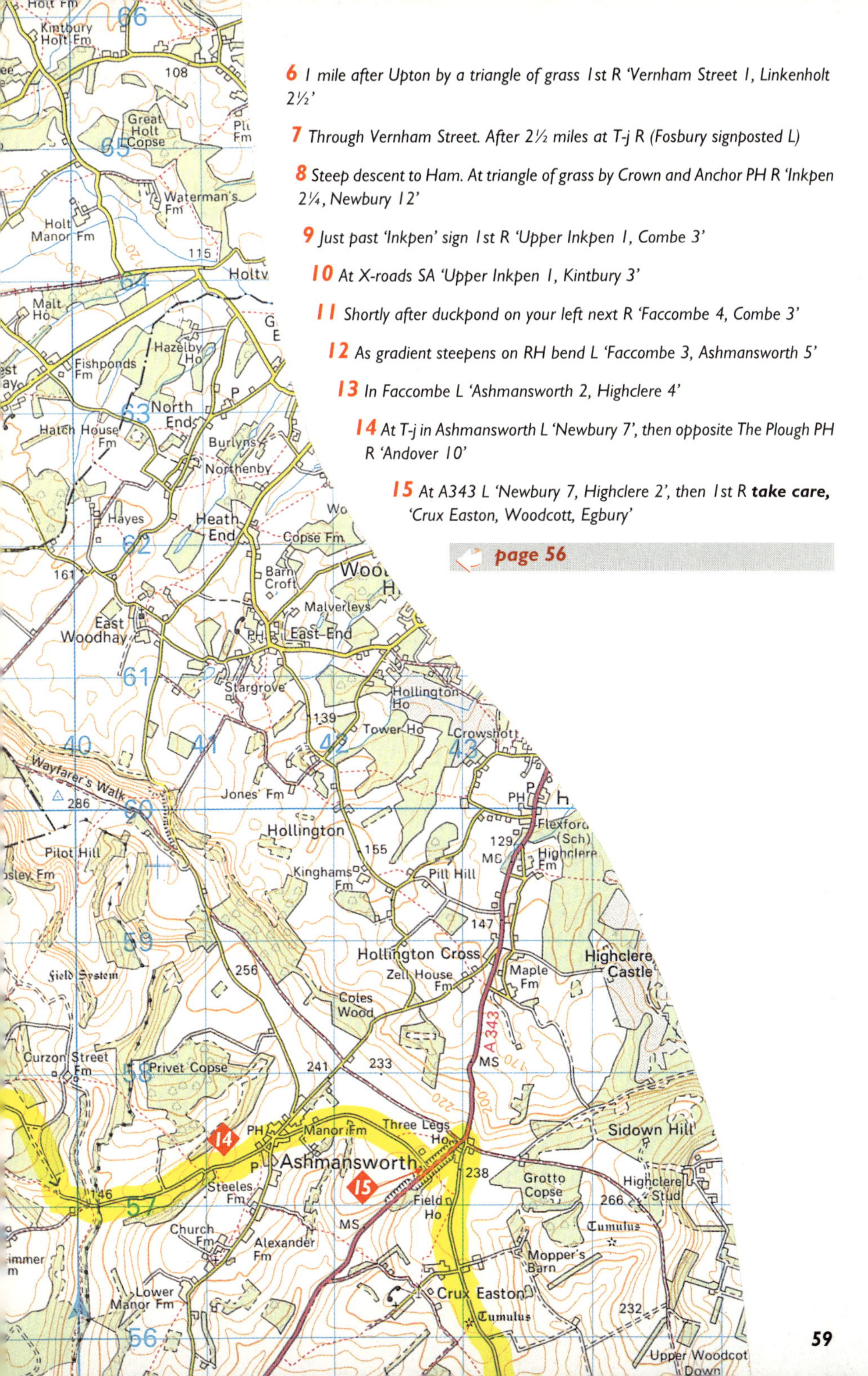

6 *1 mile after Upton by a triangle of grass 1st R 'Vernham Street 1, Linkenholt 2½'*

7 *Through Vernham Street. After 2½ miles at T-j R (Fosbury signposted L)*

8 *Steep descent to Ham. At triangle of grass by Crown and Anchor PH R 'Inkpen 2¼, Newbury 12'*

9 *Just past 'Inkpen' sign 1st R 'Upper Inkpen 1, Combe 3'*

10 *At X-roads SA 'Upper Inkpen 1, Kintbury 3'*

11 *Shortly after duckpond on your left next R 'Faccombe 4, Combe 3'*

12 *As gradient steepens on RH bend L 'Faccombe 3, Ashmansworth 5'*

13 *In Faccombe L 'Ashmansworth 2, Highclere 4'*

14 *At T-j in Ashmansworth L 'Newbury 7', then opposite The Plough PH R 'Andover 10'*

15 *At A343 L 'Newbury 7, Highclere 2', then 1st R **take care,** 'Crux Easton, Woodcott, Egbury'*

page 56

From Whitchurch to Kingsclere via Hampshire lanes and Watership Down

The ride heads southeast from Whitchurch through rolling farmland before dropping to the River Dever valley at Stoke Charity. From the beautiful village of Micheldever, the route heads north through Overton, crossing the River Test before climbing to Hannington, with its lovely green in front of the church. A descent into the delights of Kingsclere leaves you with a steep climb through woodland to the top of the Downs at Watership Down, about which Richard Adams wrote. From here, a gentle descent leads you back to Whitchurch.

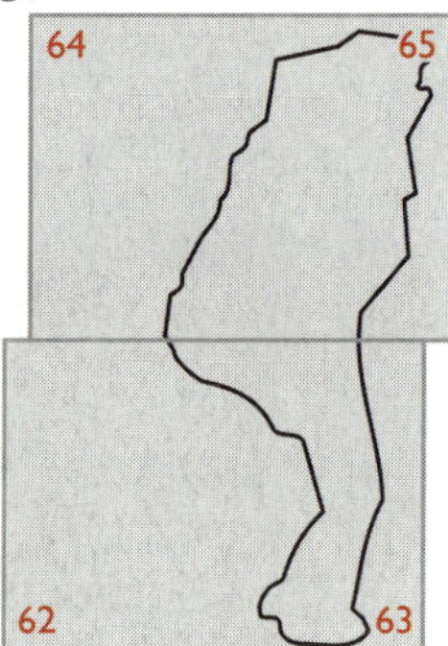

Start

The roundabout in the centre of Whitchurch

Parking: Follow signs from centre of Whitchurch to two long-term car parks

Distance and grade

36 miles

 Easy/moderate

Terrain

Undulating Hampshire downland with one gentle 400-foot climb from Overton to Hannington and a short steep one onto Watership Down, southwest of Kingsclere

Nearest railway

Whitchurch

Refreshments

Plenty of choice in Whitchurch
Greyhound PH, White Hart PH, Overton
Vine Inn, Hannington
George & Horn PH, Crown Inn, Kingsclere

Whitchurch
A303 (T)
Hunton
Micheldever
Ove

Hampshire countryside in spring

North Oakley
Hannington
Plantation Hill
Kingsclere
Watership Down
Cole Henley

1 *Leave Whitchurch on the Winchester Road 'Winchester'*

2 *Just after Harvest Home PH on your R, turn L on Micheldever Road*

3 *At T-j after 2 miles R 'Micheldever Station 3'*

4 *Go underneath A303. At T-j R 'Sutton Scotney 2½, Stockbridge 10½'*

5 *After 1 mile 1st L 'Hunton 2, Stoke Charity 2½'*

6 *In Hunton at T-j L 'Stoke Charity ½'*

7 *At X-roads L 'Micheldever 1¾'*

8 *At T-j in Micheldever L 'Micheldever Station, Overton'*

9 *At X-roads SA 'Overton 4½'*

page 64

Laverstoke Ho
Weir
Priory Fm
Freefolk
Laverstoke
B 3400
Whitchurch
The Gables
Turrill Hill Fm
Sapley Farm Ho
Burley Wood
Upper
Southfield Fm
Spring Pond Fm
Abra Barrow
White Hill
Resr
Lower Whitehill Cotts
Bramdown Copse
Knowle Hassock
New Barn Cotts
Laverstoke Grange Fm
Southley Fm
Upper Whitehill Fm
Pilgrim's Fm
Tunnel
New Barn Farm
Brickkiln Wood
Shooting Twr
Laverstoke Wood
Litchfield Grange
Tumuli
Roundwood Fm
Tufton Warren Fm
Freefolk Wood
Cobley Wood
Three Barrows
Field System
Popham Beacons
Tumuli
Landing Strip
Blind End Copse
Tunnels
Field System
Tumulus
Upper Norton Fm
Long Barrow
A 303
Kitelands
Warren Fm
Micheldever Station
Upper Cranbourne Fm
Northbrook Fm
Black W
Hunton Down Fm
Wks
Norton Manor
Hunton Grange Fm
Parkhill Fm
Cranbourne Grange
Moat
Norsebury Ring
Northbrook Ho
West Stratton
Tumuli
Wonston Grange
Hunton
Northbrook
Norsebury Ho
Cowdown Fm
Wonston
Stoke Charity
Weston Colley
Micheldever
Borough Fm
M3

10 *In Overton at traffic lights R, then 1st L 'Station, The Mill'*

11 *2nd R 'Hannington 3½'*

12 *At T-j L (NS)*

13 *Through Hannington. After 1½ miles, L 'Kingsclere Estates Ltd. Plantation Farm'*

14 *At T-j with busy A339 L (**take care**), then 1st L 'Kingsclere'*

15 *At T-j by the George and Horn PH L (NS)*

16 *At church L on Swan Street 'Overton, Whitchurch'*

17 *1st R 'Sydmonton 2½, Old Burghclere 3½', then L at T-j (same sign)*

18 *After 2 miles, at X-roads L 'Ashley Warren, Cole Henley, Whitchurch'*

19 *At T-j R 'Whitchurch 2'*

20 *At T-j with main road L to return to Whitchurch*

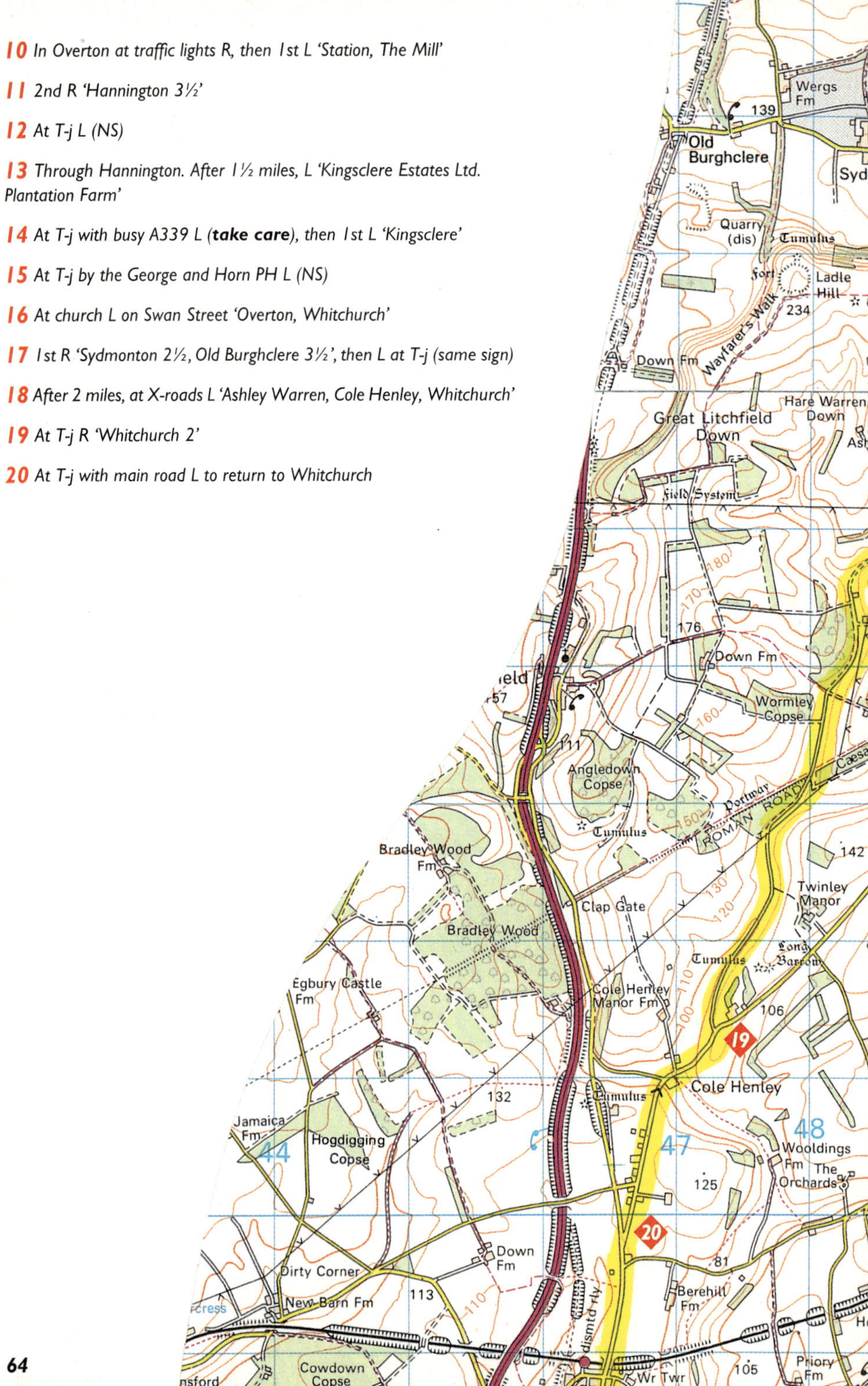

Nothing Hill
Kingsclere
Isle Hill
Bishop's Hill
Nuthanger Fm
Fossicks
Watership Down
Cannon Heath Down
White Hill
Cottington's Hill
Freemantle Park Fm
Park House Stables
Field Barn Fm
Gallops
Sandford Fm
The Old House
Plantation Fm
Plantation Hill
Portway
ROMAN ROAD (course of)
Tumulus
Tumuli
Hannington
Kennels
Walkeridge Fm
For Down
Cannon Heath Fm
Warren Fm
Hare Warren Fm
Polhampton Lodge Stud
Tidgrove Warren Fm
North Oakley
Warren Bottom Copse
Robley Belt
Belt
BASINGSTOKE AND DEANE DISTRICT
Freemantle Fm
Frost Hill Fm
Willesley Warren Fm
Ridgeway Fm
Long Barrow
Wayfarer's Walk
Frith Wood
Great Deane Wood
Little Deane Wood
Ashe Warren Ho
Deane Down Fm
New Barn
Mill
OVERTON STATION
Quidhampton
Polhampton Fm
Deane
Ashe
Foxdown
Court Fm
Sch
Wks
Lynch
Overton
Source of the River Test
Southington
Berrydown Fm
Berrydown Court
Wr Twr
Ashe Park
Cheesedown Fm
Church
Laverstoke Ho
Weir
Burley Wood
Sapley Farm
A 339(T)
B 3051
B 3400

9 Along the beautiful Test Valley from Stockbridge

The Test Valley is delightful cycling country, with easy flat lanes, lovely views of the river and a succession of attractive villages where each beautiful house seems to offer an even more dazzling display of flowers than the last. The route leaves Stockbridge southwards following the river valley as far as Mottisfont Abbey. Quiet lanes from here to Sparsholt pass through open farmland and woodland. The Test is rejoined at Wherwell and the section past Longstock House is one of the many highpoints of this ride.

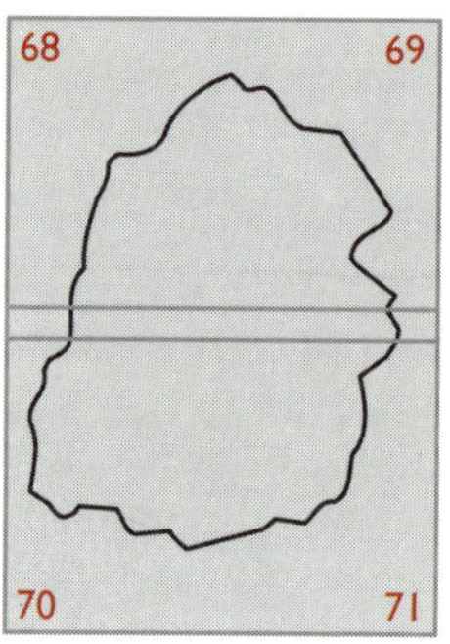

Start

Main Street, Stockbridge

Parking: As above

Distance and grade

31 miles

 Easy/moderate

Terrain

The Test Valley is flat and the countryside to the east is gentle. The highest point is to the south of Sparsholt, 400 feet higher than the River Test at Mottisfont, but none of the climbs is strenuous.

Nearest railway

Dunbridge, 1 mile from the route at Mottisfont or Winchester, 3 miles from the route at Sparsholt

Refreshments

The Boot Inn, Houghton
Morning coffee and teas at Mottisfont Post Office
Mottisfont Abbey Gardens, Mottisfont
Newport Inn, Braishfield
The Plough Inn, Sparsholt
Fox and Hounds PH, Crawley
White Lion PH, Wherwell
Peat Spade PH, Longstock

Stockbridge
Houghton
Mottisfont
Michelmersh
Braishfield
Standon

Places of interest

Stockbridge (1)

This small town is visited by those wishing to fish in the Test, an excellent game river. Interesting Victorian buildings include the Town Hall, the White Hart Inn and the Grosvenor Hotel; the oldest building is the 13th-century chancel of the old church.

Stockbridge

Houghton Lodge (1-2)

Lawns slope down to the willow-fringed river from this ornamental house. The gardens are fairly simple with beautiful snowdrops and daffodils in spring; the restored glasshouses contain vines and decorative plants.

Mottisfont Abbey (3)

Founded as an Augustinian Priory in the 12th century, the Abbey derives its name from the Saxon word 'moot' meaning council and the 'font' that wells up near the house. After the Dissolution, it was converted into a private house by Lord Sandys. It now belongs to the National Trust who created the rose gardens, for which Mottisfont is famous, within the walled kitchen garden. The house is surrounded by extensive parkland.

Crawley (11)

With timber-framed cottages and a duckpond, this village is very picturesque. The church has Norman features, the Court dates back to the 19th century and there is an interesting old pub.

Wherwell (14)

Another charming village full of timber-framed and thatched cottages, Wherwell is the site of an abbey established by Queen Elfrida, mother of Ethelred the Unready. The abbey was destroyed by the 'zeal or avarice of King Henry' and a 19th-century manor house, the Priory, now occupies the site. A few ruins remain within the grounds of the house and there are more relics inside the neighbouring Church of St Peter and Holy Cross.

Sparsholt Littleton Crawley A30 Wherwell Longstock

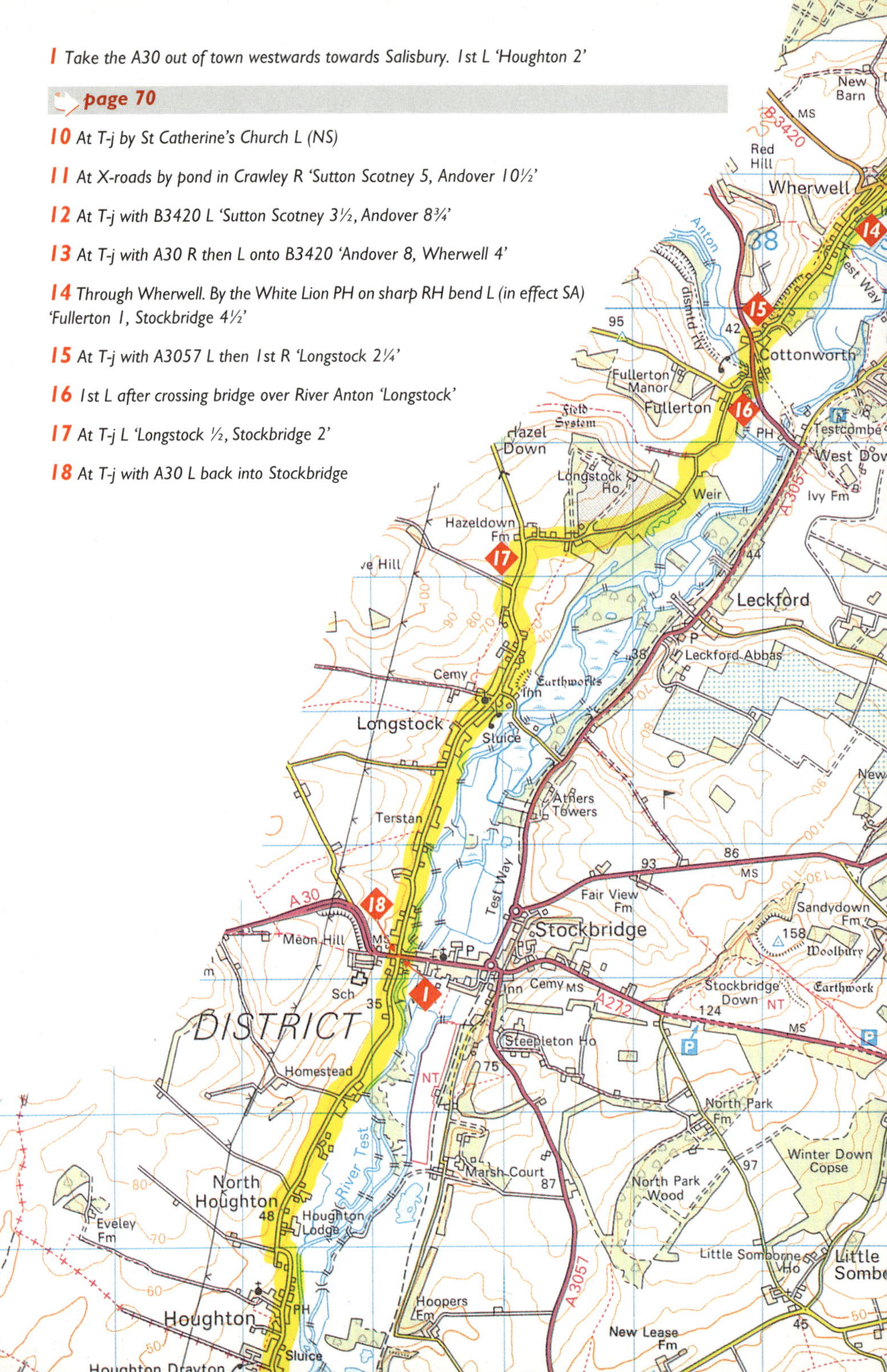

1 *Take the A30 out of town westwards towards Salisbury. 1st L 'Houghton 2'*

page 70

10 *At T-j by St Catherine's Church L (NS)*

11 *At X-roads by pond in Crawley R 'Sutton Scotney 5, Andover 10½'*

12 *At T-j with B3420 L 'Sutton Scotney 3½, Andover 8¾'*

13 *At T-j with A30 R then L onto B3420 'Andover 8, Wherwell 4'*

14 *Through Wherwell. By the White Lion PH on sharp RH bend L (in effect SA) 'Fullerton 1, Stockbridge 4½'*

15 *At T-j with A3057 L then 1st R 'Longstock 2¼'*

16 *1st L after crossing bridge over River Anton 'Longstock'*

17 *At T-j L 'Longstock ½, Stockbridge 2'*

18 *At T-j with A30 L back into Stockbridge*

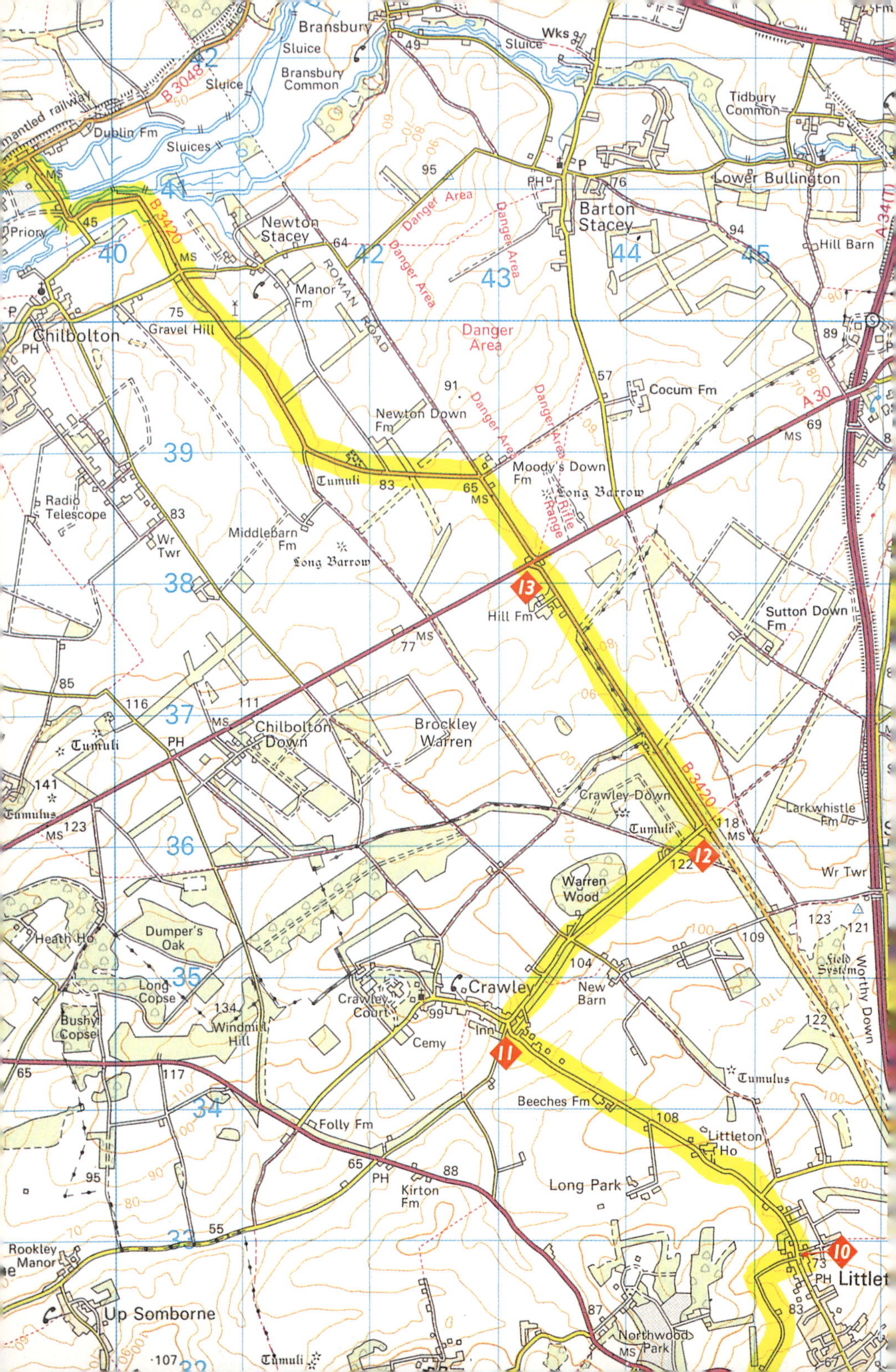

Bransbury
Sluice
Bransbury Common
Wks
Sluice
Tidbury Common
Dublin Fm
Sluices
B 3048
B 3420
Priory
Newton Stacey
Barton Stacey
Lower Bullington
Hill Barn
A 34(T)
Danger Area
ROMAN ROAD
Manor Fm
Gravel Hill
Chilbolton
Cocum Fm
A 30
Newton Down Fm
Moody's Down Fm
Long Barrow
Rifle Range
Tumuli
Radio Telescope
Wr Twr
Middlebarn Fm
Hill Fm
Sutton Down Fm
Chilbolton Down
Brockley Warren
Crawley Down
Larkwhistle Fm
Tumulus
Warren Wood
Heath Ho
Dumper's Oak
Long Copse
Bushy Copse
Windmill Hill
Crawley Court
Crawley
Inn
Cemy
New Barn
Field System
Worthy Down
Beeches Fm
Littleton Ho
Folly Fm
Kirton Fm
Long Park
Rookley Manor
Up Somborne
Northwood Park
Littlet
PH
MS
13
12
11
10

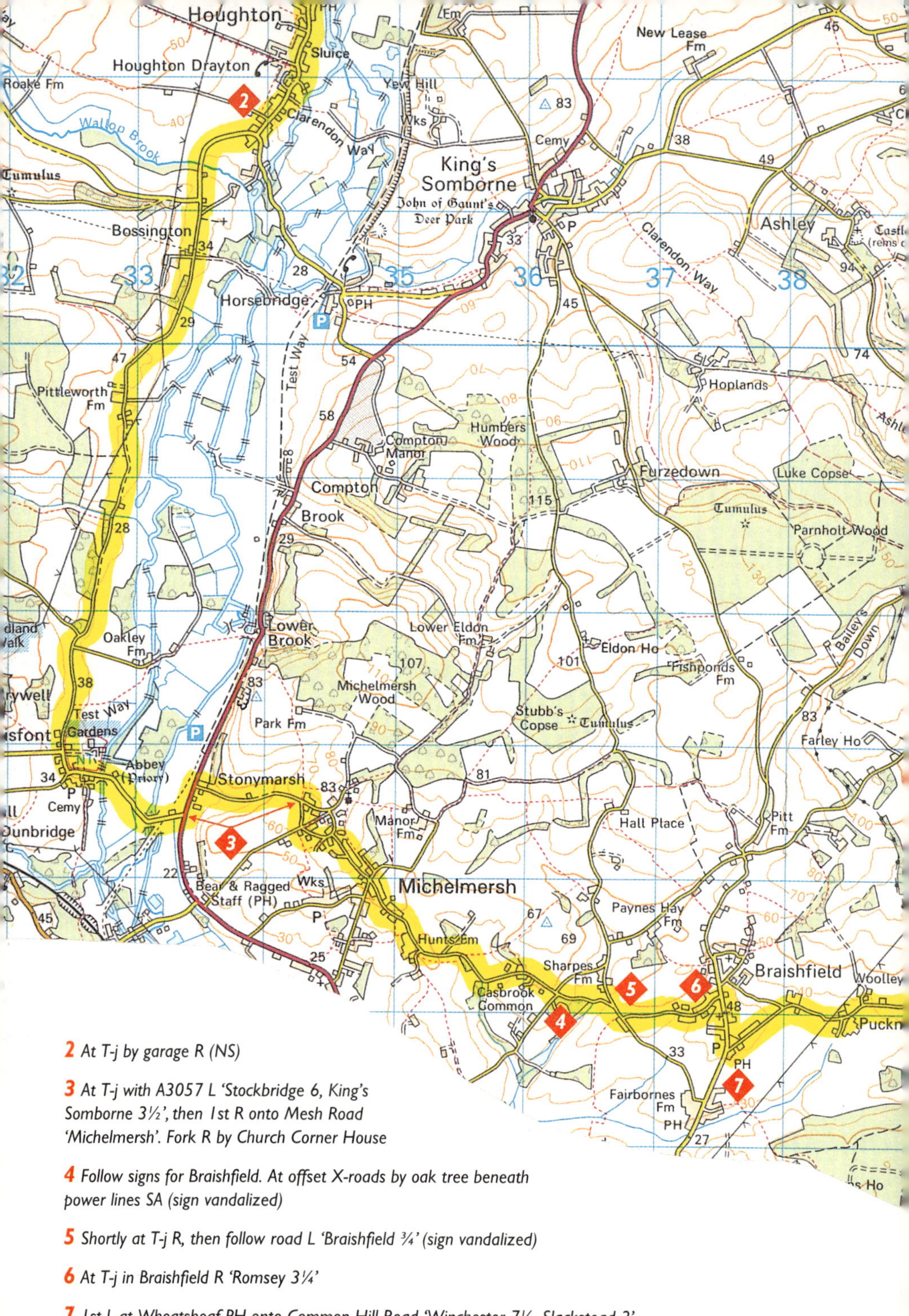

2 *At T-j by garage R (NS)*

3 *At T-j with A3057 L 'Stockbridge 6, King's Somborne 3½', then 1st R onto Mesh Road 'Michelmersh'. Fork R by Church Corner House*

4 *Follow signs for Braishfield. At offset X-roads by oak tree beneath power lines SA (sign vandalized)*

5 *Shortly at T-j R, then follow road L 'Braishfield ¾' (sign vandalized)*

6 *At T-j in Braishfield R 'Romsey 3¼'*

7 *1st L at Wheatsheaf PH onto Common Hill Road 'Winchester 7¼, Slackstead 2'*

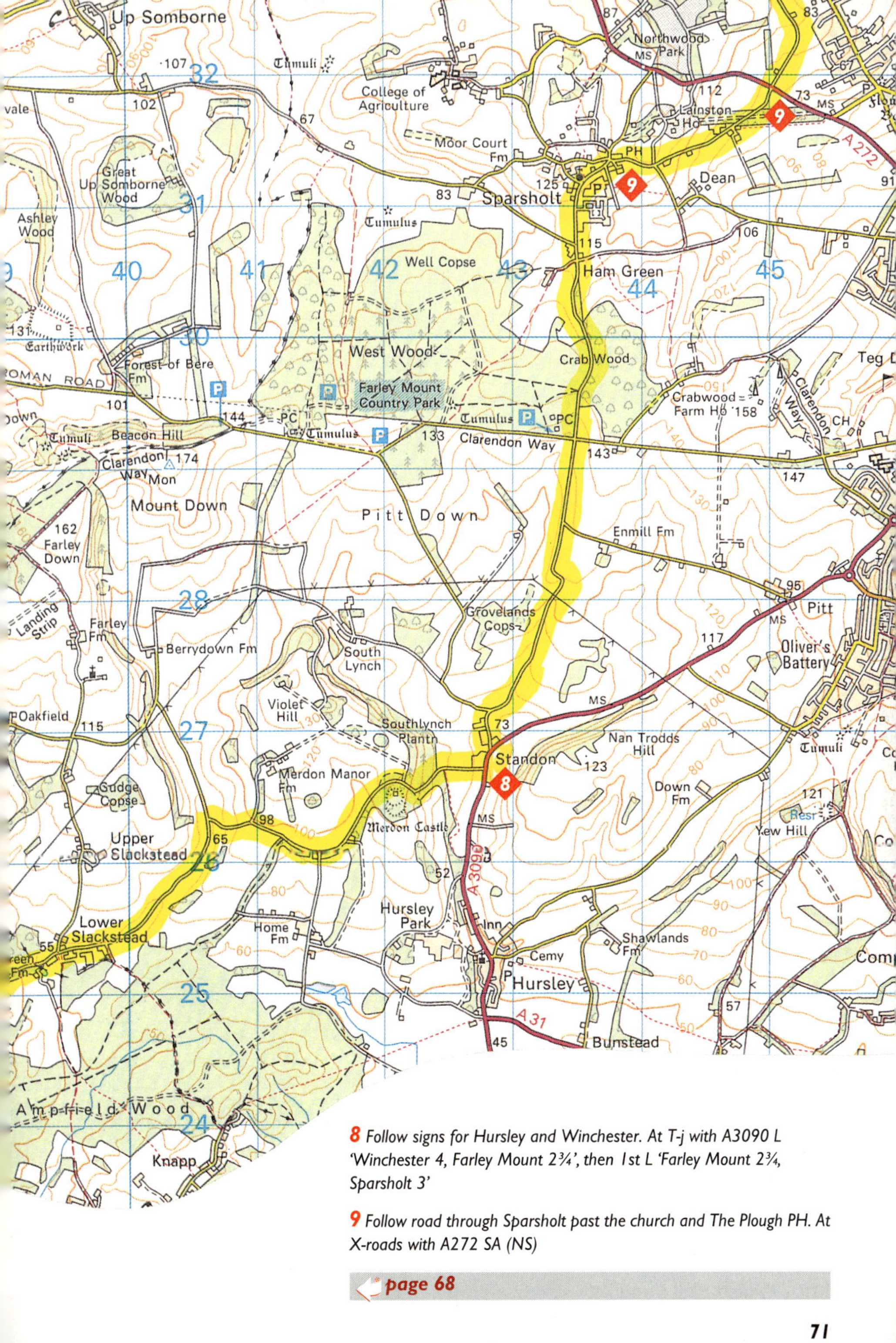

8 Follow signs for Hursley and Winchester. At T-j with A3090 L 'Winchester 4, Farley Mount 2¾', then 1st L 'Farley Mount 2¾, Sparsholt 3'

9 Follow road through Sparsholt past the church and The Plough PH. At X-roads with A272 SA (NS)

page 68

Rolling hills and woodland north from New Alresford to Odiham

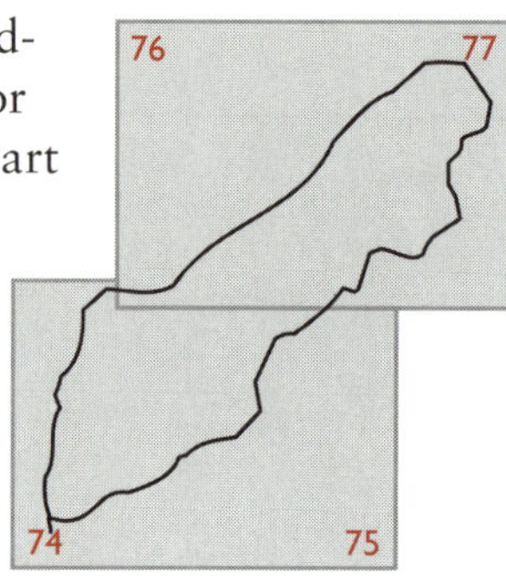

Gentle hills and woodlands are the setting for this ride in the very heart of Hampshire. New Alresford is an attractive small town with fine wide avenues and plenty in the way of refreshment. The ride passes through open countryside and woodland and few villages of any size until reaching Odiham, another town with a broad main street flanked by old brick houses. The return trip passes through similar scenery but takes in the three typical Hampshire villages of Bentworth, Medstead and Bighton.

Start

Horse and Groom PH, Broad Street, New Alresford

Parking: New Alresford station car park

Distance and grade

38 miles

 Moderate

Terrain

Mainly undulating. Despite climbs of 280 feet to Bugmore Hill, 250 feet between Preston Candover and Herriard, 400 feet south from Odiham towards Golden Pot and 230 feet between Shalden and Medstead, all the hills are fairly gentle

Nearest railway

Limited service on the Midhants Watercress Line from Alton to New Alresford or Alton, 3 miles from Golden Pot, or Hook, 3 miles from Odiham

New Alresford

Refreshments

Many pubs and tea shops in
New Alresford
Haddington Arms PH, Upton Grey
The George PH (also does cream teas),
The Bell PH, Odiham
The Golden Pot PH, Golden Pot
The Sun PH, Bentworth
Castle of Comfort PH, Medstead
Three Horse Shoes PH, Bighton

Long Sutton
Golden Pot
Shalden
Bentworth
Medstead
Bighton

Preston Candover
Bradley
Chilton Wood
Preston Down
Down Fm
Preston Grange
Chilton Manor
Chilton Candover
Lower Wield
Candover Ho
Brown Candover
The Ox Drove
Wield Wood
Upper Wield
Juniper Hill
Armsworth Hill Fm
Barton Copse
Godsfield Copse
Bugmore Hill
Newmer Fm
Armsworth Ho
Hoggs Lodge
Hattingley
Godsfield
Chapel
Heath Green
Upper Lanham Fm
Tumuli
Tumulus
Lower Lanham Copse
Abbotstone Woods
Oliver's Battery Settlement
Grove Fm
Abbotstone Down
Lower Lanham
Breach Fm
West End
Nettlebed Fm
Bighton Ho
Broadlands
Coombe Fm
Stancomb Fm
High Dell Fm
Southdowns
Bighton Manor
Bighton
Old Alresford
Old Alresford Ho
Barnetts Wood Fm
Ranscombe Fm
Gundleton
Sutton Beech Wood
Old Alresford Pond
Arlebury Park
Bighton Bottom Fm
Northside Fm
Mid-Hants Rly
Western Court
New Alresford
Ropley Lodge
B3046
Wayfarer's Walk

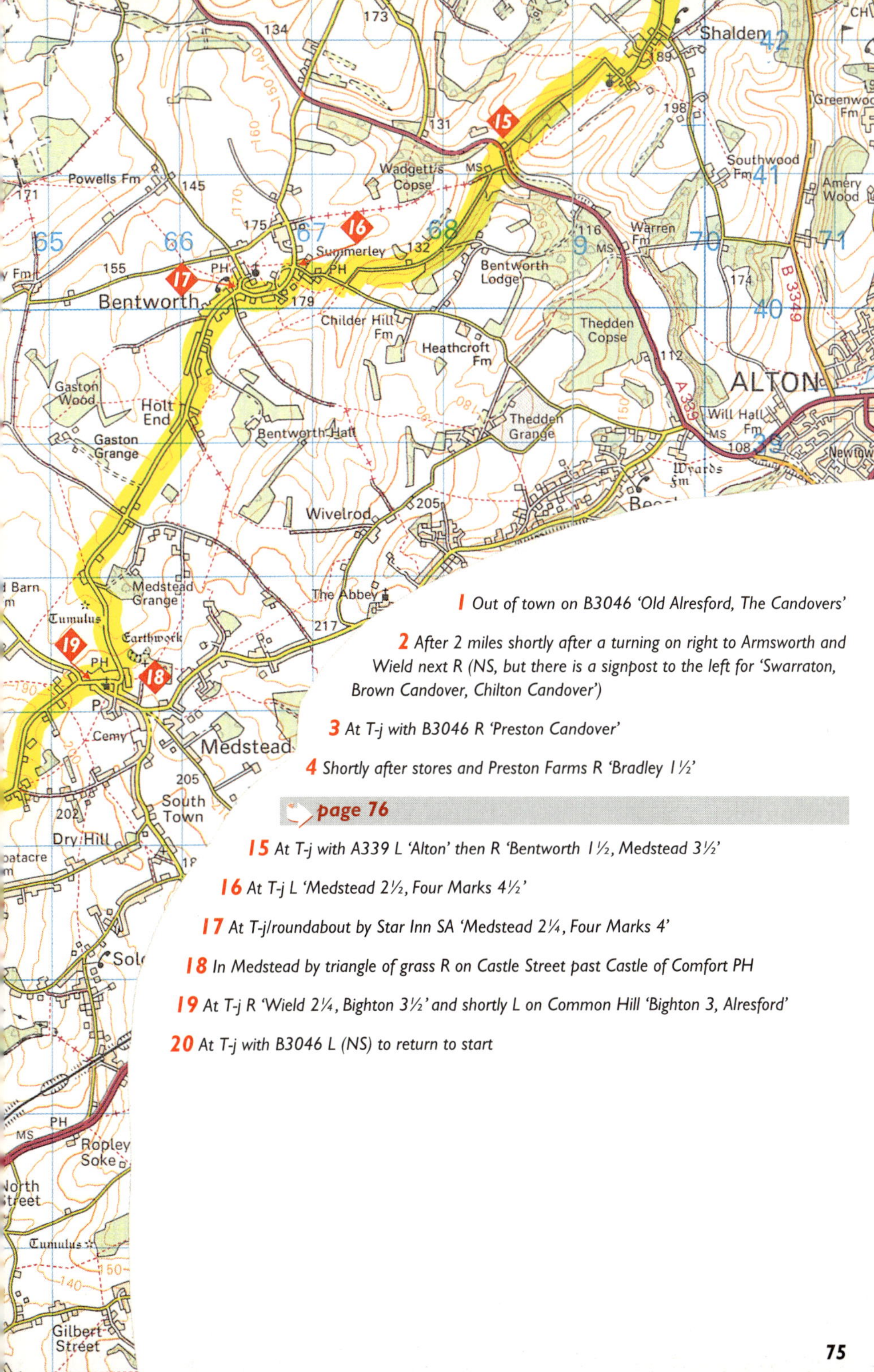

1 Out of town on B3046 'Old Alresford, The Candovers'

2 After 2 miles shortly after a turning on right to Armsworth and Wield next R (NS, but there is a signpost to the left for 'Swarraton, Brown Candover, Chilton Candover')

3 At T-j with B3046 R 'Preston Candover'

4 Shortly after stores and Preston Farms R 'Bradley 1½'

page 76

15 At T-j with A339 L 'Alton' then R 'Bentworth 1½, Medstead 3½'

16 At T-j L 'Medstead 2½, Four Marks 4½'

17 At T-j/roundabout by Star Inn SA 'Medstead 2¼, Four Marks 4'

18 In Medstead by triangle of grass R on Castle Street past Castle of Comfort PH

19 At T-j R 'Wield 2¼, Bighton 3½' and shortly L on Common Hill 'Bighton 3, Alresford'

20 At T-j with B3046 L (NS) to return to start

5 *At T-j R 'Herriard 2, Basingstoke 3'*

6 *At X-roads with A339 SA 'Weston Patrick 1½, Upton Grey 3, Odiham 6'*

7 *Through Upton Grey. Just before sign for North Warnborough R 'Odiham ¾, South Warnborough 2½'*

8 *On sharp LH bend just past telephone box, R onto West Street (no through road). At X-roads with A32 SA onto High Street*

9 *Next to Chinese restaurant opposite the bank R 'Long Sutton 3'*

10 ***Easy to miss.*** *Just after landing lights on left and emergency gates on right, R on small lane, following perimeter fence (NS)*

11 *At T-j L 'Well', then 1st R 'Froyle 2¼'*

12 *At T-j R 'Golden Pot 2¾, Herriard 6¾'*

13 *At X-roads with B3349 at the Golden Pot PH SA onto The Avenue 'Shalden 1½, Lasham 2½'*

14 *1st L just after Barn Cottage 'Shalden 1, Bentworth 2'*

page 75

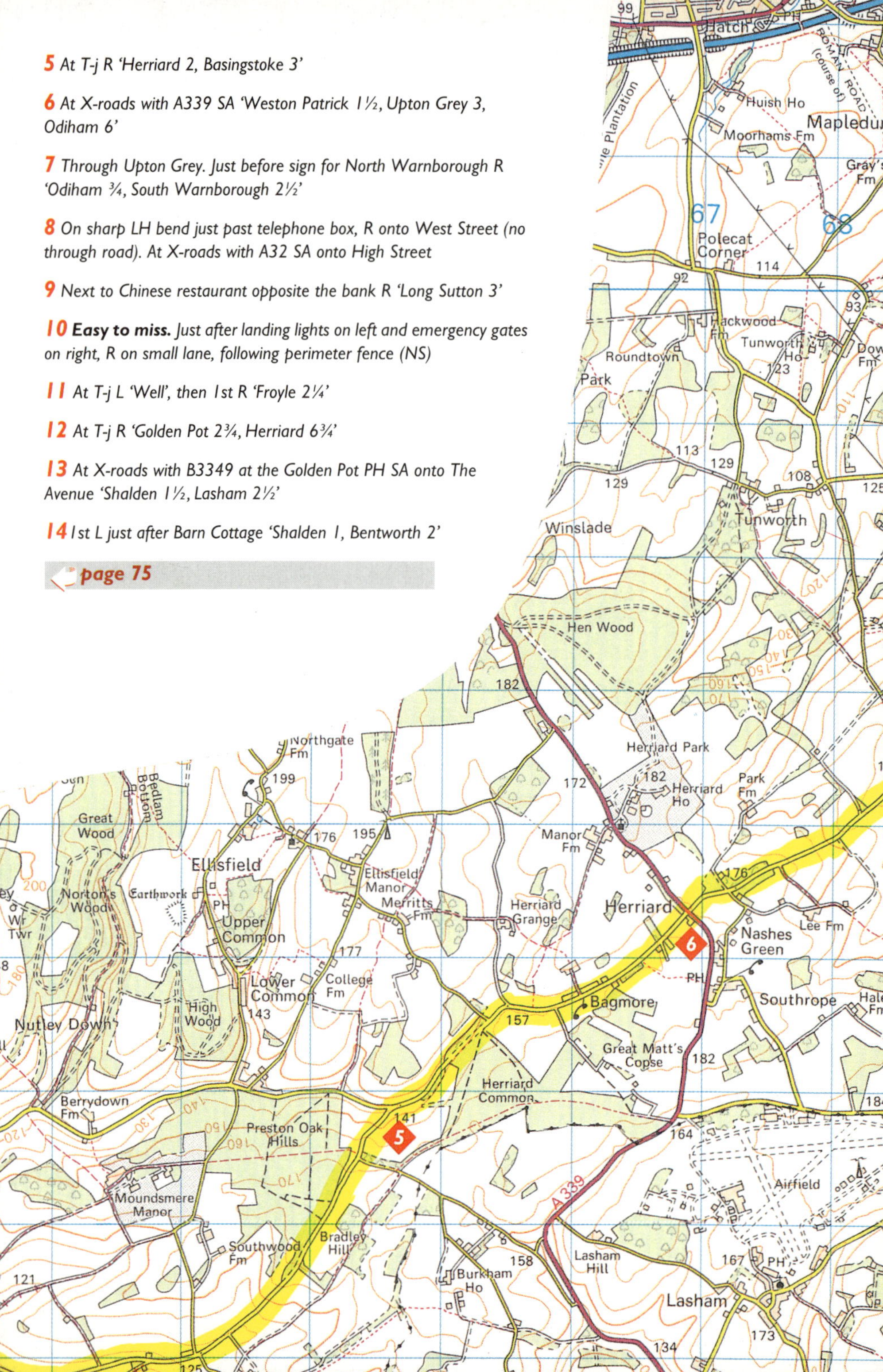

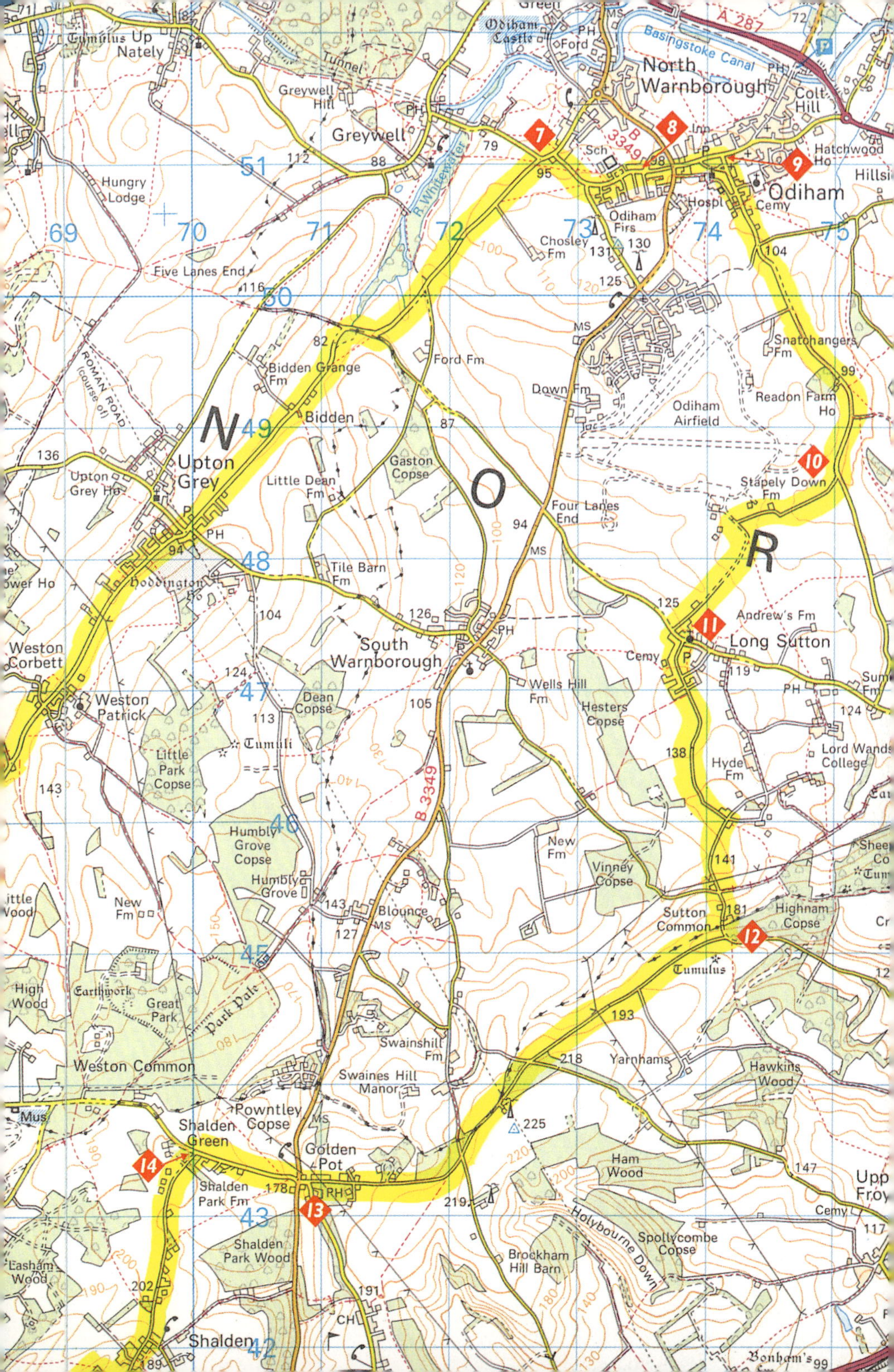

Up Nately
Tunnel
Greywell Hill
Greywell
Odiham Castle
Ford
North Warnborough
Basingstoke Canal
A 287
Colt Hill
Hatchwood Ho
Odiham
Hungry Lodge
Odiham Firs
Chosley Fm
Five Lanes End
Snatchangers Fm
Ford Fm
Bidden Grange Fm
Bidden
Down Fm
Readon Farm Ho
Odiham Airfield
Gaston Copse
Upton Grey
Upton Grey Ho
Little Dean Fm
Stapely Down Fm
Four Lanes End
Tile Barn Fm
Hoddington
South Warnborough
Andrew's Fm
Long Sutton
Weston Corbett
Weston Patrick
Dean Copse
Wells Hill Fm
Hesters Copse
Tumuli
Little Park Copse
Hyde Fm
Lord Wandsworth College
Humbly Grove Copse
Humbly Grove
New Fm
Vinney Copse
Blounce
Sutton Common
Highnam Copse
Tumulus
High Wood
Earthwork
Great Park
Park Pale
Swainshill Fm
Yarnhams
Hawkins Wood
Weston Common
Swaines Hill Manor
Powntley Copse
Shalden Green
Golden Pot
Ham Wood
Shalden Park Fm
Holybourne Down
Spollycombe Copse
Shalden Park Wood
Lasham Wood
Brockham Hill Barn
Shalden
Bonham's
ROMAN ROAD (course of)
R. Whitewater
B 3349
N
O
R
7
8
9
10
11
12
13
14

New Alresford to Bishop's Waltham, along the Meon Valley and over the Downs

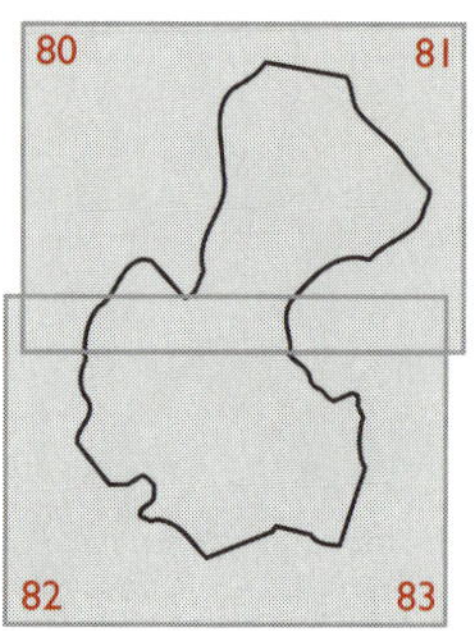

Quiet lanes in southern central Hampshire provide a delightful ride through easy rolling countryside and woodland. The route goes south through the lovely village of Beauworth, with its thatched houses and a church with a wooden steeple. Between Upham and Bishop's Waltham you pass the amazing turrets of Vernon Hill House (between instructions 10 and 11). Bishop's Waltham is a convenient halfway stop and you may wish to visit the ruins of the Bishop's Palace, the seat of several Bishops of Winchester. The ride drops into the valley of the River Meon, which it follows north to the charming village of Exton. A steep climb rewards you with very fine views from the top of Beacon Hill. The ride is mainly downhill or flat through several stretches of woodland from here back to the start.

Start

New Alresford station car park

Parking: As above

Distance and grade

31 miles

 Easy/moderate

Terrain

Undulating. Climbs of 300 feet south from Cheriton, 200 feet from Bishop's Waltham to the edge of the Meon Valley and 430 feet from Exton up onto Beacon Hill. The final one is the only hill of note and the views are fabulous

Nearest railway

Limited service on the Midhants Watercress Line from Alton to New Alresford

New Alresford
Cheriton
Beauworth
Lane End
Upham
Bishop's Waltham
Swanmore

Places of interest

New Alresford (1)

During the Middle Ages, New Alresford was one of the most important wool towns and its main street was thought to be the finest in Hampshire. Further down the hill is Old Alresford, a scattered village with an attractive pond.

Refreshments

Flower Pots PH, Cheriton
Brushmakers Arms PH, Upham
Crown PH, White Horse PH, Yew Tree tea and coffee shop, Bishop's Waltham
Hunters Inn, Swanmore
White Lion PH, Soberton
Hurdles PH, Brockbridge
Bucks Head PH, Meonstoke

Tichborne (1-2)

This pretty village comprises thatched 16th- and 17th-century houses, a small church and a Victorian manor house. An area of land known as The Crawls derives its name from a local legend: the lady of the manor, while very ill, tried to persuade her husband to do something to alleviate the poverty of the villagers; he replied that he would set aside some land to produce corn for the villagers but it would be an area no greater than that which she could crawl round. She crawled round 23 acres before dying and the villagers still receive 30cwt of corn each year.

Bishop's Waltham Palace (13)

Built by a Bishop of Winchester, this fortified palace dates from the 12th century. William of Wykeham, Bishop of Winchester and founder of Winchester College and New College, Oxford, died here in 1404. It is well worth seeing for the Gatehouse, great tower and Romanesque chapel.

Corhampton (19)

This village has an interesting and rare Saxon church with its original Saxon sundial and a slanting nave.

Soberton Droxford Exton Beacon Hill Bramdean Common A31

1 From station, take exit road out of car park. At T-j L under railway bridge

2 At end of Cheriton, on sharp LH bend R 'Winchester 7 (A272), Bishop's Waltham 7'

3 At X-roads with A272 SA 'Beauworth ¾, Bishop's Waltham 6'

4 At X-roads, just past The Milbury's PH R 'Winchester 7'

5 After 1 mile, just after a telephone box on the right L 'Lower Upham' by a letter box

6 At X-roads SA 'Blackdown ½'. Follow signs for Upham

page 83

23 After brow of hill as you start to descend, 1st R (NS)

24 At X-roads SA 'Brookwood 2½, Bramdean 4½'

25 At X-roads SA 'Woodlands 1¼'

26 At X-roads with A272 SA (NS)

27 At X-roads by telephone box L (NS)

28 At T-j R 'Alresford 3½, Ropley 2'

29 At roundabout with A31 SA 'Bishop's Sutton ½, New Alresford 2'. Follow signs for car park in New Alresford to return to start

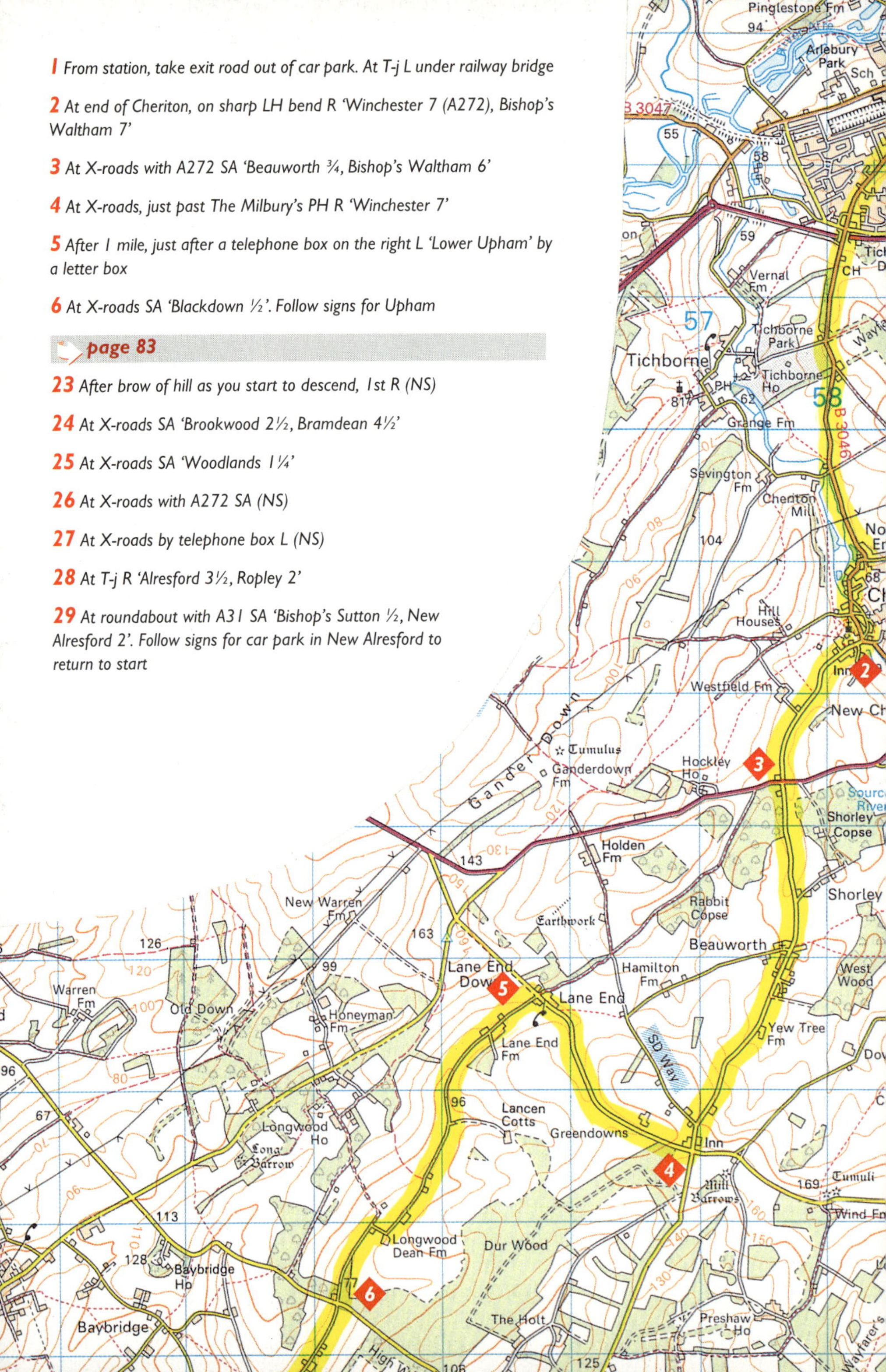

Gundleton
Sutton Beech Wood
Old Alresford Pond
Bighton Bottom Fm
Northside Fm
Mid-Hants Rly
Tumulus
Western Court
New Alresford
Bishop's Sutton
Ropley Lodge
Gilbert Street
B 3047
Ford
Ropley Dean
Ropley
A 31
White Hill
Manor House Fm
Harcombe
Scrubb Fm
Soames Fm
Wks
Common Fm
Old Park Wood
Wr Twr
Field System
Cheriton Wood
Bramdean Common
Middle Fm
Marriners Fm
Wood Fm
Wolfhanger Fm
Long Barrow
Bramdean
Woodcote Manor Ho
Slys Fm
Hinton Ampner
Hinton Ampner Ho
Tumuli
NT
Hinton Woodlands Fm
Purser's
Wayfarer's Walk
Joan's Acre
Brockwood Park
The Dean
West Meon Woodlands
Woodlands Fm
Three Horse Shoes
Kilmeston
Dean Ho
Joan's Acre Wood
Shutt's Copse
A 272
West Meon (PH)
A 32
Black House Fm
Bere Fm
Marldell Fm
Highfield
Marlands
Hayling Wood
Riversdown Ho
Wheely Fm
Lippen Cotts
Rooksgrove Fm
Tumulus
West Meon
East End
Lomer Village
Wheely Down
Warnford
1
23
24
25
26
27
28
29

Longwood Dean Fm
Dur Wood
Baybridge Ho
Baybridge
The Holt
Preshaw Ho
High Wood
Blackdown
Stony Hard Fm
Green Hill
Preshaw
Belmore Ho
Rowhay Wood
Woodcote
Ower Fm
Wordlock's Down Fm
ROMAN ROAD (course of)
Roughay Fm
Gallops
Stephen's Castle Down
White Hill
Bigpath Fm
St Clair's Fm
Upham
West Hall
Dean Fm
Franklin Fm
Bottom Copse
Upham Fm
Street End
Corhampton Down
Stroudwood Fm
Lower Upham
Stakes Fm
Highfield Fm
Dean
Ashton
Woolstreet Fm
The Hangers
Galley Down
Cross Lanes Fm
Vernon Hill Ho
Bishopsdown Stud Fm
Wintershill Hall
Roke Fm
Duncombe
Dundridge
Durley Hall Fm
Wintershill
Northbrook
Cemy
Hill Top
Hoe
Durley Street
Newtown
Bishop's Palace
Bishop's Waltham
Tumuli
Durley Manor Fm
Tangier Fm
Thickets Ho
Brooklands Fm
Durley
Mincingfield Fm
Locks Fm
Mill
Brown Heath
Clewers Hill
dismtd rly
Glebe
Calcot Ho
Forest Fm
Durley Mill
Harfields Fm
Nations Fm
Waltham Chase
Breach Hill
Bishopsmore
Hill Fm
Shirrell Heath
Wangfield Fm
Curdridge
Shedfield Grange
Hotel Shedfield
B 3037
B 3035
B 2177

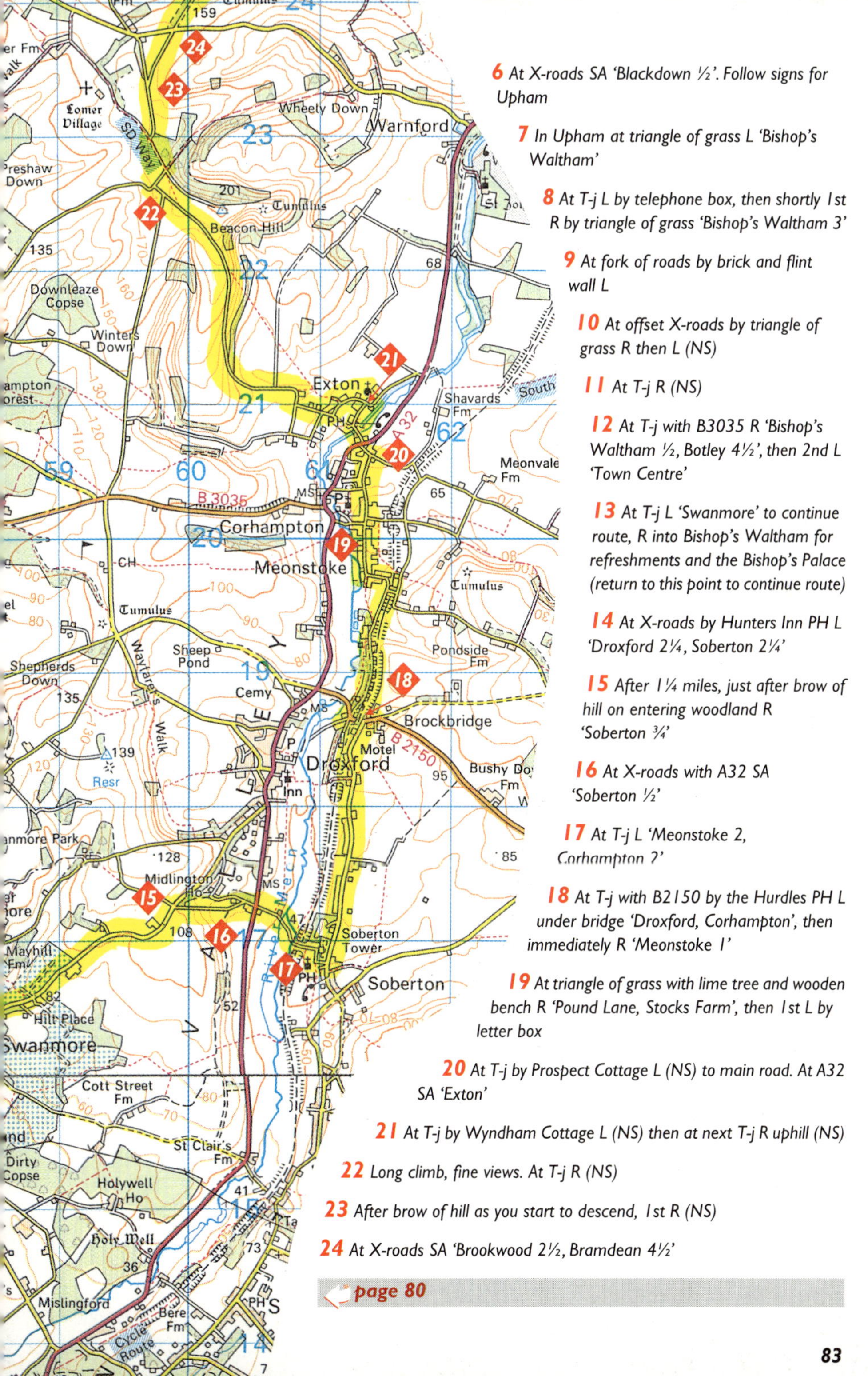

6 At X-roads SA 'Blackdown ½'. Follow signs for Upham

7 In Upham at triangle of grass L 'Bishop's Waltham'

8 At T-j L by telephone box, then shortly 1st R by triangle of grass 'Bishop's Waltham 3'

9 At fork of roads by brick and flint wall L

10 At offset X-roads by triangle of grass R then L (NS)

11 At T-j R (NS)

12 At T-j with B3035 R 'Bishop's Waltham ½, Botley 4½', then 2nd L 'Town Centre'

13 At T-j L 'Swanmore' to continue route, R into Bishop's Waltham for refreshments and the Bishop's Palace (return to this point to continue route)

14 At X-roads by Hunters Inn PH L 'Droxford 2¼, Soberton 2¼'

15 After 1¼ miles, just after brow of hill on entering woodland R 'Soberton ¾'

16 At X-roads with A32 SA 'Soberton ½'

17 At T-j L 'Meonstoke 2, Corhampton 2'

18 At T-j with B2150 by the Hurdles PH L under bridge 'Droxford, Corhampton', then immediately R 'Meonstoke 1'

19 At triangle of grass with lime tree and wooden bench R 'Pound Lane, Stocks Farm', then 1st L by letter box

20 At T-j by Prospect Cottage L (NS) to main road. At A32 SA 'Exton'

21 At T-j by Wyndham Cottage L (NS) then at next T-j R uphill (NS)

22 Long climb, fine views. At T-j R (NS)

23 After brow of hill as you start to descend, 1st R (NS)

24 At X-roads SA 'Brookwood 2½, Bramdean 4½'

page 80

12 From Petersfield west through the Meon Valley and north to Selborne

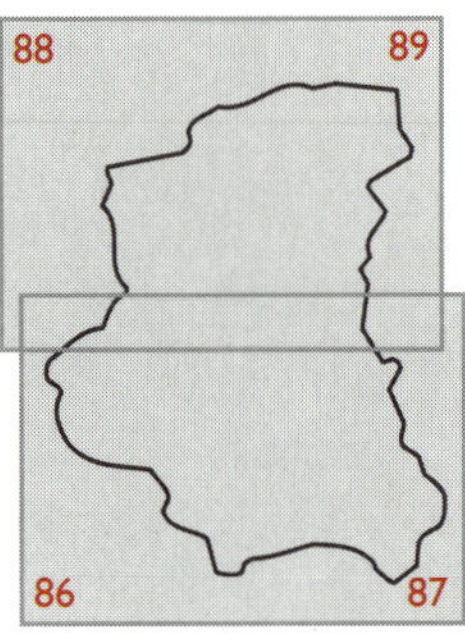

A very satisfying ride that takes in the lovely villages of Buriton, East and West Meon and Selborne and passes through downland and woodland, finishing with a descent of almost 3 miles from Warren Corner to near Petersfield. The stretch along the Meon Valley has a very special feel to it, as there are steep hills on both sides, and the church at East Meon has a very fine backdrop of the abrupt slopes of Park Hill. Selborne, the birthplace of Gilbert White, was made famous by his book, *The Natural History and Antiquities of Selborne.*

Start

Tourist Information Centre, Petersfield

Parking: Several car parks. Not cheap, except on Sundays

Distance and grade

31 miles

 Moderate

Terrain

Five climbs – 250 feet from Buriton to beneath Butser Hill, 300 feet from West Meon to West Tisted, 300 feet east from Ropley, 330 feet then another 300 feet between Selborne and Steep – and one great descent close to Petersfield

Nearest railway

Petersfield

Refreshments

Several pubs in Petersfield
Five Bells PH, Master Robert PH, Buriton
Izaak Walton PH, The George PH, East Meon
Thomas Lord PH, Red Lion PH, West Meon
Queens Hotel, Selborne Arms PH, Bush House Tea Room, Selborne

Petersfield
Buriton
East Meon
West Meon
West Tisted

Places of interest

Petersfield (1)

Now a busy market town with fine old houses, Petersfield was once an important centre of the wool trade. A statue of William III dominates the central square where the weekly market is held.

East Meon (5)

Izaak Walton, the famous angler, fished here and it is still a centre for trout fishing. The Norman church is one of the best examples of its kind in Hampshire.

Warnford (6)

Slightly off the route, Warnford is known for the large Norman tower on its 12th- to 17th-century church. Warnford Park contains the ruins of a 13th-century building known, inaccurately, as King John's House.

Chawton (18)

Slightly off the route is Chawton, the village where Jane Austen lived and wrote her final novels: *Mansfield Park, Emma* and *Persuasion.* The small cottage that was her home from 1809 until her death in 1817 is now a museum. The 17th-century manor house and the 19th-century Church of St Nicholas are situated in a park slightly outside the village. A monument to Sir Richard Knight, ancestor of Thomas who adopted Jane Austen's brother, stands in the church and is important as one of the few items to survive the fire that destroyed the previous church.

Selborne (20)

Gilbert White, the 18th-century naturalist, made this village famous with his classic study *The Natural History and Antiquities of Selborne* (1789). His house now contains a museum devoted to his work as well as some mementoes of Captain Lawrence Oates, an explorer who accompanied Scott to the South Pole. There are wonderful views from nearby Selborne Common, one of White's favourite retreats.

Ropley
Lower Farringdon
Upper Farringdon
Selborne
Warren Corner
Steep

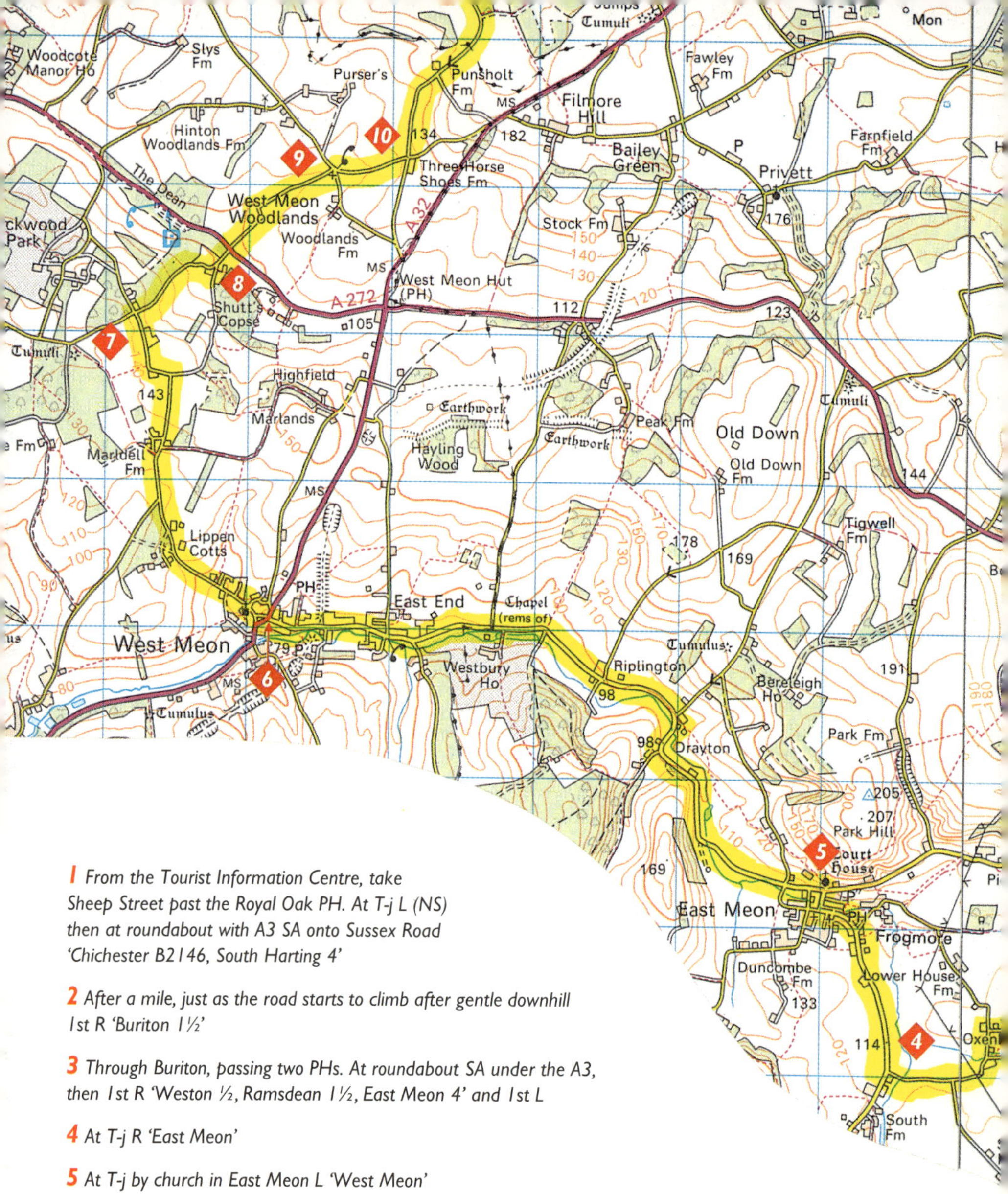

1 From the Tourist Information Centre, take Sheep Street past the Royal Oak PH. At T-j L (NS) then at roundabout with A3 SA onto Sussex Road 'Chichester B2146, South Harting 4'

2 After a mile, just as the road starts to climb after gentle downhill 1st R 'Buriton 1½'

3 Through Buriton, passing two PHs. At roundabout SA under the A3, then 1st R 'Weston ½, Ramsdean 1½, East Meon 4' and 1st L

4 At T-j R 'East Meon'

5 At T-j by church in East Meon L 'West Meon'

6 At X-roads with A32 SA onto one-way street, then shortly at T-j R (NS)

7 At X-roads after 1¼ miles by a line of copper beeches R 'Woodlands 1¼'

8 At X-roads with A272 SA (NS)

9 At X-roads by telephone and letter box SA (NS)

10 At next X-roads by a house with its left side built of red-brick L (NS)

page 88

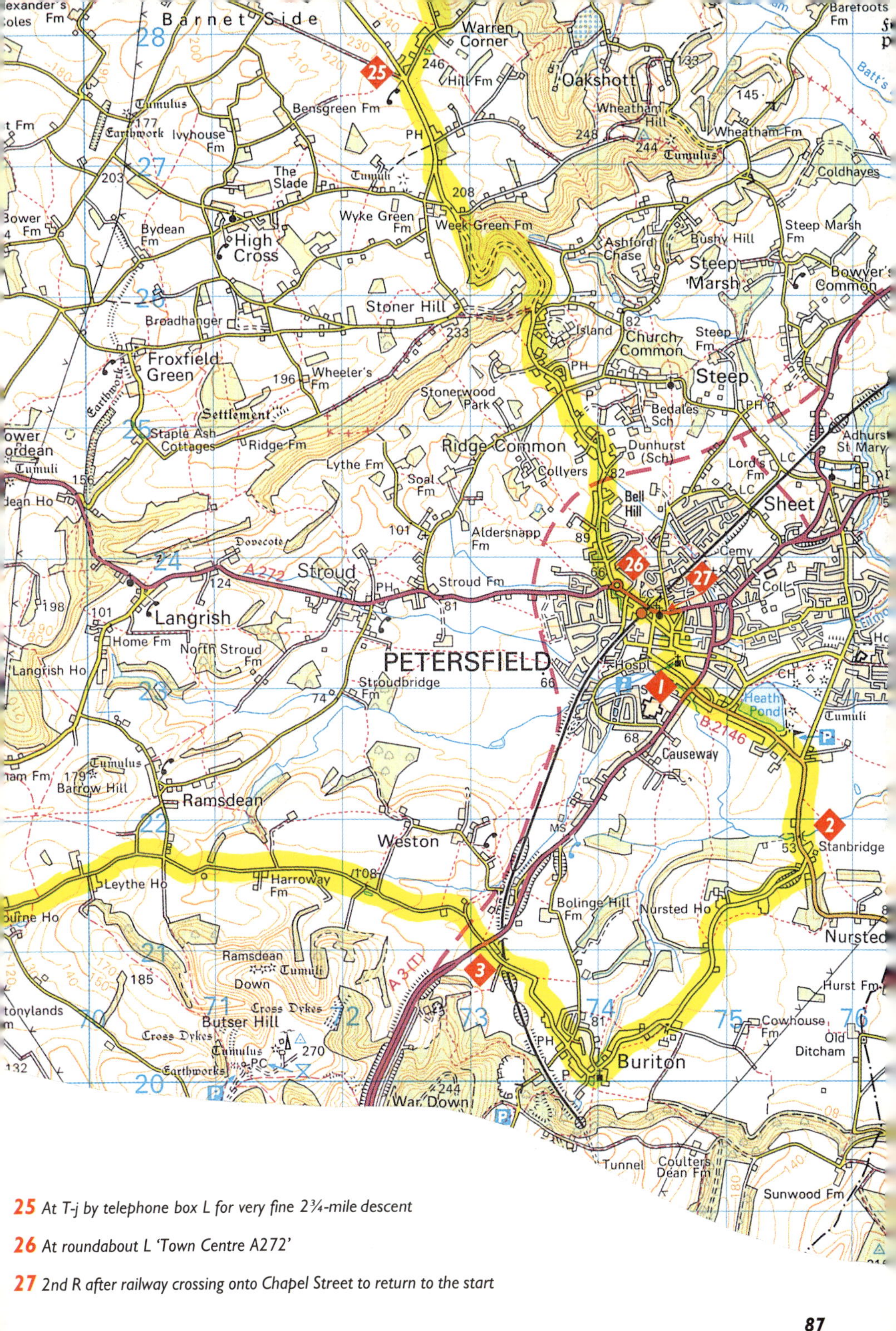

25 *At T-j by telephone box L for very fine 2¾-mile descent*

26 *At roundabout L 'Town Centre A272'*

27 *2nd R after railway crossing onto Chapel Street to return to the start*

9 *At X-roads by telephone and letter box SA (NS)*

10 *At next X-roads by a house with its left side built of red-brick L (NS)*

11 *At T-j by large red-brick houses in West Tisted L (NS)*

12 *At next T-j at end of Stapley Lane L 'Ropley, Alresford'*

13 *After 400 yards 1st R, on Church Lane, then at offset X-roads by thatched houses R, then L opposite Exeter House*

14 *At T-j R towards telephone box and letter box*

15 *After 1½ miles, shortly after Lyeway Lane to the right, on sharp LH bend, turn R on Kitwood Lane 'Kitwood, East Tisted 3¼'*

16 *At T-j at bottom of hill L 'Four Marks 1¼, Medstead 3¼', then 1st R on Willis Lane (opposite sign for Hawthorn Road)*

17 *At X-roads SA onto Brightstone Lane (NS)*

18 *At X-roads with A32 SA 'Church ½, Selborne 3, Liss 8'*

19 *At T-j with B3006 R 'Selborne ¾, Liss 5½'*

20 *At end of Selborne R 'Newton Valence 1¾'*

21 *At offset X-roads L by triangle of grass 'Hawkley 2'*

22 *After ½ mile 1st R 'Priors Dean 1¼, Colemore 2¾'*

23 *At bottom of lovely wooded descent at T-j by triangle of grass L (NS)*

24 *1st R by telephone box 'Petersfield 5'*

25 *At T-j by telephone box L for very fine 2¾-mile descent*

page 87

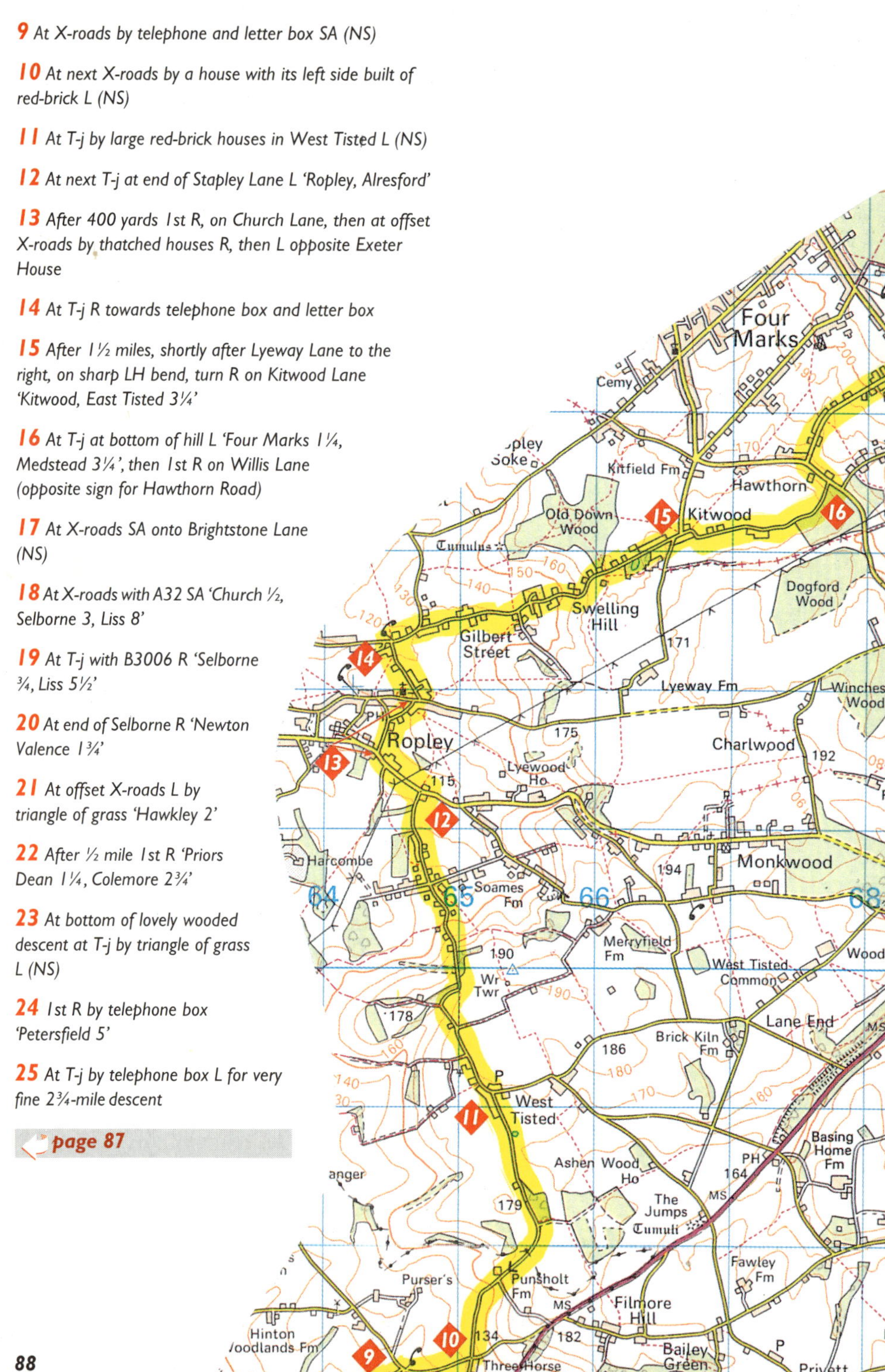

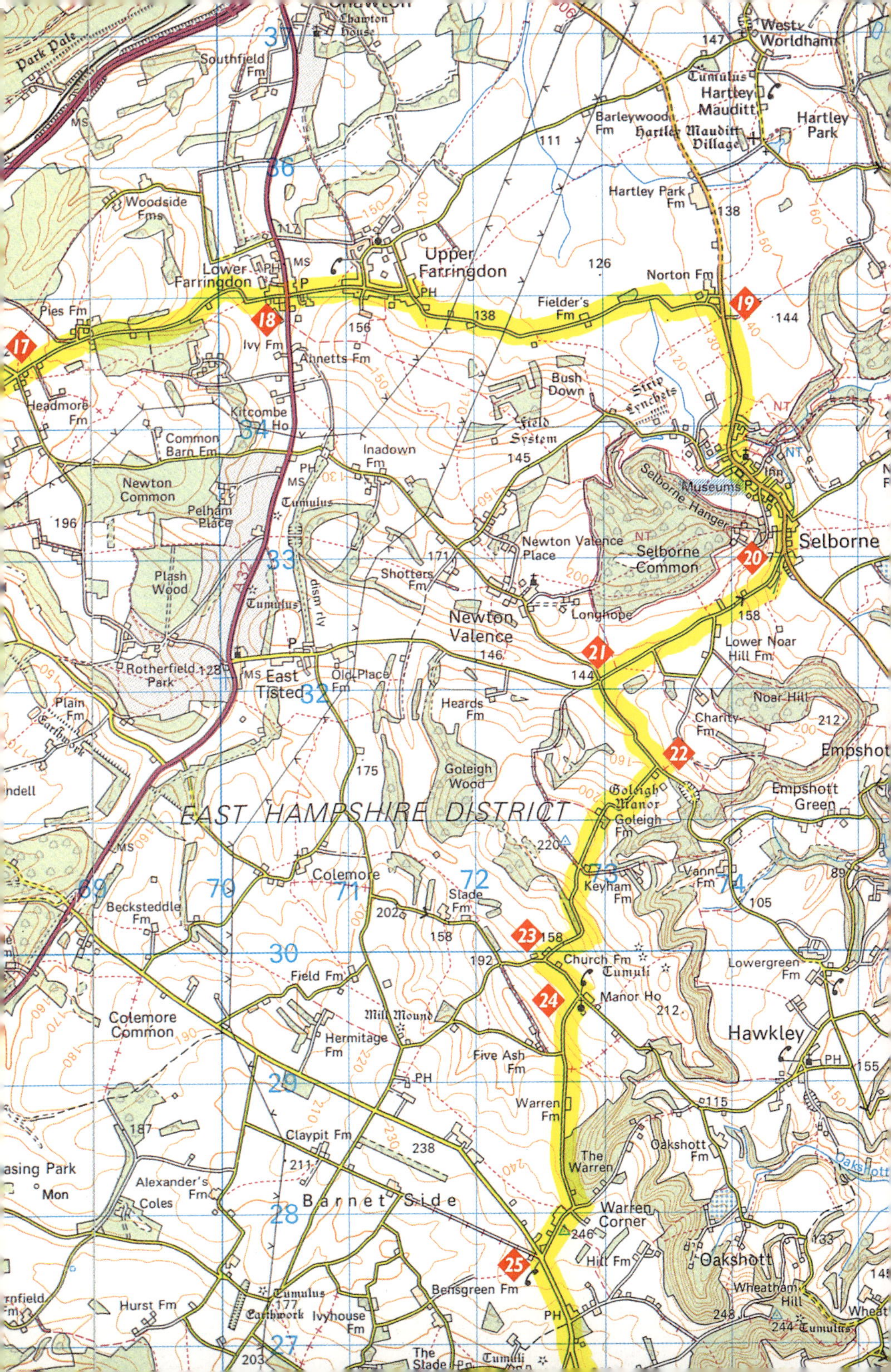

Park Pale
Chawton House
Southfield Fm
West Worldham
Hartley Mauditt
Hartley Park
Barleywood Fm
Hartley Mauditt Village
Hartley Park Fm
Woodside Fms
Lower Farringdon
Upper Farringdon
Norton Fm
Pies Fm
Fielder's Fm
Ivy Fm
Annetts Fm
Bush Down
Strip Lynchets
Headmore Fm
Kitcombe Ho
Field System
Common Barn Fm
Inadown Fm
Newton Common
Pelham Place
Selborne Hanger
Museums
Selborne
Newton Valence Place
Selborne Common
Plash Wood
Shotters Fm
Newton Valence
Longhope
Lower Noar Hill Fm
Rotherfield Park
East Tisted
Old Place Fm
Noar Hill
Plain Fm
Heards Fm
Charity Fm
Empshott
Goleigh Wood
Empshott Green
Goleigh Manor
Goleigh Fm
EAST HAMPSHIRE DISTRICT
Colemore
Slade Fm
Keyham Fm
Vann Fm
Beckstedde Fm
Church Fm
Tumuli
Lowergreen Fm
Field Fm
Manor Ho
Mill Mound
Hawkley
Colemore Common
Hermitage Fm
Five Ash Fm
Warren Fm
Claypit Fm
The Warren
Oakshott Fm
Alexander's Fm
Coles
Barnet Side
Warren Corner
Hill Fm
Oakshott
Wheatham Hill
Bensgreen Fm
Hurst Fm
Earthwork
Ivyhouse Fm
The Slade
Tumulus

13 Newport to Cowes and Yarmouth via three cycle paths

An exploration of the western half of the Isle of Wight, this ride takes in Newport, Cowes and Yarmouth,the three main centres of population on this side of the island. The Isle of Wight has an enlightened attitude towards cycling and this ride uses the three cycle paths that have been constructed: Newport to Cowes, Yarmouth to Freshwater and Blackwater to Newport. Fine views of the Solent open up from the coastal route on the north side of Cowes. Quiet wooded lanes lead inland from Cowes via Shalfleet to the picturesque port of Yarmouth. The second disused railway track leads to Freshwater, where you could lock up your bike and go for a breezy stroll along the chalk cliffs towards the Needles. The route now passes through the inland villages of Shalcombe, Brighstone and Shorwell before diving down little lanes to Atherfield and Pyle. Turning north, the ride continues via Chillerton Down and the third cycle trail back to Newport.

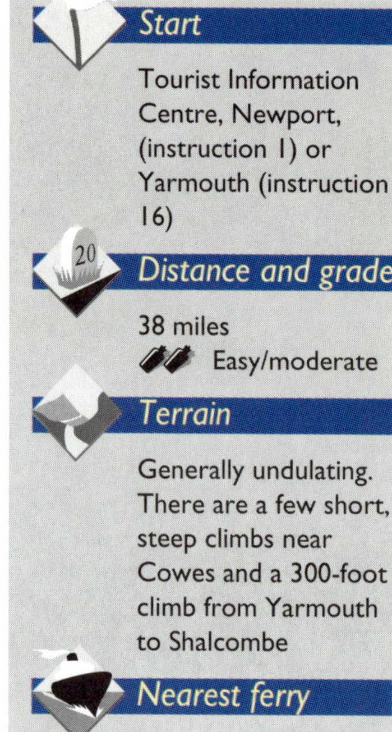

Start

Tourist Information Centre, Newport, (instruction 1) or Yarmouth (instruction 16)

Distance and grade

38 miles

Easy/moderate

Terrain

Generally undulating. There are a few short, steep climbs near Cowes and a 300-foot climb from Yarmouth to Shalcombe

Nearest ferry

Cowes or Yarmouth

Refreshments

Many places for refreshment in Newport, Cowes and Yarmouth
Sportsman's Rest PH, Porchfield
New Inn, Shalfleet *Sun Inn,* Brook
Three Bishops PH, Corner House Tea Room, Brighstone *Crown Inn,* Shorwell

Newport

Places of interest

Carisbrooke Castle (27)

About one mile to the west of the route at instruction 27. Although its general appearance is medieval, Carisbrooke was originally a Roman fort and was rebuilt as a medieval castle with the keep and curtain wall being completed in 1136. The gatehouse was added in the 14th and 15th centuries and in the reign of Elizabeth I considerable alterations were made to enable the castle to withstand artillery. The only major event in the castle's long history was the imprisonment of Charles I in 1647-48.

Carisbrooke Castle

East Afton
Shalcombe
Hulverstone
Brighstone
Shorwell
Pyle
Chillerton
Blackwater

1 *With your back to the Tourist Information Centre L towards traffic lights. At lights R. At 2nd set of traffic lights R onto High Street*

2 *Just before clock tower, L onto Holyrood Street 'Cowes via Cycle Track'*

3 *Follow in the same direction to roundabout. Turn L 'Industrial Estate, Cycle Path'*

4 *Follow through industrial estate past Royal Mail PH to 2nd roundabout and go SA*

5 *At T-j at the end of cycle path R then L on road parallel to River Medina past the Cowes Hotel*

6 *At the end of Arctic Road L 'Cowes Town Centre', then at T-j R*

7 *At T-j with Mill Hill Road L 'Town Centre', then 2nd R on Victoria Road 'Sea Front, Town Centre'*

8 *At T-j with Park Road R 'Town Centre', then L on Union Street 'The Parade'*

9 *Descend to town centre, start climbing hill then 1st R on Queens Road*

10 *Follow coastline. Shortly after Shore Road changes name to Worsley Road, R on Solent View Road*

11 *At roundabout R 'Newport, Thorness, Yarmouth' then follow road around RH bend 'Porchfield, Shalfleet, Yarmouth'*

12 *Follow signs for Yarmouth and Shalfleet. At T-j with A3054 R 'Yarmouth'*

13 *In Shalfleet at the New Inn, before the church, L on Church Lane. At T-j L (NS)*

14 *At next T-j L (NS), then 1st R on Wellow Road 'Wellow, Thorley, Freshwater'*

page 94

27 *At T-j by the Barley Mow PH L*

28 *At T-j L on continuation of Medina Avenue, then 1st R on Church Litten 'Town Centre'. At traffic lights L to return to Tourist Information Centre*

Cowes Roads
COWES
Egypt Point
Castle
Old Castle
Breakwater
Mus
Marina
Sch
Northwood Ho
CH
Gurnard
Gurnard Bay
Ferry
Hospl
Cliff Fm
B 3325
Gurnard Ledge
Coastal Path
Gurnard Pines
Cemy
Thorness Bay
Wks
Northwood
Ruffins Copse
Somerton Fm
Kingston Fm
Rew Street
Nodes Fm
RIVER MEDINA
Whipping
Sticelett
Medham Ho
Padmore H (Hotel)
Pilgrims Park
Whippance Fm
Little Thorness
Hillis Fm
Hillis Corner
Newport Cowes Cycle Way
Skinners Fm
Pallance Fm
Great Thorness
Ridge Copse
Luton Fm
Werrar Fm
Stagwell
Pallancegate
Elmsworth Fm
Crockers Fm
A 3020
Little Whitehouse
Mark's Corner
Noke Fm
Whitehouse Fm
Binfield Fm
Hillcross Fm
North Fairlee Fm
Porchfield
Parkhurst
Dodnor Ho
Parkhurst Forest
Parkhurst Prison
Rodge Brook
Lower St Cross Fm
Locksgreen
Sandhills Fm
Hospl
Signal Ho
Albany Prison
Fairlee
Forest Fm
Camp Hill Prison
Coleman's Fm
Forest Walk
Durrants
A 3054
Hunny Hill
Kitbridge Fm
Forest Side
Lower Watchingwell
Vittlefields Fm
Park Green Fm
NEWPORT
Barton
Gunville
Bulls Wood
Alvington Manor Fm
Pan
dismtd rly
Upper Watchingwell
ROMAN VILLA (rems of)
Great Pan Fm
Newpark Fm
B 3401
Great Park
Carisbrooke
Park Place Fm
Shide
Clatterford
Tennyson Trail
Priory
Stenbury Trail
Bembridge Trail
Apesdown
Carisbrooke Castle
Tumulus
Apes Down
Fords
New Close Ho
Valleys
Bowcombe Down
B 3323
Froglands Fm
Shepherds Trail
Standen Ho
Mudless Copse
Great Whitcombe
Marvel Fm
Birchfield Ho
Bowcombe
Cycle Route

17 SA onto no through road (track). At T-j with another track R and follow this for 1½ miles to road

18 At road L (NS). After ½ mile at T-j with B3399 L 'Newport'

19 After 2½ miles 1st R 'Brighstone B3399, Ventnor A3055'

20 Follow B3399 for 5 miles through Brighstone to Shorwell. At roundabout R on Farriers Way 'Chale 4½'

21 After ¼ mile, on sharp LH bend R 'Atherfield, Yafford'

22 At T-j by triangle of grass L 'Atherfield, Chale'

23 Ignoring turnings, follow this lane for 4 miles to the B3399

24 At T-j with B3399 bear L (in effect SA) 'Shorwell 2¾, Brighstone 4½, Newport 6¼'

15 At T-j with B3401 R 'Yarmouth'. At T-j with A3054 L 'Yarmouth' and follow into town centre

16 After exploring Yarmouth (or as an alternative starting point), with your back to the Tourist Information Centre L. At roundabout L on A3054 'Newport, Cowes', then 2nd R onto Mill Street just past pedestrian island

25 *After 4 miles, following signs for Newport, near distinctive red-brick clock tower of Whitecroft Hospital on sharp LH bend, R onto Sandy Lane 'Blackwater'*

26 ***Easy to miss*** *Just before joining A3020, immediately before bridge over small stream L on small path over wooden bridge to join cycle path to Newport*

page 92

From Newport to Brading and south to Niton

The Isle of Wight is a wonderful place to explore by bike. This route explores the eastern side of the island, starting with a stiff climb from Newport that gives access to a ridge over Arreton Down, with magnificent views across the Solent to the north and the English Channel to the south. A second climb takes you to the upper coastal road from Ventnor to St Lawrence, once again offering superb sea views. North from Niton the route passes over chalk downland and then along the cycle path from Blackwater to return to Newport.

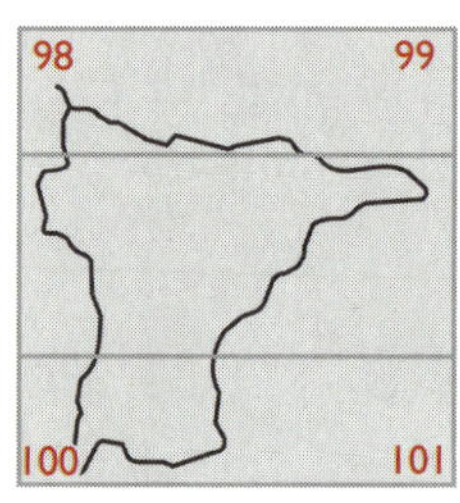

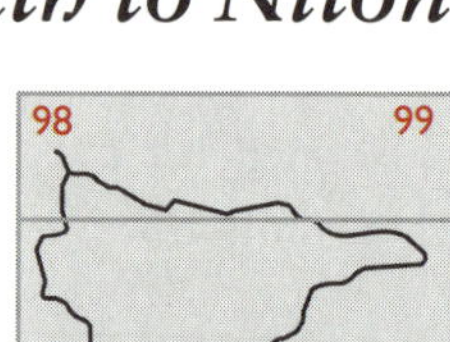

Start

Tourist Information Centre, Newport

Distance and grade

28 miles

 Moderate

Terrain

A steep then steady climb of 400 feet from Newport up to Arreton Down. A short, steep hill from Brading to Adgestone, then a longer climb 430 feet from Alverstone to Ventnor

Nearest ferry

Cowes, 4 miles from Newport via the cycle path, or Ryde, 5 miles from Brading

Nearest railway

Brading

Refreshments

Many places for refreshments in Newport and Brading
Hare and Hounds PH, Downend
Worsley PH, The Star PH, Wroxhall
White Lion PH, Niton

Newport
Downend
Arreton Down
Brading
Adgestone
Alverstone
Wr

Places of interest

Arreton Manor (4)

A 17th-century manor house containing a lacemaking collection and museum of childhood as well as contemporary furniture. In the grounds – connected to the house by a secret passageway – is the Pomeroy museum dolls house and a collection of wireless receivers dating back to the early 20th century.

Nunwell House (5/6)

A Tudor and Jacobean house with later additions. It contains period furniture in the Jacobean and Georgian wings and houses a unique collection of family militaria.

Morton Manor (7/8)

This Restoration house was built in 1680 and stands within terraced, landscaped gardens.

Appuldurcombe House

The ruins of an 18th-century mansion built for the Worsley family in the Classical style, starting in 1701. The house was irrevocably damaged in 1943 and only the shell of the house and the park – which is the work of Capability Brown – remain.

Arreton Manor

Ventnor Whitwell Niton Rookley Blackwater

1 From the Tourist Information Centre L along Orchard Street towards career office, past bus station and library. At T-j at end of Orchard Street L following one-way system

2 At T-j with Trafalgar Road L, then 1st L on Medina Avenue 'Ryde, Sandown', then 1st R on continuation of Medina Avenue 'Roman Villa'

3 At main road (A3056) SA via path onto Burnt House Lane, then 1st R on continuation of Burnt House Lane

4 Steep climb. After 2 miles at T-j L (NS), then 1st R just before Hare and Hounds PH 'Newchurch, Brading'

5 Follow the ridge road. After 2½ miles, at the top of the hill R 'Brading, Bembridge, Sandown'

6 At T-j R 'Brading, Bembridge, Sandown'

7 At traffic lights **either**: L to explore Brading (return to this point afterwards) **or** retrace route 50 yards up hill and bear L on Lower Adgestone Road 'Adgestone, Alverstone' '6'6" width limit'

8 At fork in road R, then at T-j by Adgestone Vineyard L

9 At T-j R 'Alverstone, Newchurch'

10 Follow signs for Apse Heath and Wroxhall. At roundabout SA onto Ventnor Road 'Wroxall'

11 At next roundabout SA 'Wroxall, Ventnor'

page 101

16 After 5 miles at T-j with A3020 L 'Newport', then 1st L onto Highwood Lane (after nurseries) 'Gatcombe, Chillerton, Whitecroft, Carisbrooke'

17 At T-j R 'Carisbrooke, Newport, Gatcombe, Whitecroft'

18 After 1½ miles, on sharp LH bend, 1st R onto Sandy Lane 'Blackwater'

19 **Easy to miss** Just before main road (A3020) immediately before bridge over small stream L on small path over wooden bridge to follow cycle path into Newport

20 At T-j by the Barley Mow PH L

21 At T-j at the end of this road L onto continuation of Medina Avenue, then 1st R on Church Litten

22 At traffic lights L to return to Tourist Information Centre

OF WIGHT
Whitecroft Hospital
Stone Fm
Longdown
Stenbury Trail
Merston Manor
Merstone
Haseley Manor
Langbridge
Horringford
Newchurch
Perreton Fm
Stickworth Hall
Redway
Wackland
River Yar
Hale Manor Fm
Hale Common
Gatcombe Mill
Champion Fm
Pidford
Birchmore Fm
Sheat Manor
Sibdown Fm
Chillerton
Rookley
Country Park
Pagham Fm
Bohemia Corner
Little Budbridge Fm
Bathingbourne
Branstone
Great Budbridge Manor
Kennerley Fm
Harts Fm
Rookley Green
River Medina
Lower Rill
Lower Yard
Lessland Fm
Princelett
Worsley Trail
Cridmore
Moor Fm
Bobberstone Fm
Bagwich
Godshill
Summersbury
Bachelors Fm
DISTRICT
North Appleford
Bleak Down
Bridge Fm
Model Village
Mus
Cemy
Bridgecourt
Godshill Park
Natural History Centre
Sandford
French Mill
Whiteley Bank
Beacon Alley
Sainham Fm
Winstone Fm
dismtd rly
Leechmore Fm
Worsley Trail
Redhill Fm
Yard Fm
B3327
Gt Appleford Fm
Holden Fm
Roud
Wks
Sheepwash Fm
Gatcliff Fm
Obelisk
Upper Appleford Fm
Appuldurcombe Ho (ruin)
Wroxall
Dolcoppice
Fairfields
Itchill
Stenbury Manor Fm
Stenbury Down
Gotten Manor Fm
Ford Fm
The Hermitage
Monument
Southford
Span Fm
Catherine's Down
Wydcombe
Nettlecombe
Downcourt Fm
Bierley
Rew Fm
Lowtherville
Strathwell Park
Whitwell
Week Fm
Tumulus
Kingates
Head Down
Week Down
Rew Down
Jobsons Fm
Dean Fm
Steephill
St Catherine's Hill
St Lawrence
Botanic Gardens
A3055
Niton
Coastal Path
Undercliff

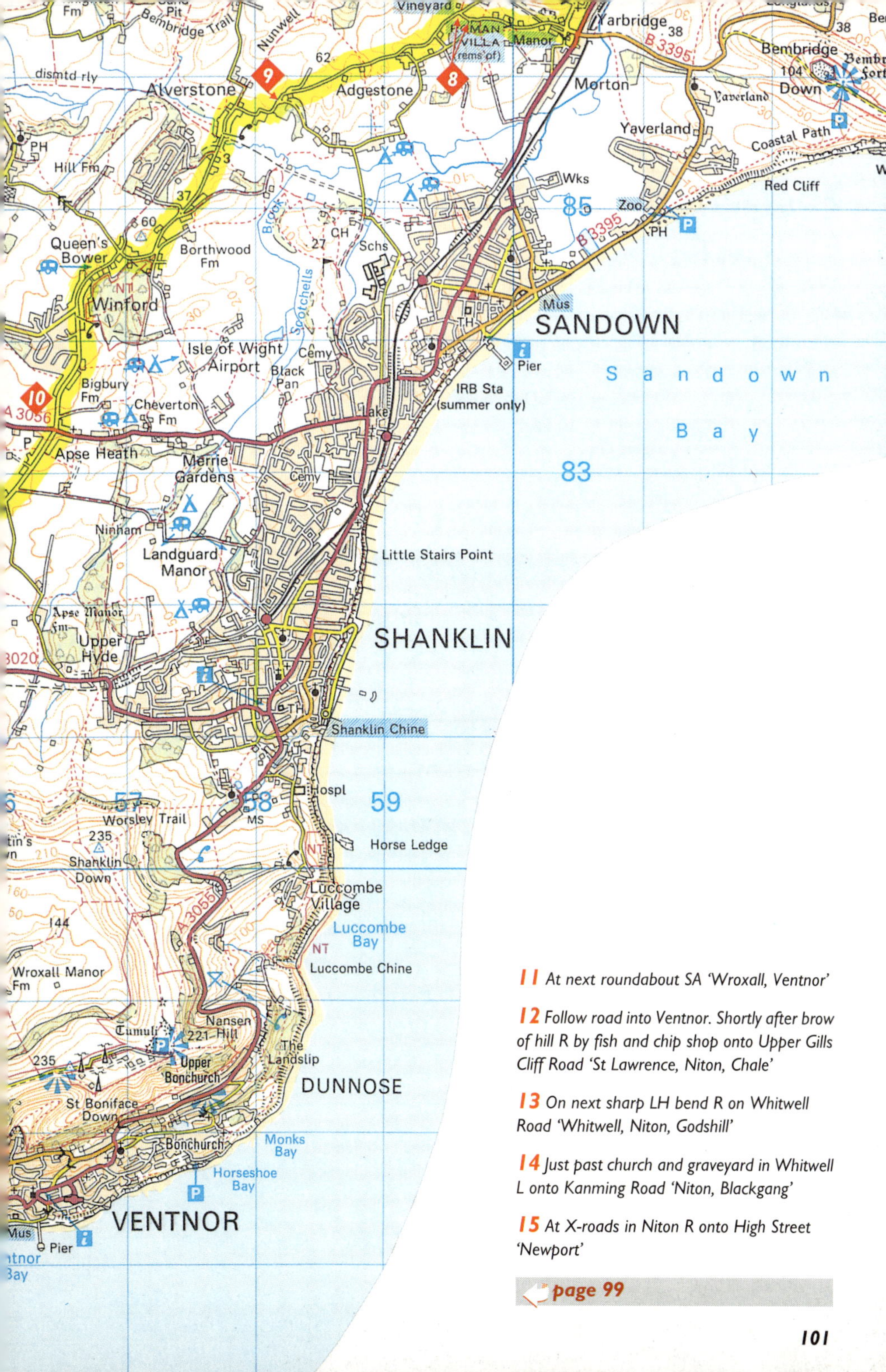

11 *At next roundabout SA 'Wroxall, Ventnor'*

12 *Follow road into Ventnor. Shortly after brow of hill R by fish and chip shop onto Upper Gills Cliff Road 'St Lawrence, Niton, Chale'*

13 *On next sharp LH bend R on Whitwell Road 'Whitwell, Niton, Godshill'*

14 *Just past church and graveyard in Whitwell L onto Kanming Road 'Niton, Blackgang'*

15 *At X-roads in Niton R onto High Street 'Newport'*

page 99

Chalk ridges and woodland tracks south of Hungerford

This ride falls into three sections: the drove road along the edge of the escarpment over the top of Walbury Hill and Inkpen Hill; the wooded tracks that lead away from the ridge, which includes a stretch of the Test Way; and a 4-mile road section between Ibthorpe and Binley to complete the circle. There are fabulous views northwards from the ridge, although the going is at times fairly rough.

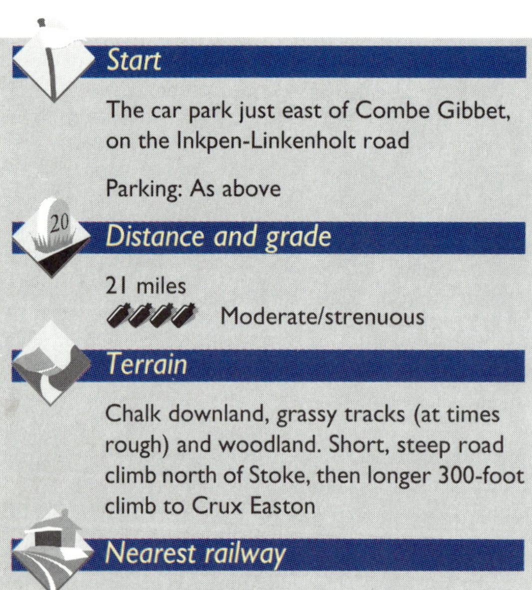

1 From the car park, take the track westwards 'Combe Gibbet'

2 Follow this track through rough and smooth for 2½ miles

3 At T-j with road L

4 After ½ mile, on sharp RH bend by a telephone box bear L (in effect SA) down no through road

5 Tarmac to Ballyack Farm. Bear R at farm sign and keep bearing R until reaching the road

6 At T-j with road bear L

7 After ¼ mile, on sharp LH bend, SA onto track

8 Go SA over two X-roads of tracks to arrive at road

9 At T-j with road L

10 On sharp LH bend, bear R (in effect SA)

11 Shortly after large wooden buildings on the right, turn L onto track just past two barns on the left

12 At T-j with road R, then L on sharp RH bend just past 'Upton' sign

13 Follow main track for 2½ miles over X-roads of tracks, ignoring turns

14 300 yards after passing large, round, black barn on your left at T-j of tracks, turn R

15 Follow this track downhill past farm to road. Turn L on lane, then L again at T-j with more major road

16 At offset X-roads with A343 R, then L by George and Dragon PH 'St Mary Bourne'

page 105

Inkpen Hill

Buttermere

Ibthorpe

Inkpen Hill
Combe Gibbet
Long Barrow
Cumulus
Ham Hill
Town Fm
Buttermere
Grange Fm
Walbury Hill
West Woodhay Down
Highwood
Fort
Wright's Fm
Summer Hill
Combe
Lower Fm
Manor Fm
Combe Hill
Test Way
Sheepless Hill
Earthwork
Rivar Hill
New Buildings
Bishop's Barn
Manor Fm
Ballyack Ho
Buttermere Wood
Rockmoor Down
Combe Wood
Hogs Hole
Tumulus
Moordown Fm
Upper Horns Fm
Henley
Pearce's Fm
Upper Row Fm
Hart Hill Down
Field System
Fosbury
Winterside Fm
Littledown
Manor Ho
Linkenholt
Manor Fm
Faccombe
Netherton
Vernham Row
Box Fm
Vernham Street
Rymer's Barn
East Down
Oakhill Wood
Vernham Bank
Vernham Dean
Sch
Vernham Manor
Grim's Ditch
Wilster Copse
Faccombe Wood
Fosbury
Upton Manor
Ankers Fm
Clinchorn Fm
Upton
Conholt Hill
Middle Conholt Fm
Conholt Ho
Conholt Park
Ambley Fm
Doyley
Rushmore Down
Hampshire Gate
Cathanger Wood
R Swift
Ibthorpe
Tangley Clumps
Whistler's Fm
Dowlands Fm
Crux Easton
Pill Heath Fm
Windmills
Tangley Bottom
Stoke
Tangley Fm
PH

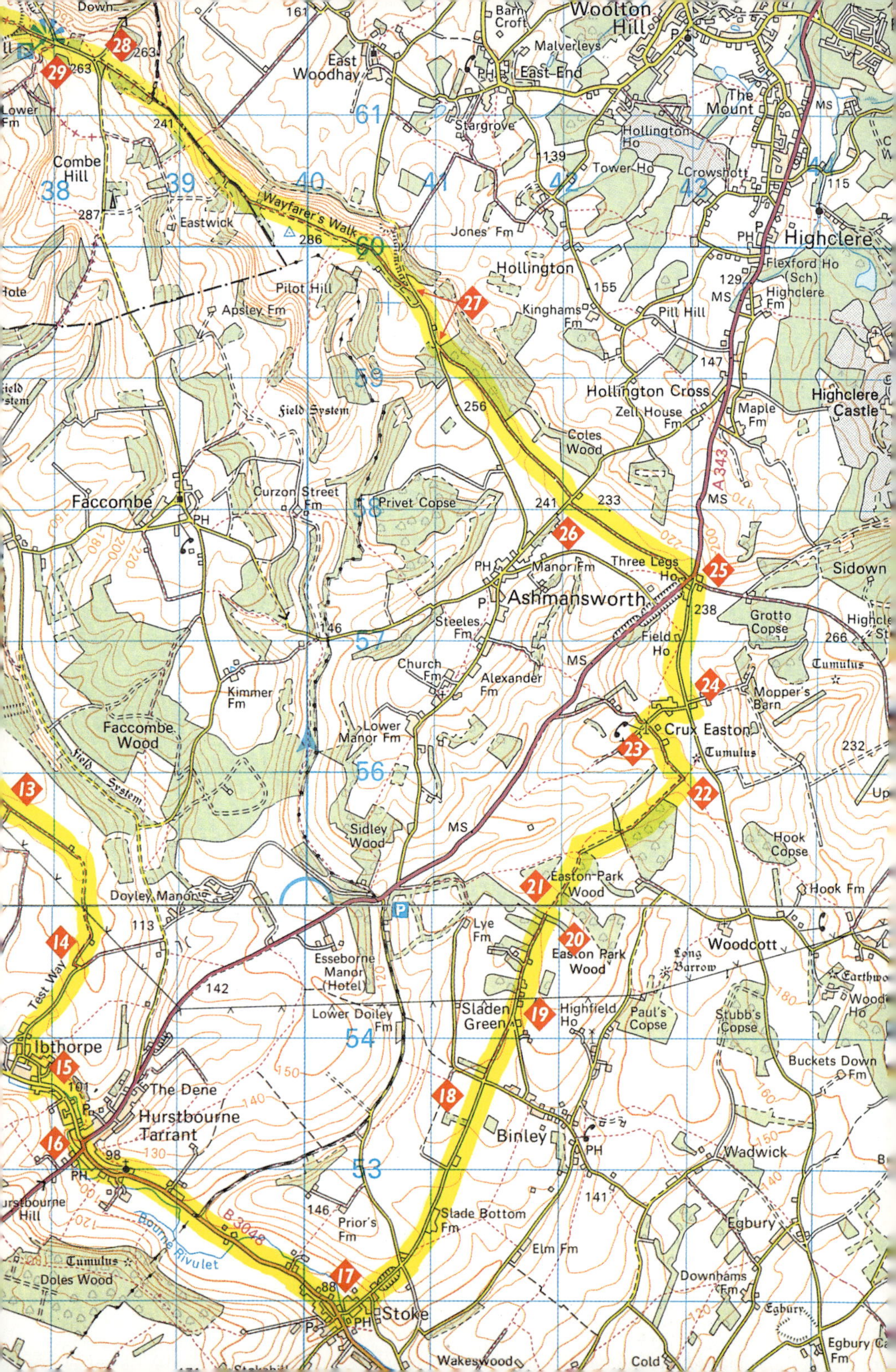

Woolton Hill
East Woodhay
East End
Highclere
Hollington
Wayfarer's Walk
Faccombe
Ashmansworth
Crux Easton
Faccombe Wood
Test Way
Ibthorpe
Hurstbourne Tarrant
Binley
Woodcott
Stoke
Highclere Castle

17 *After 1½ miles, in Stoke 1st L 'Binley 2', passing White Hart PH on your right*

18 *1½ miles after PH, on sharp RH bend, SA onto track (Binley signposted to the right)*

19 *Merge with track coming from the right and follow through woods*

20 *At sharp RH bend in woods, with a 'No public right of way' sign to your right, carry SA through DIY gate into field*

21 *Rough track improves. Follow it in same direction*

22 *Follow track round sharp LH bend towards buildings and road*

23 *SA on tarmac by house. At X-roads near telephone box R (NS)*

24 *At T-j L 'Highclere 2, Newbury 7'*

25 *At T-j with A343 SA onto grassy track*

26 *At 1st road SA*

27 *At 2nd road R, then L after 300 yards steeply uphill to track*

28 *At 3rd road L, then immediately R at T-j*

29 *On sharp RH bend after 300 yards, bear L 'Byway' to return to start*

Off-road riding tips

- Padded shorts and gloves make off-road riding more comfortable
- If there is any possibility of rain take something waterproof. Never underestimate the effects of wind-chill when you are wet, even in summer
- In wet and cold conditions keep a layer of warm clothes next to the skin – thermal underwear or wool
- Discretion is the better part of valour – do not be persuaded to do something which you feel is way beyond your abilities
- To get an early start, prepare your equipment and bike the night before
- Make yourself a checklist which you can use whenever you go off on a ride, amending it for weekends away or winter riding

A view from Inkpen Hill

Refreshments

White Hart PH, Stoke
George and Dragon PH, Hurstbourne Tarrant

Watership Down, south of Newbury

The Kennet and Avon Canal, the A4 road and the London to Hungerford railway vie for space in the valley of the River Kennet, lying between the Lambourn Downs and the Ridgeway to the north and the north Hampshire Downs to the south. It is mainly over the latter that this ride travels, with fabulous views from the ridge between White Hill and Watership Down, the setting for Richard Adams' tale about adventurous rabbits. The southern part of the ride takes you along some beautiful woodland tracks before climbing on road to the village of Hannington and a final descent to Kingsclere.

Refeshments

Crown Inn, George & Horn PH, Kingsclere
Vine Inn, Hannington

Start

The church in Kingsclere between Newbury and Basingstoke on the A339

Parking: Free long-term car park in Kingsclere, off Swan Street near church

Distance and grade

19 miles
 Easy/moderate

Terrain

Chalk downland woodland, quiet lanes. Two 300-foot climbs, both on road

Nearest railway

Whitchurch, 2 miles from the southwest corner of the route, or Basingstoke, 6 miles from route near Ibworth

Kingsclere
White Hill
Watership Down
Ridgeway Farm

Off-road riding tips

- Keep some spare dry clothes and shoes in the car to change into and carry some bin liners in the car to put dirty, wet clothes in
- Keep other possessions dry in very wet weather by carrying them in two sets of plastic bags
- If using a jet spray to clean your bike, do not aim the hose directly at the hubs or bottom bracket; clean these parts from above
- Lubricate your bike after washing it or after a very wet ride, paying particular attention to the chain
- Lower your saddle when going down steep off-road sections, keep the pedals level, stand up out of the saddle to let your legs absorb the bumps and keep your weight over the rear wheel
- Carry a water bottle in the bottle carrier and keep it filled, particularly on hot days
- Good energy foods which don't take up much space are dates, figs, dried fruit and nuts

Beech trees near Watership Down

B3051

Warren Bottom Copse

Hannington

Plantation Hill

1 *From the church take the B3051 'Whithurch, Overton', climbing 280 feet in 1½ miles*

2 *Near the top of White Hill R on Wayfarer's Walk 'Inkpen 12 miles', 'No cars or motorbikes except access'. Bear R*

3 *Follow track over gravel, then chalk, then grass with fine views to the right*

4 *Climb past the trig point, following the arrows. Descend to the road on a narrower, rougher track*

5 *At T-j with road L for 300 yards to brow of hill, then L through gate opening (orange pointer)*

6 *Follow orange pointers, bearing R onto grassy track at the entry to Sydmonton Court Estate*

7 *Track improves from grassy to hardcore as it descends the hill*

8 *At T-j with road R, then after 1½ miles just past Ridgeway Farm on the left turn L 'Whitnal Farm'*

9 *Tarmac as far as farm then good track. Bear L at fork*

10 *At X-roads of tracks L. Follow this in the same direction for 2½ miles, taking care when crossing the B3051*

11 *At T-j with next road R, then 1st L after ¼ mile 'North Oakley 2, Hannington 3'*

12 *After 600 yards at triangle of grass bear R then SA onto grassy track*

13 *This is a narrow track, which becomes broader. At junction with forestry track bear L*

14 *At X-roads L 'North Oakley 1¼, Hannington 1½'*

15 *After 1¼ miles at T-j R 'Hannington 1, Kingsclere 4½'*

16 *Follow road through Hannington. ¾ mile after village green, at bottom of gentle hill, opposite large barn on right turn L on track 'Bridleway'*

17 *At T-j of tracks bear R towards Plantation Farm. At road bear L*

18 *After 300 yards at sharp RH bend in road L downhill 'Private road, bridlepath only'*

19 *At fork in tracks bear L as far as road, then bear R onto the track ahead to descend to the B3051*

20 *At T-j with B3051 turn R to return to centre of Kingsclere*

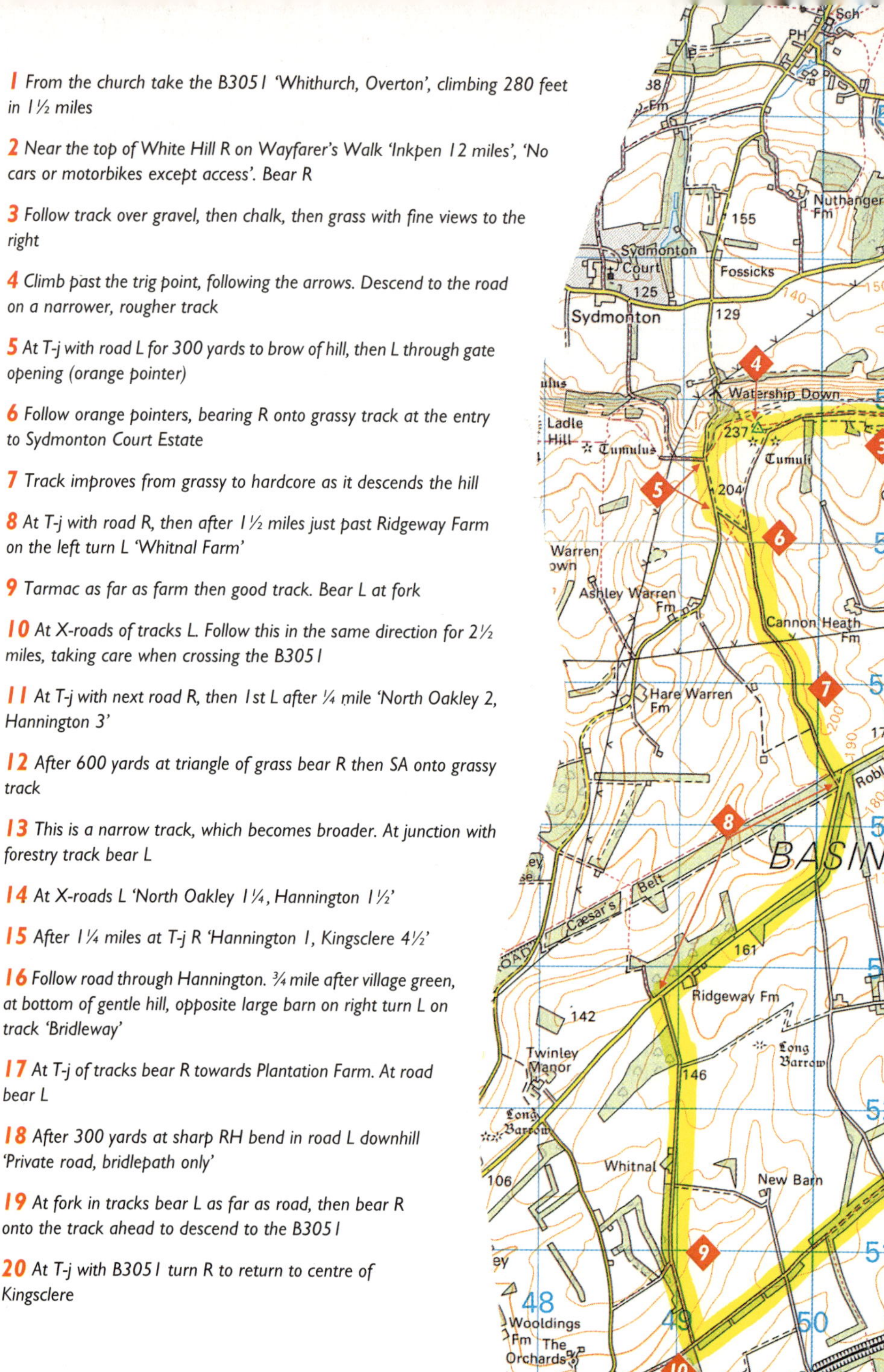

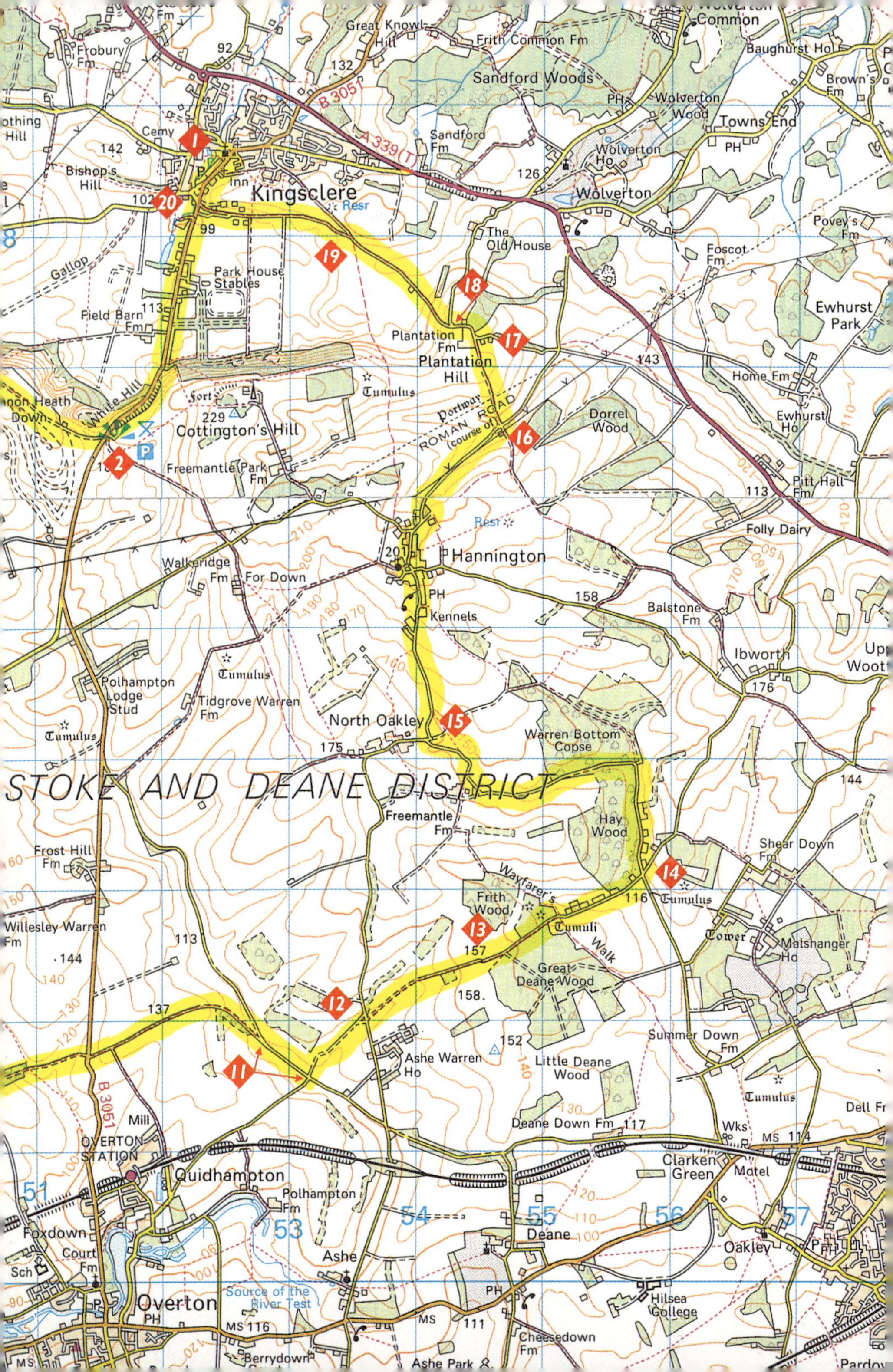
Frobury Fm
92
Great Knowl Hill
132
Frith Common Fm
Common
Baughurst Ho
Sandford Woods
B 3051
A 339(T)
Wolverton Wood
Brown's Fm
Towns End
Cemy
142
Bishop's Hill
Sandford Fm
126
Wolverton Ho
Wolverton
Kingsclere
Inn
102
99
Resr
The Old House
Foscot Fm
Povey's Fm
Gallop
Park House Stables
Field Barn Fm
113
Plantation Fm
Plantation Hill
Ewhurst Park
143
Home Fm
White Hill
Fort
229
Cottington's Hill
Tumulus
Portway
ROMAN ROAD (course of)
Dorrel Wood
Ewhurst Ho
Freemantle Park Fm
113
Pitt Hall Fm
Resr
Folly Dairy
Walkeridge Fm
For Down
201
Hannington
PH
Kennels
158
Balstone Fm
Ibworth
176
Tumulus
Polhampton Lodge Stud
Tidgrove Warren Fm
North Oakley
175
Warren Bottom Copse
Tumulus
STOKE AND DEANE DISTRICT
144
Freemantle Fm
Hay Wood
Shear Down Fm
Frost Hill Fm
Wayfarer's Walk
Frith Wood
116
Tumulus
Tumuli
Tower
Malshanger Ho
Willesley Warren Fm
113
144
157
Great Deane Wood
158
137
152
Summer Down Fm
Ashe Warren Ho
Little Deane Wood
B 3051
Tumulus
Mill
Deane Down Fm
117
Wks
MS 114
Dell Fm
OVERTON STATION
Quidhampton
Clarken Green
Motel
Polhampton Fm
51
53
54
55
56
57
Foxdown
Deane
Court Fm
Ashe
Oakley
Sch
Source of the River Test
PH
Overton
PH
Hilsea College
MS
MS 116
111
Cheesedown Fm
Berrydown
Ashe Park
1
2
11
12
13
14
15
16
17
18
19
20

3 A gentle journey in the heart of Hampshire north of New Alresford

From the friendly, attractive town of New Alresford on broad easy tracks, this ride climbs gently out of the valley formed by the River Alre and goes northeast past the watercress beds on a broad green lane towards Upper Wield. A short road section brings you to the start of another byway running parallel with the outward route, this time heading southwest, first along the Ox Drove then on the Wayfarer's Walk through beech woodland back to New Alresford.

Start

Horse and Groom PH, Broad Street, New Alresford

Parking: station car park

Distance and grade

18 miles
Easy

Terrain

One gentle 350-foot climb at the start, otherwise undulating

Nearest railway

Alton, 7 miles from Lower Wield

Refreshments

Many places for refreshments in New Alresford
Yew Tree PH, Lower Wield
Diversions off the route to:
Sun PH Bentworth
Purefoy Arms PH, Preston Candover

New Alresford
Old Alresford
Nettlebed Farm
Lower Wield
Bradley

Places of interest

Alresford House (2)

This mid-Georgian manor house was built by Admiral Lord Rodney in 1750. The grounds are now used for fruit picking and picnicking.

Off-road cycling tips

- Good equipment doesn't make you a good cyclist. The only bad cyclists are those who show no consideration to others, whether by weaving around, failing to indicate or riding on pavements in on-road situations, or by failing to follow the countryside code, and showing no respect to walkers and horseriders when off-road
- Experiment with saddle height, forwards and backwards adjustment of saddle, tilt of saddle up or down and height of the handlebars (do not exceed maximum height) until you find your most comfortable riding position
- Anticipate hills by changing into the right gear before it gets tough
- If there is an easier gear when struggling up a hill use it, and let the bike do the work not your knee joints

The Ox Drove

Abbotstone Down

Abbotstone

1 Out of town on B3046 'Old Alresford, The Candovers'

2 Immediately after church in Old Alresford R (NS)

3 After passing Kilk Lane and Upton Park Farm on your left, on sharp RH bend, L (in effect SA) onto track

4 Follow in same direction for 3 miles passing Nettlebed, then Upper Lanham Farm. The final ½ mile may be muddy (if you wish to avoid mud, turn L through Lanham Farm to road, turn R and rejoin route at instruction 6)

5 At road L, then at T-j R (sign broken)

6 At T-j R 'Lower Wield 1½, Medstead 1¾', then 1st L 'Lower Wield 1½, Bentworth 2½'

7 After ¾ mile 1st L (sign vandalized)

8 1st R after Yew Tree PH 'Bradley 1¼'

9 At X-roads, L 'Preston Candover 1¾' then after 400 yards, opposite red-brick house just past junction of farm tracks into fields L onto track 'Right of Way'

10 After 1½ miles at road SA

11 Follow this track in same direction over several X-roads of tracks, passing a large, elegant flint-and-brick house on your left and continuing in same direction on unsurfaced track

12 At road SA onto track and SA again after 50 yards 'Right of Way'

13 At T-j with major metalled track by farm buildings L, then 1st L on broad track. Follow in same direction towards line of trees, ignoring turning on right towards farm

14 At B3046 SA towards wooden barrier

15 Follow this track as it improves to join road by triangle of grass near bridge. Turn L

16 Ignore two tracks to the left. After ½ mile, at bottom of gentle slope by X-roads of farm tracks L by letter box 'Right of Way'

17 At metalled lane L. At T-j with B3046 R to return to New Alresford

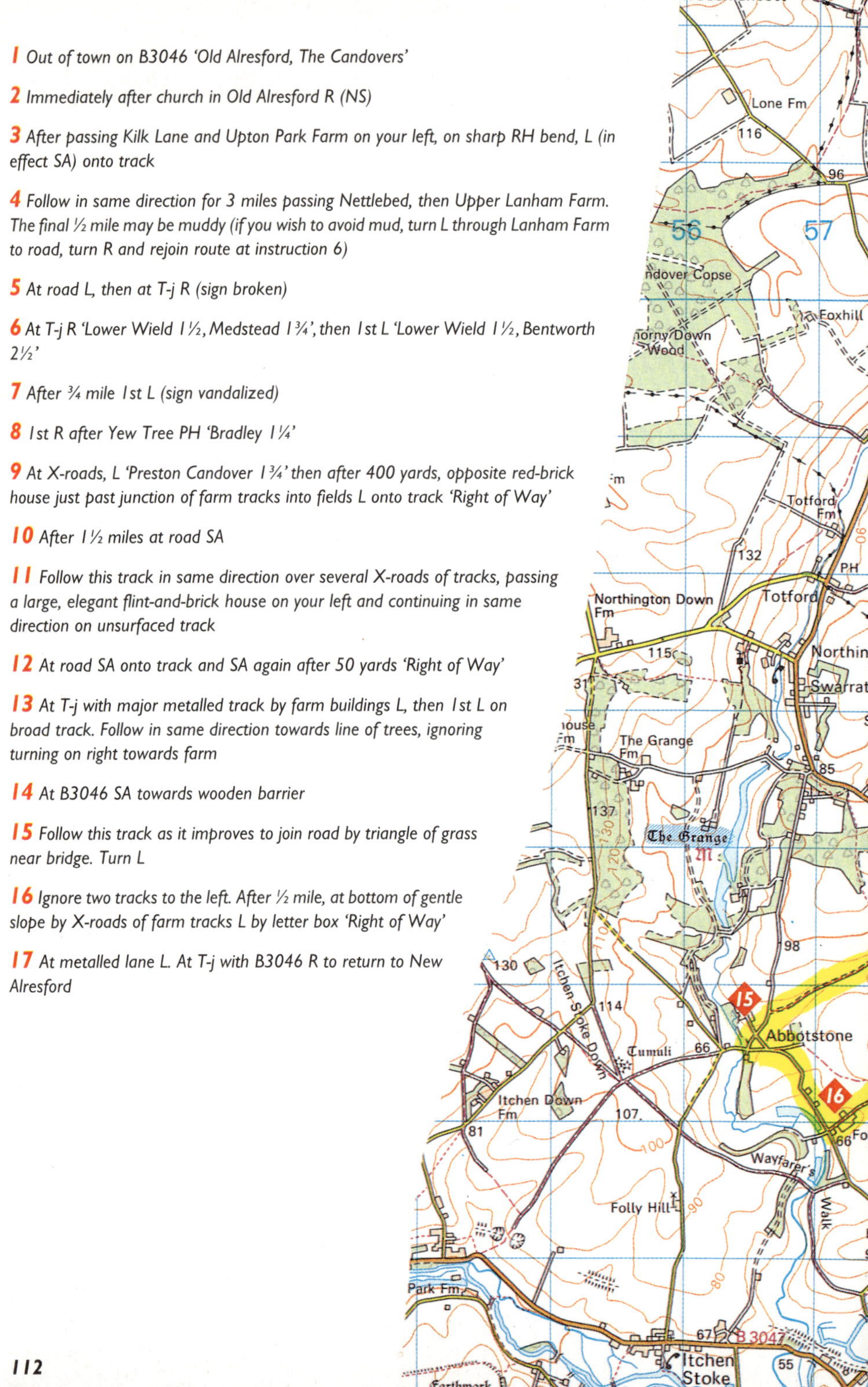

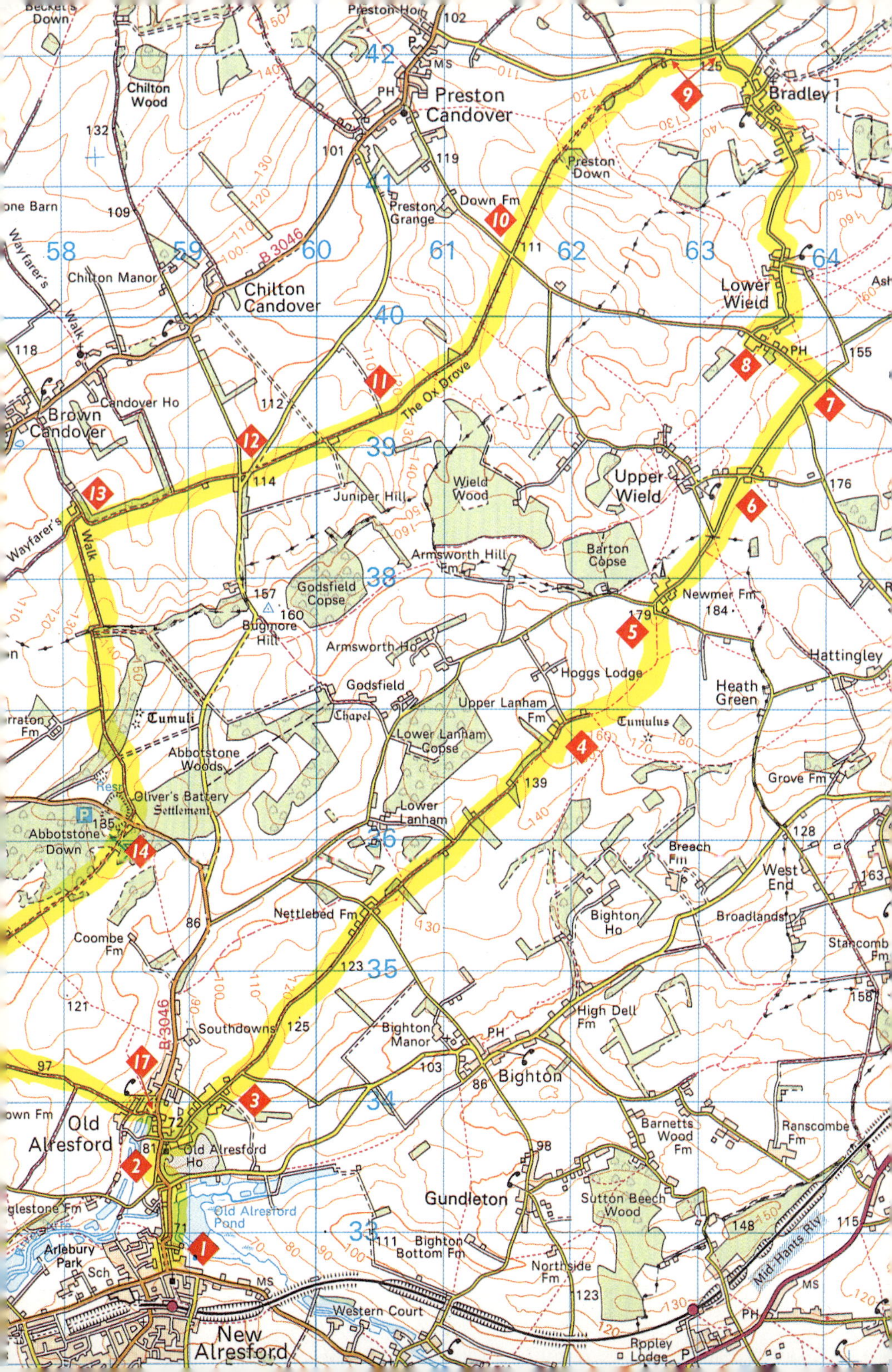

Chilton Wood
Preston Candover
Bradley
Preston Down
Down Fm
Preston Grange
Chilton Manor
Chilton Candover
B 3046
Lower Wield
PH
The Ox Drove
Candover Ho
Brown Candover
Juniper Hill
Wield Wood
Upper Wield
Wayfarer's Walk
Armsworth Hill Fm
Barton Copse
Godsfield Copse
Newmer Fm
Bugmore Hill
Armsworth Ho
Hattingley
Hoggs Lodge
Godsfield
Chapel
Heath Green
Upper Lanham Fm
Tumuli
Tumulus
Abbotstone Woods
Lower Lanham Copse
Grove Fm
Resr
Oliver's Battery Settlement
Abbotstone Down
Lower Lanham
Breach Fm
West End
Nettlebed Fm
Bighton Ho
Broadlands
Coombe Fm
Stancomb Fm
High Dell Fm
Southdowns
Bighton Manor
Bighton
Old Alresford
Old Alresford Ho
Barnetts Wood Fm
Ranscombe Fm
Gundleton
Sutton Beech Wood
Old Alresford Pond
Arlebury Park
Sch
Bighton Bottom Fm
Northside Fm
Mid Hants Rly
MS
Western Court
New Alresford
Ropley Lodge

4 Easy tracks south of New Alresford

On a fine mixture of broad and narrow tracks, this ride takes in open downland and broadleaf woodland and two crossings of the lovely River Itchen. In a couple of places the route may be slightly overgrown or, after rain and in the winter, contain some muddy sections. Forewarned is forearmed: wear clothing to cover your arms and legs, accept that your footwear – and probably your bike – will be muddy when you finish. If you want to avoid the mud take the road alternative.

Refreshments

Plenty of choice in New Alresford
Plough Inn Itchen Abbas

Start

Horse and Groom PH, New Alresford

Parking: New Alresford station car park

Distance and grade

19 miles

Easy/moderate

Terrain

Flat or undulating for the first half of the ride. One climb of 270 feet from Itchen Abbas north to the windmill by the trig point

Nearest railway

Limited service on the Midhants Watercress Line from Alton to New Alresford. Otherwise Winchester, 6 miles from the route where it crosses the A31

New Alresford

Cheriton

Places of interest

Avington Park (17)

This attractive, 17th-century country house was built in the style of Sir Christopher Wren. The Duke of Chandos altered the house in the following century and the rooms now range in style from early 18th-century to Victorian. A Georgian-style church stands in the grounds.

Near Cheriton Wood south of New Alresford

Off-road cycling tips

- Drink before you get thirsty and eat before you get hungry. Regular small amounts are better than a big lunch
- Take a compass with you for crossing moorland or in poor visibility and know how to use it
- Always thank people who make way for you

Hampage Farm

Ovington

Itchen Abbas

windmill

Itchen Stoke Down

Wayfarer's Walk

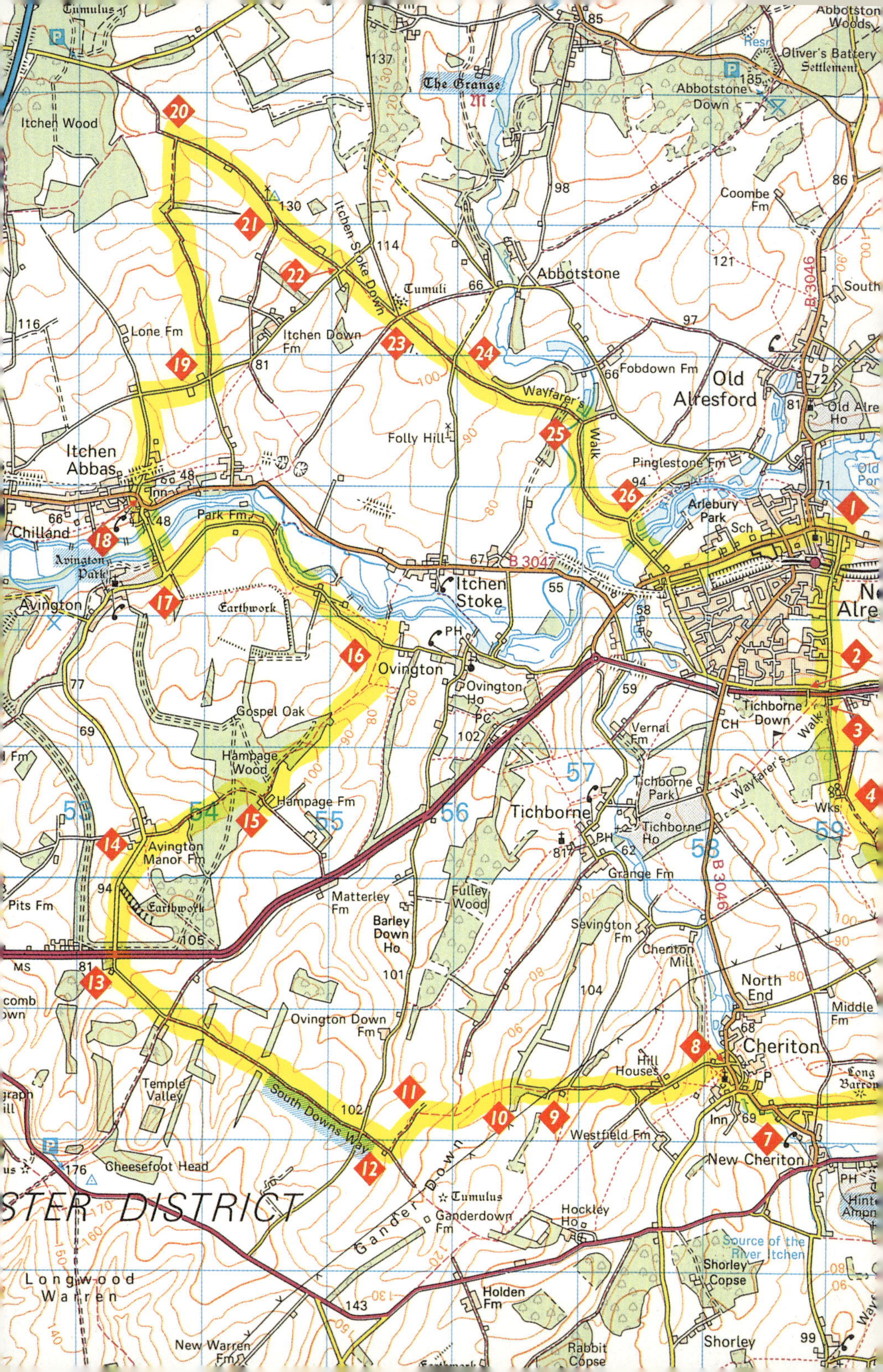

Tumulus
Itchen Wood
Abbotstone Woods
Oliver's Battery Settlement
Abbotstone Down
The Grange
Coombe Fm
Abbotstone
Itchen Stoke Down
Tumuli
Lone Fm
Itchen Down Fm
Fobdown Fm
Old Alresford
Wayfarer's Walk
Folly Hill
Itchen Abbas
Pinglestone Fm
Arlebury Park
Chilland
Park Fm
Avington Park
Avington
Earthwork
B 3047
Itchen Stoke
Ovington
Ovington Ho
Gospel Oak
Tichborne Down
Vernal Fm
Hampage Wood
Hampage Fm
Tichborne
Tichborne Park
Tichborne Ho
Avington Manor Fm
Grange Fm
Pits Fm
Matterley Fm
Barley Down Ho
Fulley Wood
Sevington Fm
Cheriton Mill
B 3046
North End
Middle Fm
Ovington Down Fm
Cheriton
Hill Houses
Temple Valley
South Downs Way
Westfield Fm
New Cheriton
Cheesefoot Head
Long Barrow
Gander Down
Ganderdown Fm
Hockley Ho
Source of the River Itchen
Shorley Copse
Longwood Warren
Holden Fm
New Warren Fm
Rabbit Copse
Shorley
STER DISTRICT

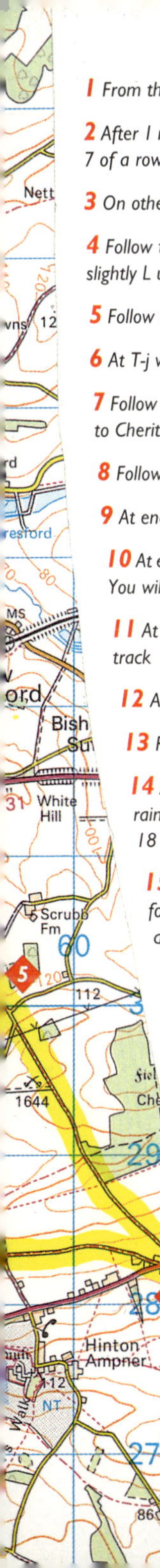

1 From the Horse and Groom PH, out of town on East Street past Peaceful Home PH. 1st R on Sun Lane

2 After 1 mile, having passed a turning left to Long Sutton and a sharp RH bend, turn L opposite numbers 6 and 7 of a row of white terraced houses between grey railings to cross bridge over A31

3 On other side of bridge L 'Bridleway, Bramdean', then 1st R 'Alresford Golf Club' (Beware golf balls!)

4 Follow this track in same direction past golf course, through wood. At junction near sewage works SA and slightly L uphill on broad track

5 Follow this main track to road. Bear R (in effect SA), then after 100 yards, on RH bend bear L (in effect SA)

6 At T-j with A272 R, then R again on LH bend by chevron

7 Follow this track in same direction over a major and minor X-roads of tracks until reaching road at entrance to Cheriton. Turn R

8 Follow road into Cheriton. Shortly after church and telephone box L on Hill House Lane (no through road)

9 At end of tarmac directly underneath powerlines, R through bridlegate into wood (maybe muddy)

10 At end of wood SA through field, aiming for a midpoint between fence on left and fence/hedgerow on right. You will pick up a more distinct grassy track, which takes you to the far LH corner of the field

11 At T-j with major (muddy) track L towards barn, then at X-roads of tracks near barn R onto more grassy track

12 At road SA

13 Follow in same direction over X-roads of tracks to A31. SA 'Ovington, Itchen Abas'

14 At bottom of hill by barn R on bridleway (**Warning!** The next section is very muddy in the wood after rain. Be prepared for this **or** if you wish to avoid it, do **not** turn R but stay on road and rejoin at instruction 18 after 2½ miles)

15 Follow in same direction over grassy X-roads in wood. At edge of wood, just before farmhouse L along forest edge 'Bridleway'. This part can be very muddy, but it does not last long and is followed by a lovely descent

16 At road L

17 After 2 miles at T-j just before 'Avington' sign R

18 Cross lovely River Itchen. At T-j with B3047 by Plough Inn L 'Kingsworthy 2½' then 1st R 'Vet Centre, School'

19 Ignore 1st left to vet centre. Take next L on track opposite road turning to right

20 At first muddy, then soon improves. At T-j R

21 Shortly after windmill fork L

22 At road, SA

23 At junction of tracks SA 'New Alresford'

24 At road SA

25 Cross stream and turn R

26 At T-j with road R. At next T-j, with B3047, L on The Avenue to return to start

5 Corfe Castle southwest to Swyre Head, returning via Knowle Hill

Here is a short ride packed with all the best ingredients: challenging climbs on firm surfaces, woodland, panoramic views from Swyre Head – the highest point on the Dorset coast – broad tracks over chalk downland, a tricky descent and an open grassy descent, and not too much mud. And then there are the cream teas to look forward to back in Corfe Castle. Particularly satisfying is the way you can see the whole course of the ride from either of the two ridges that form the northern and southern side of the route.

Start

Bankes Arms Hotel, Corfe Castle

Parking: Large car park on street leading from opposite Bankes Arms Hotel

Distance and grade

12 miles

Moderate/strenuous

Terrain

Two climbs, one of 650 feet from Corfe Castle to Swyre Head on tarmac and good tracks, particularly steep near Blashenwell Farm; the second of 450 feet from the bottom of Steeple Hill to Grange Arch, also on tarmac and good tracks

Nearest railway

Wareham, 5 miles northwest of Corfe Castle

Refreshments

Greyhound PH, Fox PH, Bankes Arms PH and a number of tea shops Corfe Castle

Corfe Castle
Blashenwell Farm
Kingston
Swyre Head
Kimmeridge

Places of interest

Isle of Purbeck

Designated an area of outstanding natural beauty, the Isle of Purbeck is a lovely peninsula that stretches from Poole Harbour to Lulworth Cove with the Purbeck Hills to the west.

Smedmore Hill above Kimmeridge

Kingston (5)

Kingston's 19th-century church is thought to be one of the best in the area; notable features are the black Purbeck marble pillars and the stone-vaulted chancel.

Kimmeridge and Smedmore House (7)

This small village with thatched and slate-roofed cottages lies near a bay renowned for fossils. The Smedmore Estate owns the bay and all the land round the village and the manor house is open to the public. Construction of the house began in the 1620s but the architecture is a mixture of styles ranging from Jacobean to Queen Anne and Georgian. Dutch furniture and paintings are on display and there is a collection of antique dolls.

Grange Arch (10-11)

Now known as Bond's Folly, this arch was built by Denis Bond in about 1740 as an imposing entrance to his house, Creech Grange. There are excellent views, sometimes as far as the Isle of Portland.

Steeple Hill

Grange Arch

Ridgeway Hill

Knowle Hill

1 *With your back to Bankes Arms Hotel SA towards National Trust shop, following road round to left 'Car Park'*

2 *At end of road SA onto no through road 'Blashenwell Farm Only'*

3 *Follow road to farm and R at the end of the farmyard 'Willwood House' (blue arrow)*

4 *Bear L at fork of tracks steeply uphill to T-j of tracks. L into wood*

5 *At road R. Follow this as far as signposts for Encombe Farms, Orchard Hill Farm. At this point L through stone pillars, then R 'No cars, bridlepath only'*

6 *Follow track gently uphill to Swyre Head, then sharply R along fence*

7 *After 1½ miles at road L, then at T-j R and after 20 yards L through bridlegate 'Range Walks, Steeple Leaze'*

8 *Shortly after next metal gate diagonally R up over brow of hill to your right towards gate in fence (no obvious track). If you miss this, and you find yourself by the firing range flagpost, head back towards the gate in fence diagonally to your left*

9 *Descend to road. Turn L 'Steeple and Creech Hill, Army Ranges'. Steeply to top and follow road round to R 'Wareham 4½. Alternative route to Lulworth'*

10 *Just beyond flagpole by car park R, then L onto track parallel with road 'Grange Arch ½, Corfe Castle 3½'*

11 *Keep an eye open for bridlegate on left to join track on other side of fence 'Cocknowle ½, Corfe Castle 2¼'*

12 *At road R, then L (both in effect SA) 'Ridge Path. Corfe Castle 1¾'*

13 *Before trig point R downhill*

14 *At road L. At A351 R 'Swanage'*

Clay Pit
King's Barrow
Hotel
Stoborough Green
Hartland Moor
Tumuli
Doreys Fm
Battle Plain
Stoborough Heath
Tumulus
Hartland Stud
Middlebere Heath
Corfe River
Three Lords Barrow
Creech Bottom
Danger Area
Rifle Range
Three Barrows
Grange Barn
Depot
New Mills Heath
Scotland
Creech Heath
Wks
Icen Barrow
Furzebrook
Furzebrook Ho
A 351
Clay Pit
Creech
Drinking Barrow
Mus
Norden
Blue Pool
Sewage Wks
Cotness
Norden Fm
dismtd rly
Whitehall
Mine
East Creech
B 3351
ISLE OF
Creech Grange
Stonehill Down
Knowle Hill
Corfe Castle
East Hill
West Hill
The Rings
Cocknowle
Great Wood
Grange Arch
Ridgeway Hill
Barneston Manor
HILLS
Church Knowle
Cemy
Corfe Castle
Challow Fm
Animal Sanctuary
West Bucknowle Ho
Bucknowle Ho
Town End
Whiteway Fm
Manor
Steeple
Lutton
Blackmanston Fm
PURBECK
Corfe Common
B 3069
Harp Stone
Bradle Fm
West Orchard Fm
East Orchard
Blashenwell Fm
Lynch Fm
Afflington Fm
Kimmeridge
Smedmore Hill
Orchard Hill Fm
Kingston
SWC Path
Toll
Gaulter Gap
Cumulus
Obelisk
Smedmore Ho
Kimmeridge Bay
Tower
Swyre Head
Encombe Ho
Coombe Bottom
South West Coast Path
Swalland Fm
Westhill Fm
Field Systems
Kimmeridge Ledges
Clavell's Hard
Rope Lake Head
Eldon Seat
Encombe Dairy
Field Stud Cent
Renscombe Fm
Houns-tout Cliff
West Hill
Egmont Point
Chapman's Pool
Emmetts Hill
Chapel
ST ALDHELM'S

6 Corfe Castle to Worth Matravers via Brenscombe Hill and the Priests Way

A ride along two ridges, the first longer, steeper and higher, takes you over Brenscombe Hill and Nine Barrow Down with magnificent views across Poole Harbour, out to sea and down into the valley. A thrilling descent drops you at the road. Several instructions and junctions later find you at the start of Priest's Way. This starts in a somewhat disjointed fashion with a surfeit of gates, but soon improves. The pub at Worth Matravers is quite a curiosity. The detour to St Alban's Head is certainly worth the effort for more superb views and a look at an amazing little chapel. The return brings the dramatic outline of Corfe Castle closer and closer, finishing with a game of dodge the gorse bush over Corfe Common.

Start

Bankes Arms Hotel, Corfe Castle

Parking : Large car park on street leading from opposite Bankes Arms Hotel

Distance and grade

13 and 4 miles. (Total 17 miles)

Moderate/strenuous

Background picture: Corfe Castle

Corfe Castle

Brenscombe Hill

Ulwell

Langton Matravers

Terrain

A steady climb of 600 feet from Corfe Castle to the top of Nine Barrow Down, and 350 feet from the railway bridge at the bottom of the valley to the highpoint of Priest's Way near Eastington Farm

Nearest railway

Wareham, 5 miles northwest of Corfe Castle

Places of interest

Corfe Castle

From its construction by William the Conquerer to its destruction by Parliamentary forces in the Civil War, Corfe Castle has witnessed many episodes in English history. William I's son, Robert, Duke of Normandy, was imprisoned here; King John, whose favourite castle it was, imprisoned his wife here in 1212 and four years later hid his crown and treasures here and Edward II, who improved and enlarged the castle, was imprisoned in it in 1326. Henry VII visited in 1496 and in 1571 Elizabeth I sold the castle to Sir Christopher Hatton, whose widow later disposed of it to the Royalist Sir John Bankes. Sir John spent most of his time in attendance on Charles I and when the Civil War broke out Lady Bankes was left to defend the castle. She held out bravely but was eventually defeated and in 1646 the House of Commons voted to demolish the building.

Refreshments

Greyhound PH, Fox PH, Bankes Arms PH and a number of tea shops in Corfe Castle Square and Compass PH, tea shop Worth Matravers

1 *With your back to the Bankes Arms Hotel R on A351 towards Wareham, then 1st R onto Sandy Hill under railway bridge (11′ 6″)*

2 *On RH bend, just past Challow Farm House on your right, L on track 'Ulwell 3¾'*

3 *Fork L 'Ridge Path, Rollington Hill ½, Ulwell 3½'*

4 *Near the top of the hill by mast at X-roads of tracks SA (blue arrow)*

5 *Follow signs for Ulwell, then at fork of tracks bear R 'Swanage, Studland'*

6 *Following signs for Ulwell again, just before mast by a gate and a fence bear R onto broad downhill track*

7 *Superb descent to road. R then 1st R by Ulwell Cottage 'Caravan Site'*

8 *Just past thatched cottage by water pump 1st R*

9 *At T-j under telephone wires R, then 1st L opposite low stone wall*

10 *At A351 R, then L on Days Road. Climb to brow of hill. Just past Casterbridge Clase on your left, turn R onto tarmac track opposite Benleaze Way (between houses no 74 and 76)*

11 *Before Bellevue Farm, on RH bend L onto track towards gate. Through gate and R onto Priest's Way 'Worth 3¼'*

12 *Go to the right of the ruin, through gate and SA through next gate*

13 **Easy to miss** *After passing through a series of gates, before losing height, keep an eye out for cattle grid on left. Cross grid on track towards grey stone farm 'South Barn'. Follow track around the back of the farmhouse 'Priest's Way'*

14 *Bear L of the barn ahead and follow Priest's Way in same direction for 2 miles, the final section being across a grazed field*

15 *At road L. Follow road past Square and Compass PH. (If you do not wish to go to St Alban's Head, turn R here and follow the second half of instruction 17.) If you are doing the full ride, carry on past tea shop towards church*

16 *At Renscombe Farm, on sharp RH bend L 'Bridleway to St Aldhelm's Head'*

17 *Go as far as chapel and return to the PH. Just before PH, bear L 'Kingston 2, Corfe Castle 4, Wareham 8'*

18 *At T-j with B3069 L 'Kingston 1, Corfe Castle 3, Wareham 7½', then R on track opposite farm 'Bridleway'*

19 *Steep descent, muddy near gate by farm. Bear R of barn. At road L, then L again on RH bend (chevrons) just past Peak House on left. 'National Trust, Corfe Common'*

20 *Wiggle your way through gorse, bearing slightly R. At road SA through another bridle gate 'Corfe Common'. Contour and bear slightly R to join road. R on road to return to Corfe Castle*

Oil Well
Wytch Fm
Depot
Wytch Heath
Rempstone Heath
Claywell
Ower Fm
Newton
Newton Bay
Goathorn
Drove Island
Goathorn Fm
Greenland
Newton Heath
Studla
New Mills Heath
Scotland
Corfe River
Heath
Cumulus
Bushey
Sewage Wks
Lower Bushey Fm
Higher Bushey Fm
Rempstone Fm
Rempstone Hall
B 3351
Rollington Fm
Brenscombe Fm
East Hill
Hotel
Tumulus
Godlingston Heath
Tumulus
Fishing Barrow
Black Do
Puckst
Aggle
Stone Circle
Kingswood Fm
Tumuli
Brenscombe Hill
Challow Fm
Corfe Castle
Mus
Cemy
Little Woolgarston
Aviary
Woolgarston
Long Barrow
Ailwood Fm
Currendon Fm
Godlingston Hill
Dean Hill
Obelis
Nine Barrow Down
Town's End
Corfe Common
Westwood Fm
Knitson Fm
Strip Lynchets
Ulwell
Godlingston Manor
Tumulus
Woodyhyde Fm
Harman's Cross
Swanage Railway
New Buildings
Purbeck Centre
Lynch Fm
Afflington Fm
Kingston
Downshay Fm
New Barn
Wilkswood Fm
Cemy
Mus
Inn
Sch
A 351
Herston
Field Study Centre
Gully
B 3069
Castle View
Coombe Bottom
Tumulus
Compact Fm
Acton
Langton Matravers
South Barn
Field Systems
Path
SWC
West Hill
Field Studies Centre
Renscombe Fm
Eastington Fm
Priest's Way
Spyway Barn
Sea Spray
California Fm
Worth Matravers
Strip Lynchets
NT
Caves
Cave
Dancing Ledge
Blackers Hole
Round Dow
South West Coast Pat
Bonvils
Emmetts Hill
East Man
Seacombe Cliff
Strip Lynchets
Winspit
West Man
Tumulus
Chapel
South West Coast Path
SY
S7

7 From Dorchester via Maiden Castle and Hardy Monument to Abbotsbury

A superb breezy ride over the chalk downland southwest of Dorchester, the route takes in fine sea views and a good refuelling stop at Abbotsbury. It starts by skirting the base of the enormously impressive hill fort of Maiden Castle before joining the Dorset Coast Path along the broad ridge track to Hardy Monument, where there are panoramic views out to sea and over the Dorset hills. A swift descent through woodland brings you to Portesham and along a disused railway to Abbotsbury – a good place to stop before a very steep climb up onto White Hill. Flint and chalk tracks and quiet lanes take you up over the ridge and down into the valley of the River Frome. A final climb from Muckleford to cross the busy A35 drops you in Martinstown, close to Maiden Castle and Dorchester.

Start

Roundabout at the west end of High Street West, Dorchester

Parking: follow signs in Dorchester or start at Maiden Castle

Distance and grade

28 miles

Moderate/strenuous

Terrain

Four major climbs : 550 feet from Dorchester to Hardy Monument, 500 feet from Abbotsbury on to White Hill, 500 feet from Long Bredy to the Roman Road on the ridge and 300 feet from Muckleford south to the A35

Nearest railway

1 From the roundabout take Albert Road southwards out of town. This becomes Cornwall Road. At 1st traffic lights SA onto Maumbury Road

2 At 2nd traffic lights R 'Weymouth', then 2nd R onto Maiden Castle Road 'Maiden Castle 1½'

3 From the car park, take the main track towards the RH edge of the hill. At the 2nd gate leave the main track, turn R uphill through field for 50 yards to join less well-defined track, which continues uphill on the RH side of the fence

4 Over the brow of the hill, through the field on main track and exit via gate onto road. Turn R, then at T-j with B3159 L 'Upwey, Weymouth'

5 Climb for ¾ mile. At brow of hill R through gateway onto track (blue arrow)

page 129

28 A T-j at bottom R, then after 30 yards R again 'Peacock Lodge ¾ Muckleford 1¼'

Dorchester
Maiden Castle
Hardy Monument
Portesham
Abbotsbury
Ashley Chase Dairy

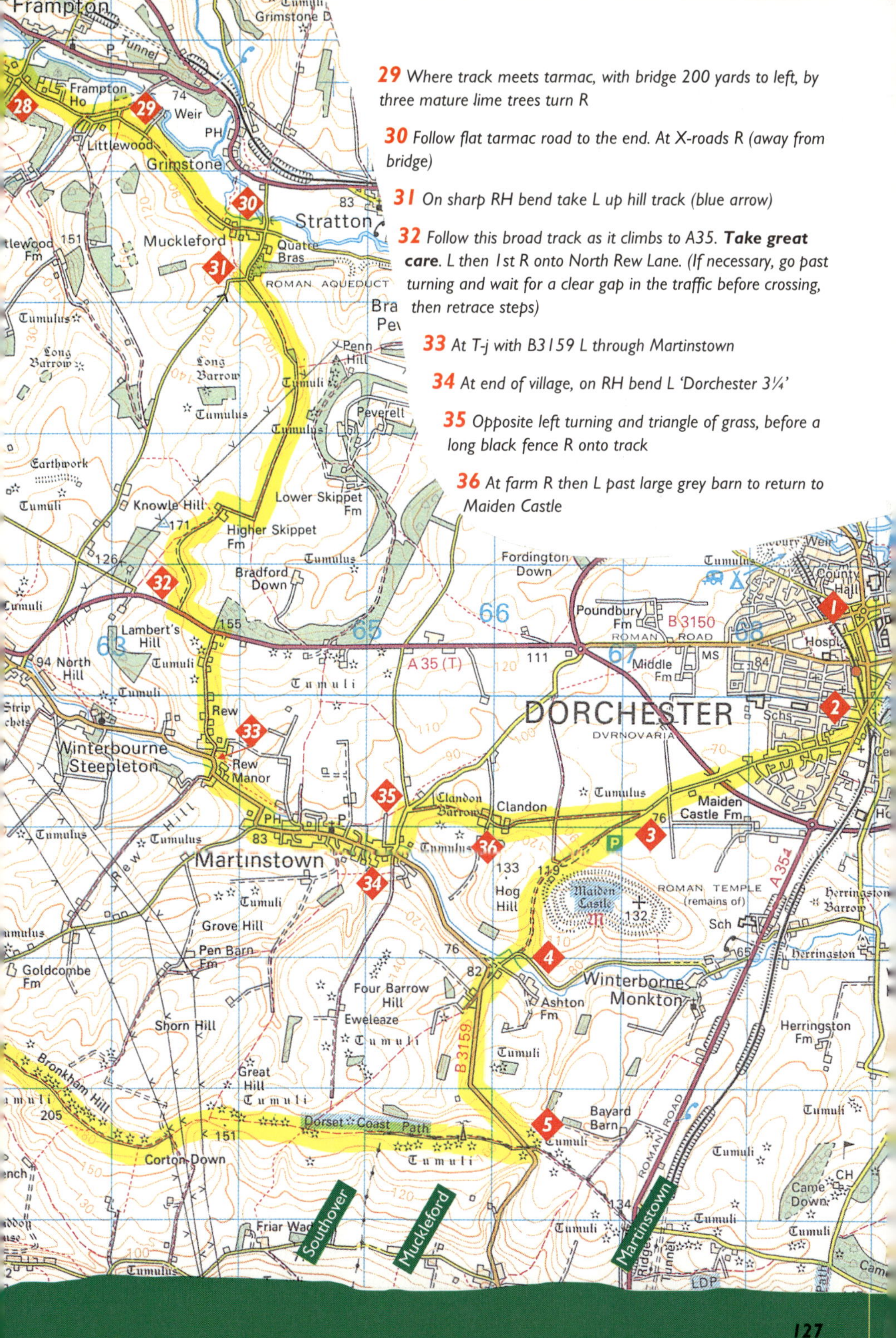

29 *Where track meets tarmac, with bridge 200 yards to left, by three mature lime trees turn R*

30 *Follow flat tarmac road to the end. At X-roads R (away from bridge)*

31 *On sharp RH bend take L up hill track (blue arrow)*

32 *Follow this broad track as it climbs to A35.* ***Take great care****. L then 1st R onto North Rew Lane. (If necessary, go past turning and wait for a clear gap in the traffic before crossing, then retrace steps)*

33 *At T-j with B3159 L through Martinstown*

34 *At end of village, on RH bend L 'Dorchester 3¼'*

35 *Opposite left turning and triangle of grass, before a long black fence R onto track*

36 *At farm R then L past large grey barn to return to Maiden Castle*

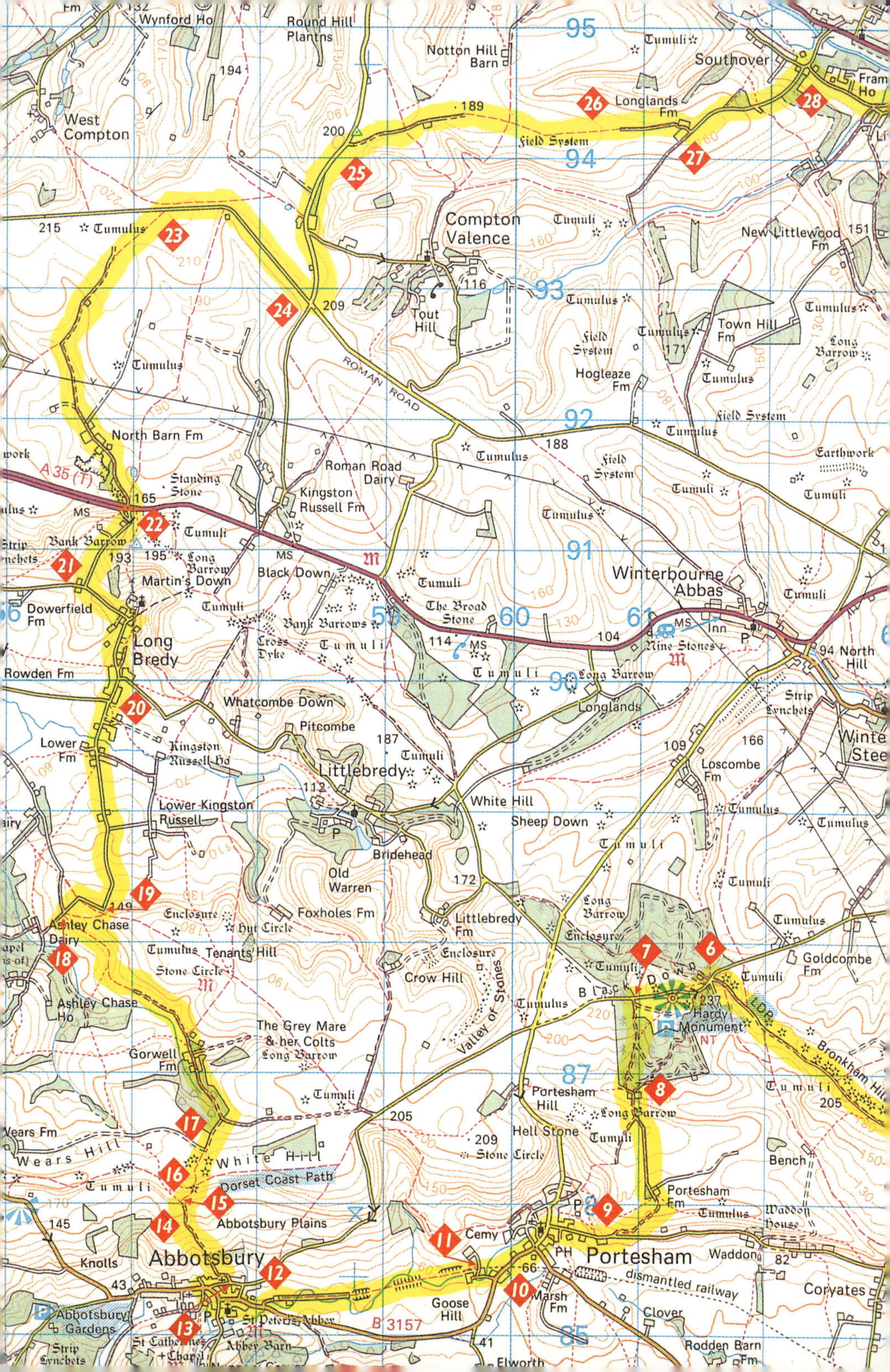

West Compton
Compton Valence
Tout Hill
Southover
Longlands Fm
Notton Hill Barn
Round Hill Plantns
Wynford Ho
New Littlewood Fm
Town Hill Fm
Hogleaze Fm
Roman Road
North Barn Fm
Roman Road Dairy
Kingston Russell Fm
Standing Stone
Bank Barrow
Martin's Down
Black Down
Long Bredy
Dowerfield Fm
Rowden Fm
Winterbourne Abbas
Nine Stones
The Broad Stone
Cross Dyke
Bank Barrows
Whatcombe Down
Pitcombe
Littlebredy
Kingston Russell Ho
Lower Fm
Lower Kingston Russell
Bridehead
Old Warren
White Hill
Sheep Down
Longlands
Loscombe Fm
Foxholes Fm
Littlebredy Fm
Ashley Chase Dairy
Ashley Chase Ho
Tenants' Hill
Stone Circle
Hut Circle
Crow Hill
Valley of Stones
Black Down
Hardy Monument
Goldcombe Fm
Bronkham Hill
The Grey Mare & her Colts Long Barrow
Gorwell Fm
Portesham Hill
Hell Stone
Stone Circle
Wears Hill
White Hill
Dorset Coast Path
Abbotsbury Plains
Portesham Fm
Waddon House
Abbotsbury
Cemy
Portesham
Waddon
Coryates
dismantled railway
Goose Hill
Marsh Fm
Clover
Knolls
Abbotsbury Gardens
St Peter's Abbey
St Catherine's Chapel
Abbey Barn
Strip Lynchets
Elworth
Rodden Barn
B 3157
A 35 (T)
Field System
Tumulus
Tumuli
Long Barrow
Enclosure
Earthwork

Places of interest

Maiden Castle

This hilltop site has been intermittently occupied for about five thousand years. The earliest inhabitants were late Stone-Age people of the Windmill Hill culture who settled at the eastern end of Maiden Castle. Iron Age dwellers were present from about 350BC and occupied a much larger area, eventually amounting to 45 acres. They progressively strengthened and elaborated their defences by enlarging and adding to the ramparts and ditches, and constructing winding, well-protected entrances of timber, stone and earth. However, Maiden Castle failed to withstand the invading Roman forces who stormed it in 43 AD. Archeologists have uncovered the graves of the defenders, many of whose skeletons show damage inflicted by sword-cuts or the missiles hurled by Roman ballistae.

6 *Follow this track for 3½ miles, towards Hardy Monument. At road L*

7 *Shortly after brow of hill L onto forestry track, just before woodland begins*

8 *Follow main track down through wood. At bottom bear R round barn, then uphill 'Portesham' towards clump of trees. Go past barn onto tarmac*

9 *Fast descent. At T-j with road R, then at T-j in Portesham L towards Kings Arms PH. At T-j with B3157 R 'Abbotsbury 2'*

10 **Take care**. *Immediately after Millmead Country Guest House R onto track*

11 *Take 2nd R through a black gate just before small black barn onto dismantled railway. At times muddy. Follow to the end*

12 *At road R into Abbotsbury. Opposite Ilchester Arms PH R up Back Street*

13 *After 200 yards, just past a row of thatched yellow stone cottages, before Spring Cottage, L up track, which becomes very steep*

14 *Follow track steeply uphill through gate. Ignore right turn to Lime Kiln, carry SA to corner of field, heading for a roof on stilts*

15 *Through next gate (by roof on stilts). Bear R uphill 'White Hill'*

16 *At next waymark R 'Inland route. Hardy Monument', through the middle of three gates, then L following the fence on your left*

17 *At T-j with major track R and follow this as it turns sharply L downhill towards wood. At tarmac L past farm*

18 *Contour on this track, at times rough, through several fields and gates to emerge at tarmac. Turn R (sign to left 'Private road, Bridleway over Private Property')*

19 *Climb steeply. As gradient flattens, take LH fork downhill, ignoring turns*

20 *In Long Bredy near a cluster of houses SA at junction with road, following signs for the church*

21 *¼ mile after no through road to church 1st R 'Dorchester 8½'*

22 *At T-j with A35 SA (white 'T' sign)*

23 *Go past buildings, ignore right turn by green barn, continue climbing gently. At T-j with lane R*

24 *At next T-j L 'Compton Valence 1, Maiden Newton 3½'*

25 *½ mile after the turning to Compton Valence, take the next R on a broad stony track by a lonesome tree*

26 *Follow along several field edges (Dorset County Council blue arrows). Maybe muddy. Track becomes enclosed*

27 *At tarmac L downhill away from farm*

28 *A T-j at bottom R, then after 30 yards R again 'Peacock Lodge ¾ Muckleford 1¼'*

page 127

Above: Maiden Castle

Chalk ridges near the Dorset coast southeast from Dorchester

Dorset seems to be blessed with a much higher proportion of good quality bridleways than most other counties in southern England. This ride uses those that follow the ridges on the chalk hills between Weymouth and Lulworth. The ride climbs from Broadmayne to join the Dorset Coast Path over White Horse Hill. It follows the ridge to the main road and soon you lose all your height before you embark on a steep road climb to the top of the white cliffs of Dorset. This stretch offers some magnificent views out to sea and along the coast. Thirsty? There is an excellent pub in East Chaldon. The return half follows the ridge along the inland hills on much rougher, grassier terrain. Swooping down to the A352, the terrain changes to a much softer agricultural character amid woodland. And then, of course, there is the ford.

Start

Osmington Drove, Broadmayne. 4 miles southeast of Dorchester on the A352, 1st R after the stores/post office

Parking : Limited parking at the start (see above). Larger car park at the end of the lane signposted 'Ringstead' off the A353 (instruction 7), but this will leave you with a steep climb at the finish

Refreshments

Black Dog PH, Broadmayne
Sailors Return PH, East Chaldon

Background picture: Durdle Door

Distance and grade

18 miles

Moderate/strenuous

Terrain

Four climbs: 350 feet from Broadmayne to White Horse Hill on firm tracks; 330 feet from the A353 to the car park on top of the cliffs, mainly on tarmac; 170 feet from near the car park to the obelisk, at times rough; 250 feet from East Chaldon to Moigns Down, mostly on tarmac but the ridge can be rough

Nearest railway

Dorchester, 4 miles from Broadmayne

East Chaldon
Five Marys
Watercombe
Warmwell

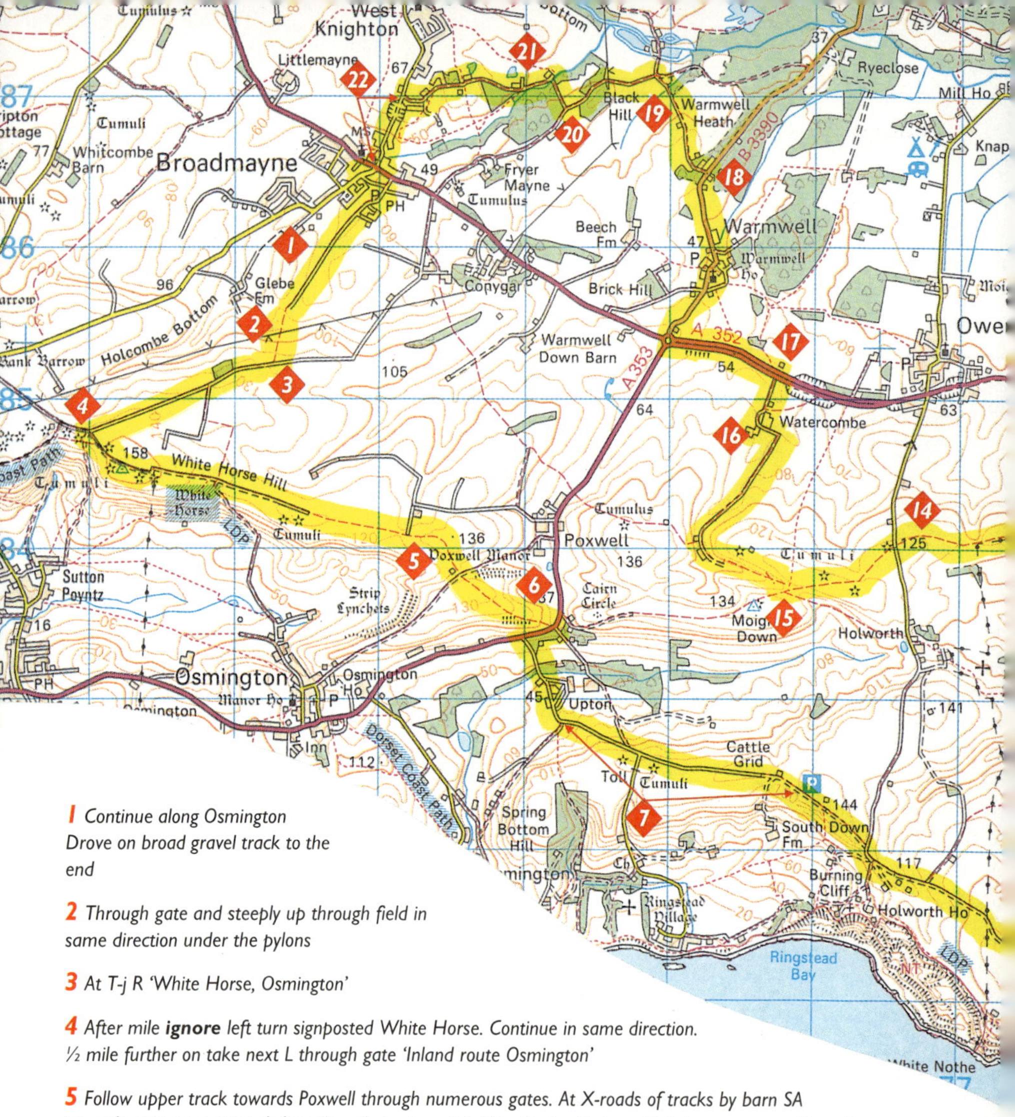

1 Continue along Osmington Drove on broad gravel track to the end

2 Through gate and steeply up through field in same direction under the pylons

3 At T-j R 'White Horse, Osmington'

4 After mile **ignore** left turn signposted White Horse. Continue in same direction. ½ mile further on take next L through gate 'Inland route Osmington'

5 Follow upper track towards Poxwell through numerous gates. At X-roads of tracks by barn SA towards gate set against skyline, then through next field to the R of telegraph pole you can see from the gate

6 Head towards small wood and buildings. Descend to busy A353. **Extreme care – dangerous crossing**: it is best to go left for 100 yards to give yourself a clear view before crossing the road. Turn R on road then 1st L 'Ringstead 1½'

7 Follow this road in same direction up steep hill, through car park then gate 'West Lulworth 5. No cars please'

8 Follow signs for Daggers Gate and West Lulworth along track then across field(s) towards obelisk. At monument R along field edge to join track on other side of fence

9 Continue towards Daggers Gate. 50 yards **before** reaching road L uphill towards barn (blue arrow)

10 At next barn R 'East Chaldon'. At gate L down into valley 'East Chaldon'. Follow blue arrows and waymarks to road

11 At road L, then follow it to the right around village green, past Sailors Return PH

12 At top of steep hill, on RH bend L through gate 'White Horse Hill 4½'

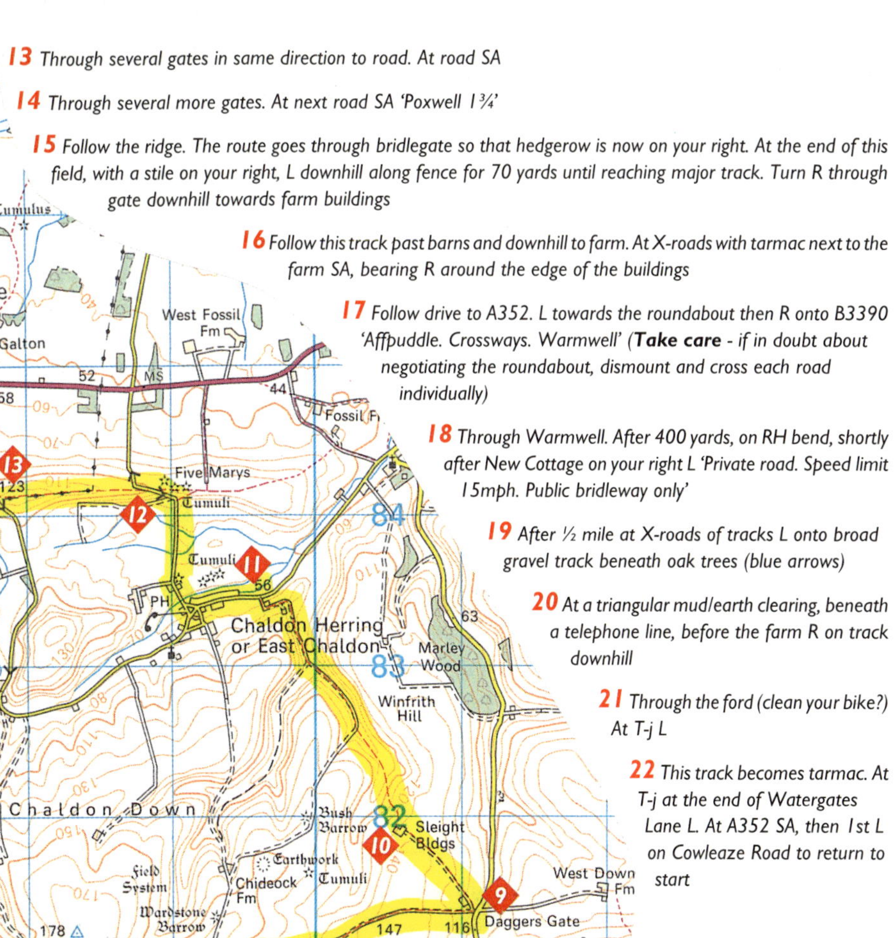

13 *Through several gates in same direction to road. At road SA*

14 *Through several more gates. At next road SA 'Poxwell 1¾'*

15 *Follow the ridge. The route goes through bridlegate so that hedgerow is now on your right. At the end of this field, with a stile on your right, L downhill along fence for 70 yards until reaching major track. Turn R through gate downhill towards farm buildings*

16 *Follow this track past barns and downhill to farm. At X-roads with tarmac next to the farm SA, bearing R around the edge of the buildings*

17 *Follow drive to A352. L towards the roundabout then R onto B3390 'Affpuddle. Crossways. Warmwell' (**Take care** - if in doubt about negotiating the roundabout, dismount and cross each road individually)*

18 *Through Warmwell. After 400 yards, on RH bend, shortly after New Cottage on your right L 'Private road. Speed limit 15mph. Public bridleway only'*

19 *After ½ mile at X-roads of tracks L onto broad gravel track beneath oak trees (blue arrows)*

20 *At a triangular mud/earth clearing, beneath a telephone line, before the farm R on track downhill*

21 *Through the ford (clean your bike?) At T-j L*

22 *This track becomes tarmac. At T-j at the end of Watergates Lane L. At A352 SA, then 1st L on Cowleaze Road to return to start*

Superb chalk ridges with sea views on the west of the Isle of Wight

You will find this magnificent ride has all the ingredients one could ask for: well-signposted, firm tracks with superb views over the island, the Solent and the English Channel, challenging climbs and broad, open descents. The western section is so good that it is repeated on the return trip. Climbing from the golf clubhouse, one soon reaches the broad chalk and flint path which gives views in all directions. A series of hills come into sight – and you will have to climb most of them! The Crown PH in Shorwell is an obvious lunch stop. The return takes in part of Brighstone Forest before rejoining the outward route for a thrilling descent with the Needles looming ever larger.

Start

Car park in Freshwater Bay at the bottom of the hill

Distance and grade

19 miles

Strenuous

Terrain

Over 2500 feet of climbing in a series of seven hills, some are short and steep, some are long and steep!

Nearest ferry

Yarmouth, 3 miles along the cycle track, or Cowes, 8 miles from the northeast tip

Refreshments

Several choices in Freshwater Bay
Divert to Brighstone *or* Shorwell *for refreshments near to the route*

Freshwater
Harboro
Limerstone Down
Lorden Copse
Chillerton Down

Off-road cycling tips

- After fixing a puncture, check the inside of the tyre for embedded thorns before replacing the inner tube. A screwdriver is useful for winkling out difficult thorns
- If your brake blocks look as though they are wearing thin, take a spare set with you. New brake blocks are much cheaper than new rims
- If there is a grating or crunching noise when you spin the wheels, pedals or cranks replace the bearings before they damage more expensive parts
- If some vegetation gets stuck in your derailleur, remove it straightaway before it does any damage
- The deepest part of a puddle on a farm track is usually where the vehicles' wheels go, so try the higher ground in the middle
- If there is any possibility of cycling in twilight or darkness, take lights with you. As a precaution in winter, take a reflective belt and/or reflective strips for ankles and wrists – being visible is what matters most
- If carrying bikes on a car, stop regularly to check they are securely fixed

Idlecombe Down
Gallibury Hump
Brighstone Down
Harboro

1 *From car park take the main road (A3055) uphill towards Ventnor. 2nd L on Southdown Road 'Freshwater Bay Golf Course', then 1st R 'Public Bridleway F 54 Freshwater Way, Compton and Tennyson Trail'*

2 *Go past golf course. At fork of tracks R (same signposts as above)*

3 *Bear R towards brow of hill to your right then stay on LH (upper) track 'Tennyson Trail'*

4 *Follow obvious main track to right of and below trig point. Descend to road. R then L onto track 'Bridleroad to Newport, Brighstone and Shorwell'*

5 *At car park/road R then L onto track (opposite road turning)*

6 *Leave the Tennyson Trail, which goes left into the wood and follow main track running to the right of the wood. You are now on the Worsley Trail. Descend to road and go SA*

7 *Follow the main track as it swings round past the mast (leave it on your right) then along the RH edge of 1st wood and LH edge of 2nd wood. Track becomes rougher. Mud by the gate*

8 *At T-j with main track L*

9 *Follow this track via gate to road. At road L then R*

10 *Very steep climb. At gate bear L. At T-j of tracks bear R towards mast (follow telephone wires at first)*

11 *Shortly, at next junction L 'Public bridleway N 136A Brighstone Forest'*

12 *At fork of tracks R 'Public Bridleway BS 4. Brighstone, Freshwater Bay, Tennyson Trail'*

13 *At 1st X-roads of tracks go SA. At 2nd X-roads, at beginning of wood, R 'Public Bridleway BS 9. Calbourne-Brighstone Rd'*

14 *At road SA. 'Public Bridleway CB 17. Brook 2, Compton 3, Freshwater Bay 5'*

15 *Climb steeply then descend as track bears L to rejoin outward trail, with magnificent views of the Needles*

16 *Return on outward route, descend to road (B3399). R then L 'Brook Down. Bridle Road to Freshwater'*

17 *Climb steeply towards but to the left of and below the trig point*

18 *On the descent across the golf course bear L at a fork of bridleways down to the road (A3055). At road R to return to start*

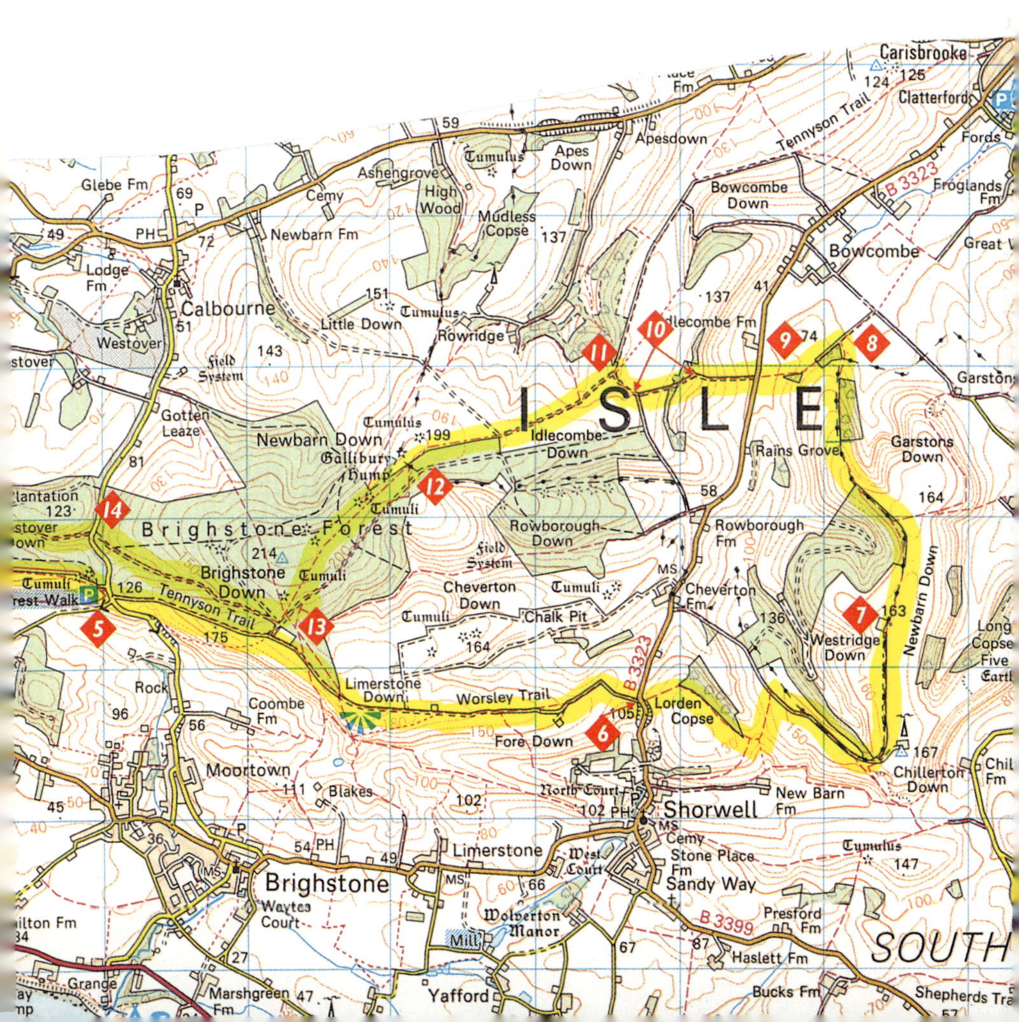

10 Rough riding on the southern downlands of the Isle of Wight

Although this ride does not approach the other Isle of Wight off-road route in terms of total height gain, it is nevertheless a tougher ride, as the steep bits are very steep and will require some pushing. Your effort is more than rewarded by the panoramic views first from the masts on Stenbury Down and then from the ridge of St Catherine's Down. There are good pub stops in Whitwell and Niton.

Start

The beginning of the cycle route from Newport to Blackwater, opposite the Barley Mow PH on Medina Avenue in south Newport

Distance and grade

22 miles

Strenuous

Terrain

Two major climbs: 650 feet from the entrance to Godshill Park to the masts and 350 feet from Niton to St Catherine's Down. Both will require some pushing, and the first can be rough in places

Nearest ferry

Cowes, 7 miles from the northern tip of the route

Nearest railway

Shanklin, 3 miles from the route at instruction 8

Refreshments

White Horse PH, Whitwell
White Lion PH, Niton

South Newport
Blackwater
Bohemia Corner
Stenbury Down
Whitwell
Nito

Off-road cycling tips

- Always allow extra time when planning a trip for delays caused by punctures or getting lost
- The same off-road route can take much longer after rain or in the winter when tracks are softer, so plan accordingly
- If using British Rail, always phone in advance to check what the regulations are for the service you wish to use and if a reservation is required
- A small elastic bungee is very useful for securing small packages to the rack or frame
- Let someone know where you are going, particularly if it is winter and you are going to a remote area.
- If you come across a blocked right of way or one you feel is in a terrible state of repair report it to the Rights of Way Department at the County Council. The most effective means is to write a letter giving grid references
- Ensure everyone has the equipment to mend a puncture (pump, tyre levers, puncture repair kit and/or spare inner tube). With four other tools: a reversible screwdriver, a small adjustable spanner, a set of appropriate allen keys and a chain link extractor you have all you need. All this fits in a small pouch, worn around your waist or attached under the saddle
- The right attitude is much more important than expensive equipment
- The success of the day can be judged by how soon you would like to go out again!

Catherine's Down
Upper Appleford Farm
Chillerton
Blackwater

1 With your back to the Barley Mow PH SA onto Stenbury Trail/Cycle Path alongside the stream

2 At T-j with road L, then at T-j with main road (A3056) R, then L after ¼ mile 'Public Bridleway SA 36. Godshill'

3 At end of tarmac bear L through gate into field. At X-roads with major track SA into field

4 At other side of field R along field edge. Through 2nd field. R then L around 3rd field (may be muddy). At T-j with major track L 'Public bridleway'

5 After ½ mile, on sharp RH bend by white railings and chevrons L 'Public bridleway A 22. Great Budbridge Manor'

6 At T-j with stone track at end of row of cypress trees R 'Public bridleway A 49, Godshill', then L (house ahead)

7 Shortly, at corner of field take the RH track along the RH edge of field towards hill with mast

8 At T-j with A3020 L, then R 'Godshill Farm Park. Public bridleway'

9 Where main road bears sharply left SA (blue arrow on yellow background) 'Private road. No unauthorised vehicles'

10 At arch R 'Public bridleway GL 49. Stenbury'. Steep climb

11 Follow beneath top of hill to X-roads of bridleways near wire fence gates. SA 'Public bridleway GL 49, Stenbury Down, Ventnor'

12 Very steep climb, at times rough, towards mast. Just before mast L through bridlegate onto service road

13 As road bears L downhill bear R on track. At fork of bridleways (LH track is signposted V 63 bear R 'Public bridleway')

14 At next fork bear R again 'V57, Nettlecombe'

15 At T-j of bridleways R, then L on 'NT 119, Nettlecombe, Whitwell, Niton'

16 Follow signs for Whitwell. At car park R, then L before pond 'NT 5 Whitwell'. Along field edge. Aim towards 4-way signpost and towards Whitwell.

17 Through two squeaky metal gates. Bear L at 2nd gate towards bridge over stream

18 At road L then R 'Bridle and footpath only'. Past cemetery. At house R into field to continue in same direction

19 At T-j by Lower Fields R. At next T-j R. At T-j at the end of Town End L onto Rectory Road and follow to end

20 At T-j with A3055 R 'Newport', then after ¾ mile 1st L on Crocker Lane 'Private road, Public bridleway T 66. Head Down, Chale'

21 Steep climb on tarmac then track. Contour around hill, bearing R towards monument shaped like the letter 'i'

22 At monument L through bridlegate, then at T-j after short descent R 'GL 60, Appleford'

23 At next T-j with major track R

24 At road R, then L opposite road turning on right 'Private Road, North Appleford' (later 'GL 11, Rookley Green, Cridmore')

25 At farm R 'Public footpath GL 10' then at bottom L 'GL 11, Cridmore'

26 Follow through field, at first close to wood on left then to hedgerow on right. Over a small concrete ford through stream

27 Keep following blue arrows as track improves past farm. Follow road to T-j by triangle of grass. Turn R

28 At next T-j R 'Newport', then L 'Leading to Brook Lane, G8, Newbarn Down' At X-roads SA

29 At road R 'G 6, Gatcombe'. Shortly after sharp RH bend (Snowdrop Lane on left) L 'G 6, Carisbrooke'

30 Steep climb on concrete then along field edge. At X-roads with major track R

31 At road bear L (in effect SA). At end of Rectory Lane L, then R on Sandy Lane 'Blackwater'

32 Just before T-j with main road (A3020) L onto path over stream onto cycle path to return to start

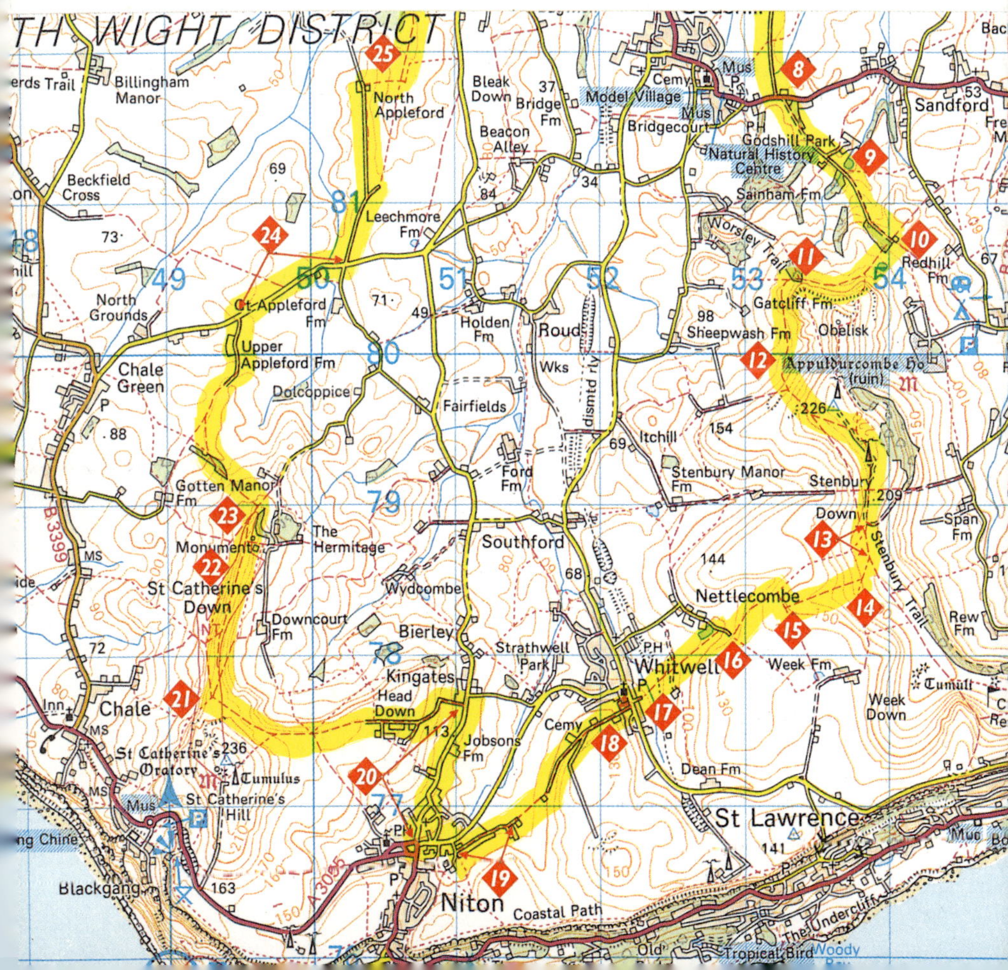

Cycle TOURS

I wish to order the following titles

	Price	Quantity	Total
Avon, Somerset & Wiltshire ISBN 0 600 57913 1	£9.99		
Gloucestershire and Hereford & Worcester ISBN 0 600 57914 X	£9.99		
Dorset, Hampshire & Isle of Wight ISBN 0 600 57915 8	£9.99		
Kent, Surrey & Sussex ISBN 0 600 57916 6	£9.99		
Postage and packing	Free		
		Grand total	

Name (block capitals)

Address

Postcode

I enclose a cheque/postal order for £

made payable to **Reed Book Services** or

Please debit my ☐ Access ☐ Visa ☐ American Express account

number

by £ Expiry date

.... Signature

• **Free postage and packing** • While every effort is made to keep prices low, the publisher reserves the right to increase prices at short notice. • Your order will be dispatched within 28 days, subject to availability.